Tokyo

From sleepy fishing village to samurai capital to vibrant global metropolis, Eiko Maruko Siniawer takes readers through Tokyo's rich history, revealing four centuries of transformation deeply woven into its fabric. This accessible guide introduces a world of shoguns and Kabuki theater, riots and earthquakes, wartime devastation and reconstruction, booms and busts, bright lights and skyscrapers, all viewed through the lived experiences of those who have inhabited and shaped a city of distinctive neighborhoods and different personalities. Emphasizing the city's human heart, Siniawer conveys a vivid sense of time, culture, and place through ten moments that have shaped Tokyo's many lives.

Eiko Maruko Siniawer is Class of 1955 Memorial Professor of History at Williams College, specializing in the history of modern Japan. Her previous publications include *Ruffians, Yakuza, Nationalists: The Violent Politics of Modern Japan, 1860–1960* and *Waste: Consuming Postwar Japan.*

Ten Moments That Shaped

Structured around ten evocative moments in a city's past, these concise and engaging volumes allow readers to discover the rich histories of cities around the world. Our expert authors combine vivid historical detail and insightful analyses to tell the story of each city in an accessible and compelling manner.

For a list of titles in the series see
www.cambridge.org/10-moments

Tokyo

Eiko Maruko Siniawer
Williams College

CAMBRIDGE
UNIVERSITY PRESS

CAMBRIDGE
UNIVERSITY PRESS

Shaftesbury Road, Cambridge CB2 8EA, United Kingdom

One Liberty Plaza, 20th Floor, New York, NY 10006, USA

477 Williamstown Road, Port Melbourne, VIC 3207, Australia

314–321, 3rd Floor, Plot 3, Splendor Forum, Jasola District Centre,
New Delhi – 110025, India

103 Penang Road, #05–06/07, Visioncrest Commercial, Singapore 238467

Cambridge University Press is part of Cambridge University Press & Assessment,
a department of the University of Cambridge.

We share the University's mission to contribute to society through the pursuit of
education, learning and research at the highest international levels of excellence.

www.cambridge.org
Information on this title: www.cambridge.org/9781108845762

DOI: 10.1017/9781108990882

First published 2025

A catalogue record for this publication is available from the British Library.

Library of Congress Cataloging-in-Publication Data
NAMES: Siniawer, Eiko Maruko, author.
TITLE: Tokyo / Eiko Maruko Siniawer, Williams College, Massachusetts.
DESCRIPTION: Cambridge, United Kingdom ; New York : Cambridge University
Press, 2024. | Includes index.
IDENTIFIERS: LCCN 2024006188 | ISBN 9781108845762 (hardback) | ISBN
9781108965002 (paperback) | ISBN 9781108990882 (ebook)
SUBJECTS: LCSH: Tokyo (Japan) – History. | Tokyo (Japan) – Civilization.
CLASSIFICATION: LCC DS896.6 .S56 2024 | DDC 952/.135–dc23/eng/20240208
LC record available at https://lccn.loc.gov/2024006188

ISBN 978-1-108-84576-2 Hardback
ISBN 978-1-108-96500-2 Paperback

CONTENTS

FIGURES

MAPS

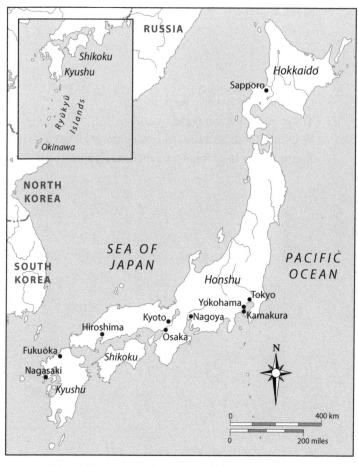

Map 1 Contemporary Japan. Map by David McCutcheon
FBCart.S www.dvdmaps.co.uk

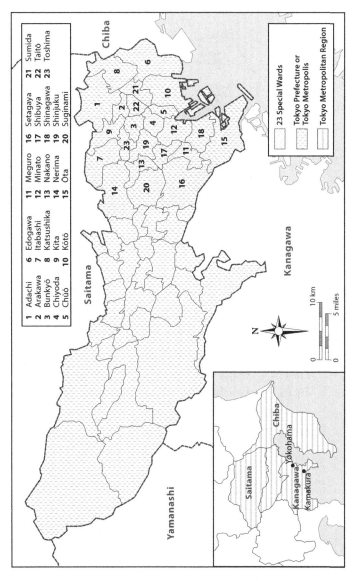

Map 2 Tokyo metropolitan region. Map by David McCutcheon FBCart.S www.dvdmaps.co.uk

1	Adachi	6	Edogawa	11	Meguro	16	Setagaya	21	Sumida
2	Arakawa	7	Itabashi	12	Minato	17	Shibuya	22	Taitō
3	Bunkyō	8	Katsushika	13	Nakano	18	Shinagawa	23	Toshima
4	Chiyoda	9	Kita	14	Nerima	19	Shinjuku		
5	Chūō	10	Kōtō	15	Ōta	20	Suginami		

23 Special Wards

Tokyo Prefecture or Tokyo Metropolis

Tokyo Metropolitan Region

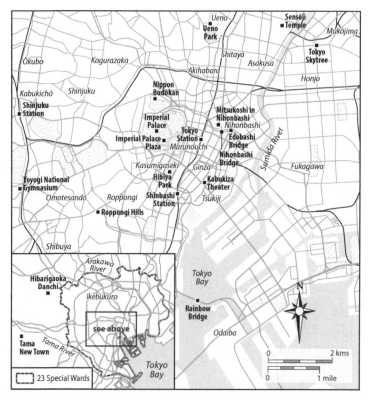

Map 3 Neighborhoods and sites in contemporary Tokyo.
Map by David McCutcheon FBCart.S www.dvdmaps.co.uk

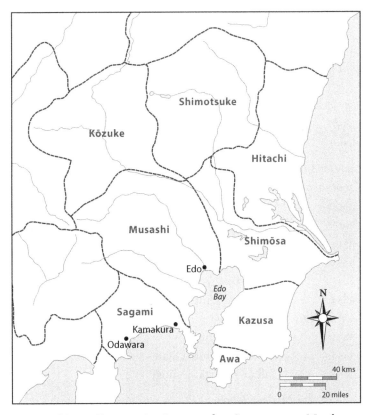

Map 4 Kanto region in premodern Japan, c. 1590. Map by
David McCutcheon FBCart.S www.dvdmaps.co.uk

CHRONOLOGY

1185–1600 Medieval Japan

1457	Ōta Dōkan built Edo Fortress
1590	**Tokugawa Ieyasu officially entered Edo Castle**

1600–1868 Early Modern Japan

1600–1868	*Tokugawa Period or Edo Period*
1600	Battle of Sekigahara
1603	Tokugawa Ieyasu granted title of shogun
1714	**Ejima-Ikushima Incident**
1853	**American warships appeared at mouth of Edo Bay**
1854	Japan and United States signed Treaty of Kanagawa
1855	Ansei earthquake
1858	Japan and United States signed Harris Treaty
1868	Fall of Tokugawa shogunate

1868–Present Modern Japan

1868–1912	*Meiji Period*
1868	Meiji Restoration
	"Edo" renamed "Tokyo" (Eastern Capital)
1872	**Shinbashi–Yokohama Railroad Line opened**
1894–1895	Sino-Japanese War
1904–1905	Russo-Japanese War
1905	**Hibiya Riot**
1910	Korea annexed as Japanese colony

1912–1926	*Taishō Period*
1923	**Great Kanto earthquake**
1926–1989	*Shōwa Period*
1931	Japan invaded Manchuria
1937–1945	Asia Pacific War
1937	**Prayer event in colonial Seoul**
1945	American firebombing of Tokyo
1945–1952	American occupation of Japan
1960	**Crown Prince Akihito and Princess Michiko visited Hibarigaoka apartment complex**
1964	Tokyo Olympic Games
1981	***Somehow, Crystal* released**
1989–2019	*Heisei Period*
1995	Aum Shinrikyō sarin gas attacks
2011	Great East Japan earthquake, or 3.11
2016	**Prime Minister Abe Shinzō appeared as Mario at Rio Olympic Games**
2019–Present	*Reiwa Period*
2021	Tokyo 2020 Olympic Games

PROLOGUE

IN a city of neighborhoods with distinct pasts and different personalities, the intimate Kagurazaka district feels like a treasure trove of stories and experiences to anybody who wonders about its history. Standing at the foot of Kagurazaka and peering up its main street, you can start to see the many elements of Tokyo's vibrant tapestry. This corner of the sprawling capital has an urbane warmth thanks to its modest scale, with only a few buildings that extend above three or four floors and a relatively slender, tree-lined central avenue that's blocked off on weekends for strolling pedestrians (see Figure 0.1). With perceptive eyes, you'll notice the café specializing in Japanese-style sweets and the bakery offering French desserts, the convenience store and the stationery shop, the upscale wine bar and the fast-food burger joint. Even when I was on a graduate student's budget over twenty years ago, I'd take refuge in my favorite haunts – stealing away to the Japanese pub at the top of a steep flight of stairs, pondering what I'd found in the archives while lingering over a baguette sandwich, and risking burns from molten liquid spurted by a clam cooked on a tabletop grill at a lively seafood place. To this day, I think about the daily lives of the commuters who come to work in the neighborhood's offices and establishments, and about the Tokyoites who call Kagurazaka home, who shop at the grocery store and pharmacy, visit the bank, go to the local barber, and while away time at the pachinko parlor.

To look at Kagurazaka more closely, to bring some knowledge of the neighborhood's history to bear on its present, is to understand how inextricably and deeply the past is bound to

Figure 0.1 Kagurazaka at night. Photograph by Higuchi Hiroshi. Courtesy of Stockbyte/Getty Images.

contemporary Tokyo. The hill or *saka* (*zaka*) that helps define Kagurazaka and endures in its name reflected the defensive logic of a town that was built around a castle, when this capital of warrior government was still called Edo and the Tokugawa family at its head sought to keep their samurai enemies at bay. Early in the 1600s, when the reigning Tokugawa shogun constructed the outer moat around his castle town, gates and watchtowers were erected at strategic locations. At one such point, just beyond the outer moat in what is now Kagurazaka, a dangerously steep hill was created to prevent assailants from riding horse-drawn carriages across the bridge and toward the castle (see Figure 0.2). The shogun also stationed here his direct samurai retainers, or vassals, to guard the northwest flank of his stronghold. While the hill was somewhat smoothed in the 1870s when there was no longer a castle or a shogun to protect, the characteristic slope remained. And the

Figure 0.2 Kagurazaka in the late Tokugawa period. Hiroshige, *Ushigome Kagurazaka no zu*, c. mid-1800s, woodblock print. National Diet Library Digital Collection, accessed July 29, 2023, https://dl.ndl.go.jp/pid/1306169.

moat-cum-canal still flows at its base. Since the mid-1990s, a small wharf used for many decades by the Tokyo Aquatic Club also came to house the Canal Café, an Italian restaurant along the water that graces Kagurazaka with the sounds of live jazz on summer evenings.[1]

Still very much evident, the bones of the neighborhood (and the city) were set by the Tokugawa in the 1600s and were given life by a growing number of Edoites. The needs of the samurai in Kagurazaka fueled and shaped the development of the area over the coming centuries. Catering to residents' spiritual lives, Buddhist temples and Shinto shrines thrived, with several enduring in some form into the present. You can visit Akagi Shrine from the mid-1500s and contemplate its recent renovation by the renowned architect Kuma Kengo, who also designed the adjoining upscale apartment complex, and you can stop before Zenkokuji temple, which relocated here in the 1790s, and imagine the samurai who lived near its grounds. You might also hear echoes from shrines of the music, or *kagura*, they have long played, and which gave the neighborhood the first part of its name – Kagurazaka, or hill of the music of the gods. Over time, this samurai area also drew more and more townspeople, the artisans and merchants who made a living by providing the goods for day-to-day life. Their shops can be glimpsed today in the local businesses selling freshly roasted tea, making Japanese confections, or tailoring kimonos. By the mid-1800s, Kagurazaka was a patchwork of sizeable estates belonging to higher-ranking samurai, smaller estates of lower-ranking samurai, shrines and temples, and the more modest homes of townspeople.[2]

If you venture off the main street and into the neighborhood's alleyways, you'll find winding passageways covered with cobblestones and graced here and there with a discreet door that leads to a *ryōtei*, or exclusive, high-class, Japanese restaurant. The few *ryōtei* that remain are vestiges of Kagurazaka's history as an entertainment district which housed an unlicensed pleasure quarter in the Tokugawa days, then in the late 1800s, a flourishing of teahouses, restaurants, and geisha houses that sprung up in estates vacated by samurai when samurai were no more. Enlivened by the opening of a nearby railway station in 1895, and the good fortune of surviving a massive earthquake in 1923, the bustling shopping streets and nightlife of Kagurazaka drew various Tokyoites for decades, from politicians to writers and artists, and students from the nearby university. The feel of this entertainment quarter is evoked today in the residual maze of narrow alleys and through architectural nods to this past in buildings both old and new, from the black wooden walls that line walkways to the latticework that

Figure 0.3 Narrow alley in Kagurazaka. Photograph by author, July 7, 2023.

• ● •

embellishes doors and windows (see Figure 0.3).[3] Most palpable is the spirit and vitality of the neighborhood which lives on through the Tokyoites who enjoy its cafés, shops, bars, festivals, and restaurants.

• ● •

We start with Kagurazaka not just because it's one of my favorite neighborhoods in Tokyo, and one I hope you'll have a chance to visit, but also because it demonstrates so elegantly the visibility of the past in the present. There are some who claim that the past doesn't exist in contemporary Tokyo, that it's been obliterated by earthquakes and fires, world war, and new construction. But the history of Edo and Tokyo, of Edoites and Tokyoites, has indelibly shaped how and where people live, work, and play in the metropolis. It explains why you see in Kagurazaka low wooden structures and high-rise apartments, subway riders and pedestrians, Japanese restaurants and French cafés, asphalt roads and cobblestone walkways, chain stores and family shops. This history shouldn't be reduced to some vague notion of "tradition" which assumes there's something essential and unchanging baked into the city's cultural DNA. Nor is there any reason to think that this history is somehow mysterious or unknowable, that we can't understand this past deeply and empathetically. The history of this city is as complicated, and as accessible, as any other. Over centuries, the many lives of Edo/Tokyo have been changed by people with diverse and conflicting desires, beliefs, and concerns. Exploring the historical experiences of the city's residents reveals how flawed the presumption is that there's some fundamental difference between "Eastern cities" and "Western cities." Edoites and Tokyoites have interacted with ideas, people, and things from around the world; figured out how to move around a growing city; designed and constructed, lived and worked in buildings of many shapes and sizes; found ways to enjoy themselves; and made and sold, shopped and bought. The history of Tokyo, entangled with Japan's experiences of imperialism, colonialism, democracy, fascism, and capitalism, offers its own particular variations on very familiar themes.

Before we begin delving into this history, it might be helpful to orient ourselves in time and place. Our story opens centuries before Tokyo became the megacity we know today, and before Japan became a modern nation with a strong centralized state, clearly delineated borders, or even a cohesive sense of itself as Japan. The Kanto Plain on which Edo and then Tokyo took shape wasn't thought of as being in the north, with Kyoto and Osaka in the south, as might be assumed from a quick look at a map. Still today, the Kanto area which encompasses the Tokyo metropolitan region is referred to as eastern Japan, distinct from

Figure 0.4 Nighttime view from the Kinshi neighborhood of Sumida ward. Photograph by Satō Shintarō, 2009.

the Kansai region in the west. In the premodern period, these lands on the eastern edge of the realm were far from the center of things; they were nothing more than an unremarkable backwater. If, before the 1600s, you had asked an aristocrat on the streets of Kyoto about the Kanto Plain, they might have shrugged their shoulders and mumbled about how its fields and fishing villages probably wouldn't ever amount to very much.

1

Founding the Shogun's Capital

O N a clear day in the late summer of 1590, the ambitious warrior Tokugawa Ieyasu strode across the expansive Kanto Plain. Rimmed by mountains and the waters of the Pacific, this area in the eastern reaches of the Japanese realm had recently become his dominion – a reward for his contributions to the seizure of land from rival samurai. To consecrate this sizable acquisition, Ieyasu had planned his ceremonial trip for this particular date, considered auspicious for coinciding with the first harvest of new grain. Around midafternoon he stopped at a temple for a meal, and a short while later he made the approach to his new home. People had gathered along the route, and regional powerholders had assembled to witness this occasion: the ascendant Tokugawa Ieyasu's official entrance into the castle at Edo.[1]

When Ieyasu stepped foot in the castle, on the spot where the Imperial Palace now stands in the middle of what is now Tokyo, he laid eyes on a building that was more of a fort than a command center suitable for a warrior of his stature. He was, after all, a shrewd and skilled samurai who had amassed might and wealth by aligning himself with the preeminent warlords of the era, first Oda Nobunaga and then Toyotomi Hideyoshi. By 1590, Ieyasu was a principal vassal of Hideyoshi, who was well on his way to consolidating control over much of the realm and bringing an end to over a century of almost constant warfare between feuding samurai. But while Ieyasu was bestowed much of the Kanto region by Hideyoshi, he didn't inherit an imposing castle that projected his newfound power. The footprint of what would become the three central enclosures of the castle did exist. But the fortification wasn't encircled by a stone wall, just an earthen embankment about three meters tall covered with grass. In a handful of spots around this perimeter, simple wooden gates allowed passage. The floors were made of dirt in some places; in others, the ground was covered with planks salvaged from old ships. And the roof wasn't tile, but a patchwork of wood shingles and thatch.[2]

Looking out from this modest fortress perched atop a bluff, someone other than Ieyasu might have found it difficult to envision this land as the site for their military headquarters and castle town. To the southeast was the Hibiya Inlet whose waters at the time lapped close at the castle's feet. Scattered along the shores of this inlet of Edo Bay were fishing villages of thatched-roof homes. To the northwest were hills and to the east marshy lowlands, leaving little space to house an army or build much of anything. And there was no abundant source of drinking water. It's hard to know from the scant sources on medieval Edo just how many people called it home, much less how exactly they lived. What's certain is that Edo was distant from the bustling capital in Kyoto and the centers of Hideyoshi's power. For Ieyasu, the granting of this land in the east removed him from the Tokugawa family's hereditary base to the west. Given all of these drawbacks to the Kanto region, Hideyoshi's transfer of Ieyasu may not have been a generous reward so much as a farsighted attempt to contain a potential competitor.[3]

But Ieyasu had his reasons for choosing to settle in Edo and not in the historical Kanto strongholds of Kamakura or Odawara further south. Perhaps he appreciated Edo's location at the innermost point of the bay, a strategic position that was easily defensible and protected from naval assault. Or its link to other areas by way of major roads like the Tōkaidō that ran down the coast to Kyoto.[4] Whatever his rationale, Tokugawa Ieyasu treated the allotment from Hideyoshi as an opportunity to bend upward the arc of his career and transform Edo into a proper castle town befitting one of the realm's most powerful warriors.

• • •

The breathtaking metamorphosis spurred by Tokugawa Ieyasu in the late sixteenth century was a pivotal chapter in the story of the place that would become early modern Edo and then modern Tokyo, but it was not the first. This sprawling area already had a long history of multiple lives, as people and things and ideas from elsewhere came and left their imprint on the Kanto Plain. In its very early incarnation, well before there was any sense of a politically organized realm, this land was the stomping ground of animals. Elephants and large deer came from Eurasia when the Japanese archipelago was still a crescent-shaped mass attached to the continent, and they tread upon the soil that hundreds of thousands of years later would sit below Tokyo. (In the mid-1970s, three elephants would be discovered more than twenty meters below ground by crews building a subway line near Hamachō Station.) Giant mammals like the Palaeoloxodon elephant were eventually overhunted by people who followed the same route from the continent as the animals and plants before them. And around the time that ocean waters severed the crescent from the continent and broke it into a string of islands, about 12,000 years ago, people became less nomadic and started to lead more settled lives on the Kanto Plain.

When the seeds of a political body were sown, it wasn't here in the east but in the west. And there the realm's administrative center of gravity would remain for more than a millennium.

3

Over the 600s and early 700s, an emergent state in the western region now known as the Kansai adapted Chinese legal codes as the basis for its rule, the monarch came to be called *tennō*, or emperor, and the nascent entity came to be known as Nihon, or Japan. Distant from this kernel of governance, the Kanto existed in its own sphere and followed its own rhythms, coming more gradually to agriculture, bronzeware, and political organization. But as the state's administrative apparatus developed, the province of Musashi was established and its borders defined to include almost all of today's metropolis of Tokyo as well as neighboring Saitama prefecture to the north and parts of Kanagawa prefecture to the south. The Kanto was still at the edges of the realm, but it was no longer beyond administrative reach.

In its medieval incarnation, Musashi province and the greater Kanto Plain became a prime arena for warriors jockeying for land, wealth, and power. These conflicts were part of a larger story of the rise of samurai, who came to challenge and would eventually usurp the political strength and authority of the state in the west. In the mid-800s to mid-1000s, these warrior families had emerged through military service to the emperor, who was the sovereign ruler at the apex of the governing imperial court in Kyoto. Court politics, culture, and intrigue were a world unto itself that revolved tightly around the capital. From this vantage point, the province of Musashi was a distant frontier, imagined as unpopulated and backward, beyond civilization and culture. Even the name Kanto, meaning "east of the barriers," was a description from the perspective of Kyoto. With some disdain for life outside of the capital, a court aristocrat who was appointed to serve as a governor was more likely to make his home not in the province but in Kyoto and to oversee his land from afar, hiring warriors to serve not just as guards but also as administrators. These empowered warriors came to eclipse the

court aristocrats in the provinces and became ever more powerful in areas such as the Kanto.[5]

One such Kanto warrior, a man named Chichibu
Shigetsugu, decided at some point in the 1100s to set up residence
in a strategic spot – on a bluff overlooking an inlet. Inspired by this
location, he changed his name from Chichibu to one meaning
"mouth of an inlet." And he conferred upon the land around him
this new name: Edo. The Edo family became formidable warriors
in this region after the first samurai government, or shogunate,
was founded in the 1180s at Kamakura in the southern Kanto. The
Kamakura shogunate tipped the balance of power away from the
emperor and the imperial court in the long-established capital of
Kyoto and toward the samurai, like the Edo family, of the Kanto
region.

In the mid-1400s, the Kanto became the stage for a civil
war between samurai in which one warrior family after another
gained and then lost dominance. One such family was the Uesugi,
who erected the castle at Edo that Tokugawa Ieyasu would claim
over a hundred years later. In 1457, the Uesugi decided to shore up
their position on the plain and commanded a chief retainer – Ōta
Dōkan – to build and administer the fortress at Edo. For this, he
would become a fixture in stories told about the history of Tokyo.
In the mid-1950s, a bronze statue of Ōta Dōkan was created to
commemorate the putative five hundredth anniversary of the
founding of Tokyo. This likeness now resides in the soaring
glass and steel trussed atrium of the Tokyo International Forum,
a strangely incongruous reminder of the medieval past. In Ōta
Dōkan's day, Edo Castle was both a military fortification and
a social hub. The fortress had three enclosures that were separated
by a deep moat and encircled by a barrier. There were archery
grounds where warriors gathered each morning to test their skills
with the bow and arrow. And Dōkan hosted gatherings for guests

who together composed *renga* or linked verse poetry. Near the castle, fishing boats and merchant ships would dock, bringing wares from other provinces and even overseas. There was rice from Awa, tea from Hitachi, bamboo arrows from Echigo, and copper from Shinano, as well as fish, lacquer, and medicines.

As the civil strife of the mid-1400s stretched into a prolonged period of almost unceasing war, the Kanto continued to witness the fortunes of competing samurai families wax and wane. It was the Hōjō of Odawara who were losing their grasp of Edo and its fortress when Toyotomi Hideyoshi launched his campaign to wrest control of the region. In early 1590, as his forces advanced and dealt one crushing blow after another, the castle at Edo fell quickly to the Toyotomi assault.[6]

• ● •

After Tokugawa Ieyasu received the surrendered Hōjō provinces and officially took claim of Edo in 1590, he oversaw its transformation from a strategic outpost into a full-fledged medieval castle town, designed to function as his military headquarters and the administrative center of his territory. Over the next ten years, Edo pulsed with the efforts of those who came to remake this modest place into a regional powerhouse.

One of the first orders of business was to tackle the shortcomings of the built and natural environments by repairing the castle and laying the groundwork for the town. The footprint of the castle's core was expanded, and over a dozen Buddhist temples to its west were relocated to make room for the construction of its western compound. Paired with these renovations were infrastructure projects, many of which sought to control the water of this swampy land crisscrossed by rivers. To create more buildable soil, the Hibiya Inlet was partially drained and filled with dirt from the excavation of a moat around the castle's new western enclosure. To ease the transport of goods by boat, new waterways were dug. Prime among them was a canal called the Dōsanbori that connected the Hirakawa River to the center of Edo, making it possible for things like rice to be sailed down the river and through the canal to arrive near the castle's main gate. To ease travel over land, bridges were built. And to provide drinking water for the town's residents, Ieyasu ordered the development of a system of waterworks.

The town that developed around the castle was shaped by the logics of military defense and the societal supremacy of samurai. At a time when Toyotomi Hideyoshi was demanding that clearer distinctions be made between samurai, farmers, and townspeople, areas of Edo came to be designated for particular occupational groups and began to form distinct identities. Direct retainers of Ieyasu charged with defending the castle lived on its northwest flank, lower-ranking vassals were placed close around the castle, and those of higher rank were given larger estates on the periphery. Townspeople who catered to the various needs of the samurai set up shop and home along the Dōsanbori canal, with specific neighborhoods specializing in certain goods and services like lumber and shipping. There was a periodic market where people could shop, and a brothel. Townspeople also took up residence in already established villages and squeezed around the samurai homes, temples, and shrines in the periphery.[7]

As laborers, lumberers, boatmen, and merchants set the pillars of the castle town, Tokugawa Ieyasu protected and strengthened Edo through a combination of adept management of his relationship with Hideyoshi, administrative skill, and a dose of good luck. In the years following their defeat of the Hōjō, Ieyasu continued to prove himself a dependable vassal to Hideyoshi. He spent a year and a half in Hizen province, on the island of Kyushu, which was a base for Hideyoshi's invasion of Korea in 1592. Ieyasu helped organize the massive number of soldiers and laborers mobilized for the assault but avoided deployment to the peninsula as one of the half million soldiers who fought against Korean and Chinese troops in the devastating six-year conflict. Instead, he spent some of this time with Hideyoshi in Osaka and near Kyoto. When in Edo, he tended to ceremonial responsibilities like holding banquets and to administrative tasks like promoting vassals, issuing licenses, and distributing fiefs.[8] When Toyotomi Hideyoshi died in 1598, Tokugawa Ieyasu was well positioned to fight for the reins of power and emerged as the leader of one of the two camps competing for control of the realm. At the decisive Battle of Sekigahara in 1600, Tokugawa Ieyasu's "eastern army" defeated the rival "western army." The consolidation of power started by Oda Nobunaga and advanced by Toyotomi Hideyoshi culminated in the victorious Tokugawa, and Japan was as unified as it had ever been. In 1603, Ieyasu was granted by the emperor the title of shogun (literally "generalissimo"), making him the foremost military ruler of the realm and ushering in the era of the Tokugawa shogunate and the elevation of Edo from a castle town to the shogun's capital.

• ● •

The triumphant Tokugawa family cast the foundation and frame of early modern Edo. Doubling down on Edo as their base, the Tokugawa reenvisioned it as the seat of their rule – Edo was to be the military headquarters, administrative nucleus, and political hegemon of a unified realm. For the first time in over a thousand years, the political and administrative center of gravity would unequivocally be in the east. Power was to be concentrated in the Tokugawa family and its warrior government at Edo, drawn away from the imperial court in Kyoto and from the daimyo lords around the country. A daimyo was a samurai who governed one of the 260 some domains across the land, ostensibly serving the shogun but also exercising autonomy and amassing power through rule of his domain. The Tokugawa shogunate sought to control and weaken the daimyo not just to assert its political supremacy but also to ensure that its newly established order would endure. We now know that Tokugawa rule would last for over two and a half centuries and that this period would be characterized by relative peace. But in the early 1600s, after over a century of almost constant warfare, the stability so recently won seemed fragile. To prevent disorder and assert authority, the first few Tokugawa shoguns – Ieyasu (r. 1603–1605), Hidetada (r. 1605–1623), and Iemitsu (r. 1623–1651) – built mechanisms and symbols of their power into the city of Edo.

The consolidation of power in the shogun's capital created a tremendous centripetal pull toward Edo that was felt across the realm. People, money, natural resources, and goods streamed into the town, sometimes by government coercion and sometimes by sheer magnetism. This potent combination of force and opportunity propelled the construction and growth of a city that was, in these early Tokugawa decades, a very male and quite rough and tumble place to be. There were the many samurai who were called to the military capital to serve as warriors and government bureaucrats, as well as thousands of masterless samurai who, without a lord to employ and pay them, came in search of work.

Edo Castle was the lodestone of the shogun's capital: a visual symbol of the shogunate's power, authority, and centrality. The very process of building this castle served as a way for the shogunate to control daimyo, drain domain coffers, and generally flex its muscle, mobilizing people and resources on a vast scale. Laborers were requisitioned by the shogunate for its various engineering and construction projects, with each domain's contribution calculated by its tax base. These men dug canals, built bridges, leveled Kandayama hill in the north, and used that soil to completely fill the Hibiya Inlet and create today's area of Nihonbashi from Shinbashi to Hamachō. Peasants came to work as day laborers, and carpenters, painters, lacquerers, stonemasons, plasterers, and metalworkers spent decades renovating the castle. With stone scarce on the Kanto Plain, major daimyo further west were ordered to provide 1,120 pieces of large stone for every hundred thousand *koku* of rice capacity in their domains. To send a single large stone to Edo, stonemasons first had to extract the block, weighing up to several tons, from a quarry in the mountains; then about a hundred laborers pulled it to the port where it was loaded onto a ship that could carry only one or two stones per trip; seamen took a week or so to transport this cargo to Edo; and laborers met the stone at the recently created wharves at Edo Harbor and pulled it to the castle, directed by men who rode atop the block, waving flags and beating drums to coordinate the whole effort. The expense of paying and feeding thousands of men, the cost of the stone itself, and some of the burden of procuring the 3,000 or so transport ships were borne by the daimyo.

Most of the timber for the castle was also provided by daimyo. Carpenters would first determine the dimensions of the logs they needed; given the immense scale of the castle, some of the logs had to be more than thirty meters long and over one-and-a-half meters in diameter. Foremen then found the right trees and lumberers cut them, in places like the northern Kanto and to the west in present-day Nagano and Shizuoka prefectures. A log might then be carried over land by hundreds of men to a river, perhaps one that had been dammed to create a current strong enough to carry such weight. The timber was then rafted right into Edo or else to a spot where it could be loaded onto a ship that traveled the last leg of the journey to the city. This tremendous undertaking – the labor and sheer amount of lumber required for Tokugawa construction projects – depleted both the financial and natural resources of domains. It has been estimated that three Tokugawa castles alone, in Edo, Nagoya, and Sunpu where Ieyasu retired, exhausted about 6,800 acres of prime forest. By the mid-1600s, the flurry of building in Edo and elsewhere had consumed forests across the archipelago from the southern island of Kyushu to the northern reaches of Honshu.[9]

From the work of many thousands of men emerged a castle that emanated the strength and ensured the defense of the shogunate. A stunning addition to the main compound was a five-story keep measuring over fifty-seven meters in height from the base of its stone foundation walls, which still exist today, to its iron-tiled roof. Taller than any ever built in the realm, the keep towered over the expanded, multiple enclosures of the castle which included decorative reception halls, the shogunal residence, and the "great interior" or inner chambers for the shogun's wife and concubines, and female attendants.

With the castle at its center, a spiral pattern spun outward and ordered the space of the city, its rough shape influenced by topography as well as cosmology and military strategy (see Figure 1.1). Giving this shape some structure were the canals-cum-moats that radiated outward to an outer moat roughly fifteen kilometers long. Along this canal system at over thirty strategic points were huge, heavily guarded and fortified gates which served as both monumental structures and defensive checkpoints.

The spiral pattern informed where people lived and how the character of their neighborhoods developed, with samurai of higher status closest to the center and townspeople of lowest status on the outskirts. In the innermost part of the curve, to the east of the castle, were the mansions of those domain lords considered

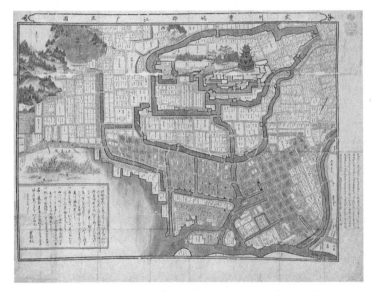

Figure 1.1 Map of Edo spiral. *Bushū Toshima gun Edo no shō zu*, 1632, hand-colored manuscript copy of printed map. Courtesy of the Tokyo Metropolitan Library.

most trustworthy by the shogunate; these were the so-called *fudai* daimyo who had been on the side of Tokugawa Ieyasu even before the Battle of Sekigahara in 1600. Next, moving clockwise to the south of the castle in what is today the area from Marunouchi to Kasumigaseki, were the domain lords whose loyalty to the shogunate was suspect; these were *tozama* daimyo who had fought against Ieyasu at Sekigahara and had since acceded to Tokugawa rule. Mirroring the way that domains were distributed across the realm, the dependable *fudai* were kept closer than *tozama* to the seat of power. Then, to the west and north were samurai of lower rank than the domain lords, mainly bannermen and housemen who, as direct retainers of the Tokugawa, were tasked with shoring up defenses on this vulnerable flank of the castle. Finally, in the outermost part of the spiral were the townspeople, the artisans and merchants who lived and worked in the crowded neighborhoods on the lowlands by Edo Bay.[10]

The daimyo who inhabited the inner ring of the spiral had been drawn to Edo first by Tokugawa enticement and then by shogunal coercion. Shortly after the Battle of Sekigahara, daimyo who came to Edo to win Ieyasu's good graces were rewarded with grants of land close to the castle on which to build their residences. After Ieyasu assumed the position of shogun, it became customary for daimyo to split their time between the capital and their domain, often leaving family members in Edo while they were away as an act of deference to shogunal power. In the mid-1630s, the shogunate made this system of "alternate attendance" mandatory, requiring all 260 some daimyo to spend every other year in Edo in service to the shogun. To ensure that a daimyo would not misbehave while back in his domain, he was compelled to leave his wife and most of his children in the capital under the gaze of the shogunate. The alternate attendance system swelled the population and fueled the physical growth of the city. Wives and daughters of daimyo, and sons who were not heirs, spent most or all of their lives in Edo. A permanent staff and their families were also kept in the capital. For small and medium-sized domains, this might be several hundred people; for larger domains, at least 1,000 and up to several thousand people. There were also 250,000 to 300,000 people, a quarter to almost a third of the city's population in the early 1700s, who traveled with their daimyo and stayed for the year in Edo.

To house all of these people, perhaps as many as a thousand daimyo compounds were built in the city. On the land closest to the castle was the domain's main compound with its administrative facilities, spacious quarters for the lord and his immediate family, sprawling gardens, and residences for chief officials and high-ranking retainers (see Figure 1.2). The daimyo

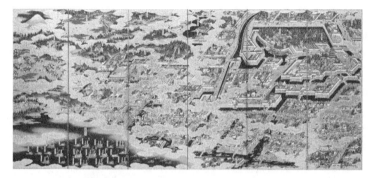

Figure 1.2 Edo Castle and daimyo estates. *Edo zu byōbu*, seventeenth century, left screen of six-panel folding screens, color and gold on paper. Courtesy of National Museum of Japanese History.

mansions of the early 1600s were grand and ornate with extravagant gates and reception spaces, intended to display power and to impress the early shoguns who regularly visited the domain lords. The front gate to the residence of the *fudai* daimyo from Hikone, for example, was about eighteen meters long and glittered from the gold leaf on its roof eaves, ridge tiles, and rhinoceros sculptures. In addition to the primary mansion, daimyo also built a secondary compound further from the castle.[11]

Within its walls, a daimyo estate buzzed with the activity of a veritable army of people who kept the domain's outpost in Edo running smoothly. Retainers managed personnel, handled shipping, performed secretarial and budgetary work, dealt with purchasing and storage, and guarded the estate. There were food tasters, tea masters, hairdressers, stable masters, and doctors. The domain compounds also drew in and recruited people from Edo and outlying rural areas to work as servants. It may be that at certain points in the Tokugawa period as much as 10 percent of the city's population consisted of servants to samurai – men and

14

women who filled a variety of positions in the household. Young women worked as pages, personal assistants, and attendants. There were also servants who carried palanquins, gardened, cleaned, cooked, ran errands, handled correspondence, fought fires, and served as bodyguards.

Keeping and hiring so many people in Edo was a large financial burden for the domains, which also shouldered the lion's share of the costs for their trips to and from the capital. The financial expenses of alternate attendance consumed half to three-quarters of a domain's total disposable income. Travel alone amounted to 5 to 20 percent of a domain's budget, depending on its distance from the capital. On the route to and from Edo, the retinue paid for lodging at inns in post stations, food either brought with them or bought on the road, and a variety of miscellaneous expenses like river crossings, tips, and straw sandals that lasted only four or five days of the journey made largely on foot. To make purchases along the way, notoriously heavy cash boxes replete with metal coins had to be carried. So physically demanding was the task of going to Edo that some domains instructed their retainers to prepare by getting into shape; others gave the travelers a break from their regular work before and after the trip to rest their bodies. Exerting high physical and financial tolls, the alternate attendance system together with the construction of the city were mechanisms by which the shogunate sapped human, natural, and financial resources out of the domains and into its growing capital.[12]

In the outermost curve of the spiral was the city's commercial hub – the districts for townspeople. In one sense, this area inhabited by artisans and merchants was laid out like that for samurai, with considerable shogunate attention to occupation. Because the shogun granted land to those who served him and stipulated that people in similar occupations should live close together, neighborhoods emerged based on trade. There were wards for smiths, coopers, carpenters, plasterers, sawyers, founders, gunsmiths, scabbard makers, and indigo dyers. But in most other ways, this space for artisans and merchants, in the lower rungs of the status hierarchy, was markedly and visibly different from that of the samurai elite. While the daimyo occupied the hilltops and high grounds of the city, or so-called Yamanote, the townspeople lived in Shitamachi, below the castle on the eastern lowlands and soil that had filled the Hibiya Inlet. While daimyo compounds sprawled across prime real estate and, with other samurai residences, claimed over 70 percent of land in the city, the commoner districts were densely packed. By the early 1640s, around 300 commoner blocks were squeezed into 10 to 15 percent of the city's land, from Kanda through the area around the Nihonbashi bridge to the Kyōbashi bridge. And while daimyo mansions were lavish, the houses of townspeople were modest in comparison even as they became more substantial over time. Commoners lived in simple structures with straw roofs, and then in two-story tile-roofed homes. Occasionally, a three-story building could be spied on the corner of a block.[13]

While some townspeople had called Edo home since the Hōjō days, others were pulled to the capital by its expanding commercial possibilities (see Figure 1.3). Among them were merchants from the western provinces of Ise and Ōmi who opened Edo branches of their retail stores to sell everything from tea to paper and cotton cloth. One such entrepreneur, Nishikawa Jingorō, hung out his shingle in Nihonbashi in 1615, offering specialty products from his native Ōmi like mosquito nets and the top layer of tatami mats. Other craftsmen and merchants were brought or called to the castle town by Ieyasu as purveyors for his samurai. One such man was a fisherman named Mori Magoemon from Tsukuda village, in today's Osaka prefecture, who was given

Figure 1.3 Activity around Nihonbashi bridge. *Edo meisho ki,* 1662, in Asai Ryōi, Ōno Hiroki, and Miura Jōshin, *Edo meisho ki: Zen 7-kan ao byōshi: zen, kō hen: Keichō kenmonshū: Zen 10-kan,* vol. 2 (Tokyo: Edo Sōsho Kankōkai, 1916), 6. National Diet Library Digital Collection, accessed August 2, 2023, https://dl .ndl.go.jp/pid/952976.

by Ieyasu a small island as well as fishing rights in the nearby waters of Edo Bay. In return, Magoemon agreed to supply Ieyasu's men with fish, and in 1603 his family secured permission to sell their surplus catch to townspeople. A decade later he opened a shop, and by the early 1640s his neighborhood of Nihonbashi bustled with people selling all manner of goods from the sea. Of the fourteen or so fishmongers who established themselves here, about half were affiliated with Magoemon's original group from Tsukuda village. For this, Magoemon and his men came to be regarded as the founding fathers of what would become the famed Tsukiji Fish Market. The goldsmith Gotō Mitsutsugu too was summoned to this eastern area of Edo, from Kyoto. Gotō was entrusted by the shogunate with minting and then inspecting gold coins in what was the earliest incarnation of the gold mint. To further address the shogunate's currency needs, in 1617 the Daikoku family from Izumi province, now in Osaka prefecture, was directed by the shogunate to establish in the Kyōbashi area the silver mint – or *ginza*.[14]

Sex work was given a specially delineated, and ordered, space in Shitamachi. To the northeast of Nihonbashi, farther from the city's center, a dedicated area for prostitution was created in 1618. An officially sanctioned "pleasure quarter" was the idea of a brothel keeper named Jin'emon who along with his fellow petitioners argued that granting them a plot of land and a monopoly on the sex trade would serve the shogunate's interests of maintaining social and political stability. Convinced, the shogunate allocated to these brothel owners some marshy land which they turned into a district named Yoshiwara, encircled by a moat and thick plaster walls and accessible only by its one entrance, the Great Gate. The women who worked within these boundaries were physically confined and legally defined, placed into the newly created category of "prostitutes" and so controlled differently than other women who, like the bathing girls in the many bathhouses across the city, sold sex outside of the regulated space of Yoshiwara.[15]

• • •

18

From the prostitutes on the periphery to the shogunate officials at its core, the people who lived and worked in the spiral of Edo hungered for a whole array of goods that were brought into the shogun's capital from across the realm. Some necessities of the city's growing population came from relatively nearby, like the vegetables, fruits, firewood, charcoal, rice, and rice bran from the Kanto region. As the land just west of Edo was nourished with water from the Tama River carried by new irrigation canals, it became more fertile and yielded barley, wheat, millet, buckwheat, and *daikon* radishes. From beyond the city's backyard, regional specialties were imported to provide daimyo compounds with tastes from home like dried bonito from Yokosuka domain or fermented soybeans from Odawara domain. Forged too were economic links between the shogun's city and the imperial capital at Kyoto as well as the burgeoning commercial and financial center of Osaka. From Kyoto came combs, wigs, cosmetics, pottery, household furnishings, and military supplies. Some of these goods were transported and sold by merchants who kept their headquarters and did their wholesale purchasing in Kyoto but operated as retailers in Edo. One notable Kyoto-based merchandiser was the Mitsui family who, in 1673, opened in Edo their landmark Echigoya store, the forerunner of the Mitsukoshi department store. From and through Osaka came cotton, oil, sake, vinegar, and soy sauce. The young capital's growing consumption demands not only propelled the movement of goods and established economic connections across the realm but also had an impact on the fate of towns, cities, and regions well beyond Edo. Hand in hand with the alternate attendance system, the needs of Edoites helped stimulate the growth of castle towns and transform Osaka into the country's preeminent market and bank. And over time, the city's seemingly insatiable appetite prompted farmers to shift toward monoculture for export to Edo, making them more vulnerable to hardship when their crops failed.[16]

Many of the goods that made their way to Edo were transported by sea, particularly on cargo ships that traveled between Osaka and Edo Harbor. Managed by shipping agents, these vessels doubled and then quadrupled in capacity as commercial relationships thrived. In addition to the water routes that connected Edo to the world beyond, and the newly created waterways that moved things within the city, the Tokugawa shogunate promoted the development of a network of highways and roads that linked its capital to the rest of the realm. The point of origin of this transportation system was the Nihonbashi bridge, constructed in 1603 in the area east of the castle over what was then the lower section of the Hirakawa River, later renamed the Nihonbashi River. From the Nihonbashi bridge radiated the system's main arteries that snaked down along the coast to Kyoto, westward through the center of the realm to Kyoto, and northward. By the 1630s, the shogunate had developed the main structure of this network and made clear its official character. Priority was given to governmental, rather than private, traffic and communications. And the highways were another means by which the shogunate exerted control over domains. Not only had they been built at the expense of the domains they traversed, but local residents were responsible for transporting Tokugawa officials and goods through their domain's territory. The Tokugawa also established checkpoints at strategic locations, designed to surveil everyone's comings and goings. Originally geared toward restricting the movement of those who had opposed Ieyasu in 1600, the checkpoints were also intended to contain the traffic of guns, prevent the wives and children of daimyo from absconding from Edo, and regulate travel. Travel permits were required for most people; this was especially onerous for women, who faced stringent restrictions and so often took to side roads to avoid checkpoints.[17] With both people and goods, the Tokugawa allowed and even encouraged movement when it served their interests and imposed strict controls when it could undermine their power and authority.

The shogunate applied this logic not just to exchanges between Edo and the rest of the realm but also to Japan's relationships with the rest of the world. Tokugawa Japan was not isolated from or closed off to the outside world, as it is often described. Rather, the shogunate calibrated its approach to any given country based on an assessment of its threats and benefits. In this calculus, those countries perceived as a danger to the Tokugawa were treated with hostility and kept at arm's length. Especially worrisome to the shogunate were Western European countries with a strong Catholic missionary tradition like Spain and Portugal; their religion was seen as socially and politically subversive, so they were banned. Other places, viewed with some suspicion but not considered aggressive, were deemed acceptable trading partners. The Dutch, who had arrived in the early 1600s, were allowed to stay and serve as a conduit for European ideas and goods because they made it a point to highlight the potential gains from trade while downplaying their Christianity. They were, however, Christian nonetheless, so were restrained to a small manmade island off the coast of Nagasaki, far from Edo. Relations with China were approached with similar apprehension; the shogunate would not establish a formal diplomatic relationship with a country that insisted on displays of deference, but it did authorize trade with China through both Nagasaki and the southern domain of Satsuma. And the Chinese merchants in Nagasaki maintained a healthy trade in goods between Japan and Southeast Asian countries like Vietnam. With those places that demonstrated respect for Tokugawa authority and thus conferred legitimacy to the regime, the shogunate didn't hesitate to pursue diplomatic and trade relationships. The Ryukyu Kingdom, or what is now Okinawa prefecture, dispatched diplomatic envoys to the shogunate and preserved its status as an active trading partner, contributing to the traffic of Chinese goods through Satsuma domain. Similarly, Korea sent major embassies of hundreds of people to Tokugawa Japan, bearing gifts and goodwill. The shogunate established a trading outpost in Pusan, and the domain of Tsushima handled the immense volume of trade between the two countries.[18] All told, even with its abundance of caution, the Tokugawa approach to foreign relations allowed European exchanges through the Dutch and trade relationships with much of Asia.

• ● •

Just before the retired shogun Tokugawa Ieyasu died in 1616, over twenty-five years after his official entrance into the dilapidated castle at Edo, he might have marveled at how his castle town was being transformed into his family's capital, the bastion of Tokugawa power. He might have sensed that Edo was well on its way to becoming the largest city in the realm, one that would eclipse the size of Kyoto and Osaka by the mid-1600s.[19] But it's hard to imagine that Ieyasu understood how various aspects of the city he helped mold would endure over the coming centuries – how topography, waterways, and the spiral layout would push against the imposition of a neat grid pattern onto the landscape; how the maze of houses would grow more dense; and how the building at the center of the city would remain an important political symbol. Even the farsighted Ieyasu couldn't possibly have foreseen how the hundreds of thousands of people who came to Edo would make the city their own, shaping its politics, fueling its economy, and creating its own popular culture, forever altering life in the shogun's capital.

2

Becoming the City of Edoites

IN 1714, word of a scandal involving a celebrity, elite misbehavior, and illicit sex buzzed around Edo. Inquiring minds and curious theater enthusiasts swapped stories about the unfolding drama of a famous Kabuki actor, a woman from the shogun's inner chambers, and a displeased shogunate. The affair was set in motion earlier in the year when women of the inner quarters of the castle were sent to pay respects at two temples on behalf of the shogun's mother, Gekkōin. Among the women was one of Gekkōin's high-ranking attendants – Ejima – who had been dispatched to Zōjōji, a prominent Buddhist temple and Tokugawa family mausoleum. It was reported that the women quickly took care of their official responsibilities, changed out of their castle wardrobes and into fashionable kimonos, and went off to watch performances by some of the most popular Kabuki actors of the day at the Yamamuraza theater, not far from the location of today's Kabukiza theater in the Ginza area. Once there, the women of the castle enjoyed themselves in reserved second-floor boxes. The group of merrymakers dove into a hundred lunch boxes and consumed much sake. At one point, heavy with drink, they invited some of the actors to join their party, including one of the stars on this theater's billboard – Ikushima Shingorō – known for his good looks and skill with love scenes. They then continued their festivities at a teahouse and the private residence of the theater manager, not heading back to the castle until after their curfew.[1]

The women's belated return triggered a shogunate investigation into the matter which allegedly unearthed a long-term relationship between Ejima and Ikushima Shingorō. Punishment was severe. Fifty-seven women were expelled from the castle, Ejima and others were banished from Edo, Ikushima and others were exiled, and a few of the men involved were executed. The manager of the Yamamuraza theater lost his license, shuttering the venue; the three remaining licensed Kabuki theaters in the city had to suspend performances for a few months, nine productions at temples were aborted, and restrictions were placed on teahouses.[2]

That women of the castle went to the Kabuki theater was not reason enough for the shogunate to act so decisively. Although conservative moralists frowned on such behavior, the women's patronage of Kabuki and samurai enthusiasm for performances were open secrets. This was not the first time that Ejima and her colleagues had gone to the theater, and they were known to have taken other excursions out into the city, to view flower blossoms or visit the Yoshiwara pleasure quarters. But it may very well be that this time the shogunate wanted to make an example of the offenders who were deemed to have crossed social boundaries too brazenly. The fraternizing between the women and the actors was one step too far, a violation of shogunate expectations of a purely spectatorial Kabuki audience and a clear status divide between women of the castle and lowly actors. The theater manager had not only failed to oversee his actors and prevent any trouble but had actually encouraged the socializing. Then, of course, there was the purported affair between Ejima and Ikushima which would have been considered illicit – a sexual relationship between a chief attendant of the shogun's inner quarters and an actor, technically a societal outcast and morally an ostentatious spendthrift in the eyes of the shogunate. Flouting status distinctions, Ejima and Ikushima stood accused of subverting the social order right under the shogun's nose.[3]

In the Ejima-Ikushima incident, as it came to be known, the shogunate sought to reinforce societal boundaries at a time when they were being crossed not just in the realm of theatergoing but also in the flourishing popular culture of Edo. There was Kabuki, a boisterous form of entertainment with lively singing and dancing, bold makeup, and dramatic costumes. There was also an expanding print culture with posters and mass produced books, celebrities and fandom, and exciting stories told in many forms. This urban culture had a particularly Edo flair, marked by the inescapable presence of the shogunate and the city's large population of samurai. But it was also shaped by the energies and concerns of a growing number of townspeople, the artisans and merchants of commoner status who were below samurai on the social ladder. By the 1720s, there were almost as many commoners as samurai in Edo.[4] So from around the early eighteenth century, the relatively young city came to foster an urban culture that offered allures for both the elite warrior and townsperson, reflecting broader transformations of a town born of shogunal visions and samurai needs. As townspeople tried to claim spaces, establish institutions, and create amusements ever mindful of shogunate authority and samurai prestige, the shogun's capital also became the city of Edoites – the residents of many different backgrounds from many different places who tried to make Edo their home.

• ● •

By the 1720s, a staggering number of people counted themselves among the residents of Edo. With a population of about one million, the city was likely the largest in the world at the time, rivaled closely only by Beijing. Edo was almost twice as populous as London, the largest of the early modern European cities.[5] The tremendous growth in the population and physical presence of Edo over the seventeenth century occurred despite devastating fires that plagued the city with such regularity and seeming uncontrollability that they, along with street fights, came to be known as one of the quintessential "flowers of Edo" (see Figure 2.1). With a major conflagration striking about every six years, with smaller blazes in between, fire was a defining element of life in Edo: a cause of terrible loss as well as a catalyst for tensions over how fires should be prevented, debates about who should fight them, regulations about architecture, and decisions about the use of space in the city.[6] Largely manmade disasters, fires fueled negotiations between the shogunate and various townspeople who had different interests and competing visions for their city.

Earlier in the Tokugawa period, for a good part of the 1600s, there hadn't been much of this kind of negotiation; the shogunate had acted swiftly and unilaterally to remake its capital in response to serious fires. The first of these was in 1601, when flames laid waste to half of the fledgling city, including parts of the castle. Especially ferocious was the Meireki fire of 1657, so destructive that it would come to be called one of the "three great fires of Edo," along with the Gyōninzaka fire of 1772 and the Heiin fire of 1806. In 1657, a parched Edo, starved of rain for almost three months, became tinder for one blaze which began at a small temple and then another, a cooking fire at a samurai residence. The fires consumed whole swaths of the city, about 60 percent of its area, ultimately claiming the lives of around 108,000 people. The main keep and living quarters of the castle, 160 estates of domain lords, and over 750 compounds of bannermen and housemen were decimated. The homes of townspeople, crammed tightly together and typically roofed with wood shingles, were particularly vulnerable; about 50,000 such houses were destroyed. So too

Figure 2.1 Fire at a bathhouse. Kichōsai, *Chinka anshin zukan*, 1854. National Diet Library Digital Collection, accessed August 2, 2023, https://dl.ndl.go.jp/pid/2542652.

were 350 temples and shrines, 9,000 rice granaries, and 60 bridges. The Nihonbashi bridge in the center of the commercial district burned, as it would nine more times over the next two centuries.[7]

As construction resumed only a few weeks after the Meireki fire, the shogunate redefined space in the city, now weighing the aims of fire containment and fiscal restraint more heavily than military defense and visual symbolism. To create firebreaks and more open areas in the city center, the estates of some domain lords were relocated further out from the main enclosures of the castle. And all daimyo were directed to build a supplementary residence on the outskirts of the city to relieve congestion and to serve as a safe haven in case fire threatened or consumed their primary and secondary compounds, many of which were also moved. To alleviate the overcrowding of merchant and artisan neighborhoods, the townspeople's districts on the east side of the city were extended from Shiba in the south to Asakusa in the north, and land further east, across the Sumida River, was opened up for settlement by residences, warehouses, lumberyards, and stores. The landmark Ryōgoku bridge was built over the Sumida River to encourage this expansion into the Honjō and Fukagawa areas. Nearly all of the temples and shrines in the heart of the city were transferred to its northern outskirts and the Yoshiwara licensed pleasure quarters were relocated to Asakusa, behind Sensōji temple.[8] All of this movement outward created new spaces on the outskirts of the city where townspeople's houses, merchants' shops, amusement areas, and religious institutions were interwoven in vibrant neighborhoods. One site that epitomized this mingling was Sensōji temple, which became a place for not just religious observance but also commercial opportunities, consumption, and popular entertainment. The relocation dictated by the shogunate after 1657 seeded the outward sprawl of the city such that by the 1720s the footprint of Edo had grown from about eight to roughly fifty square kilometers.[9]

As the shogunate exercised its authority in the aftermath of the Meireki fire, townspeople pushed back. Expressing their own views and asserting their own interests, some commoners disregarded regulations while others protested shogunal mandates. One contentious issue was the government's building codes intended to make houses more resistant to fire. Of particular concern to the authorities were the residences of townspeople who, while comprising almost half of the city's population, were crowded into a little over 10 percent of its land. Tenements, or long rows of houses, packed many people tightly together. They were typically one or one-and-a-half stories high (sometimes two toward the rear, away from street visibility, in violation of city regulations), not six as was common in Europe. But they were built mostly of wood, making them highly flammable. It's not terribly surprising that merchant and artisan neighborhoods, along with the theater district, were the areas most often ravaged by fire. In response, the shogunate encouraged commoners to daub their roofs with mud – a plea that was largely ignored. When in the 1720s townspeople were exhorted by samurai officials overseeing commoner quarters, or city magistrates, to adopt terracotta roof tiles as well as lacquered timber and clapboard siding, they resisted because of the cost of such renovations. For the next three decades, city magistrates tried various strategies to compel adherence, ultimately reaching a compromise with the townspeople: fire-retardant building codes would have to be followed for any reconstruction after a fire, the costs of which would be offset by tax exemptions and small subsidies.[10]

Another site of negotiation between the authorities and townspeople were the firebreaks created by the shogunate after the Meireki fire – land that was to remain empty, absolutely free of shops and residences. This vacant space was intended to make it harder for embers to reach key structures or tightly packed neighborhoods, to function as escape routes in emergencies, and to serve as a gathering space for fire victims. But despite shogunal efforts and edicts, these spaces didn't remain vacant but filled with merchants and entertainers who pressed the boundaries of what the shogunate would allow.

One firebreak of perennial contention was in a lively commercial area known as Edobashi which extended from the foot of the Nihonbashi bridge eastward to the base of the Edobashi bridge. Here you would find the quarters for vegetable sellers (Aomonochō) and lumber merchants (Hon Zaimokuchō) as well as general merchandisers and managers of wharves and other things marine. After the Meireki fire, which utterly destroyed this area, the shogunate tasked the residents of Aomonochō and Hon Zaimokuchō with tending to both the Edobashi bridge and the firebreak. Burdened by the substantial expenses of these responsibilities, these two quarters soon began to lease space in the firebreak to seasonal merchants who sold vegetables, herbs, and plants in the summer and fall, and others who peddled satsuma oranges in the winter. These vendors were later joined by dealers of pine branches used for New Year's decorations and sellers of what were named "Western melons" or watermelons. The leaders of Aomonochō and Hon Zaimokuchō then began to lease land in the firebreak for more permanent, year-round establishments: shops that sold face powder, rouge, fragrances, soaps, hair accessories, socks, and sundries; teahouses that offered a hot beverage and snacks to shoppers and others; fortune tellers; firewood vendors; and used booksellers. The shogunate was well aware of these establishments in the compromised firebreak and allowed the two quarters to keep them open, but it also called upon its authority to impose conditions. All of the shops had to be stalls; they couldn't be a combination of a shop and a residence as was typical in merchant neighborhoods. They were to be built such that they could be taken down quickly in the event of a fire. And no one was to live in the firebreak.

By the early 1700s, Aomonochō and Hon Zaimokuchō were renting space in the firebreak to more than 100 stalls but still seemed to be short on revenue. When the two quarters moved to conclude yet more leases in 1707 to maximize earnings, they provoked a three-sided conflict involving different groups of townspeople and the shogunate. The dispute pitted the leadership of Aomonochō and Hon Zaimokuchō against the owners of established stalls who didn't want any more competition and staunchly opposed the granting of leases to additional businesses. For its part, the shogunate acknowledged that the two quarters needed income but also sought to preserve the integrity of the firebreak. In a decision that simultaneously granted concessions, limited privileges, and affirmed shogunal authority, the government allowed all established shops to continue operating but placed a permanent cap on the number of businesses at 107 stalls. It also confirmed the ban on combined shop-residences and imposed on stall owners the responsibility of firefighting around Edobashi. And, in a reflection of its concern with the maintenance of social order, the shogunate also required all stall owners to sign a written oath guaranteeing that they would abide by laws and the norms of decorum – to not fight, be rude, or stand about idly.

In the 1730s, townspeople pushed still further what was permissible in the firebreak. In 1732, two merchants who were also town elders, or merchants entrusted by samurai higher-ups with city administration, sought permission to convert two of their storehouses into "residential warehouses." With the assent of the city magistrates, the enterprising Kitamura Hikoemon and Naraya Ichiemon promptly knocked down the storehouses and built their "residential warehouses," a deceptive euphemism for housing rented by merchants. Indeed, the structures that they constructed were in the style of merchant housing complete with tiled roofs and clapboard planks. By the later decades of the 1700s, people were living in the firebreak, stalls had been rebuilt as ordinary shops, and a Shinto shrine to the guardian deity of Edobashi had been erected. Entertainment was provided in the streets and at storytelling halls, archery galleries with "arrow-pulling maidens," and "teahouses."[11]

The firebreak at Edobashi wasn't unusual in its transformation from an empty space to a vibrant merchant neighborhood and public area for selling, buying, living, worshipping, and playing. By the early 1800s, many firebreaks across the city had been appropriated by everyone from itinerant peddlers and street performers to daimyo seeking land for construction. Through a series of negotiated settlements between the government and various Edoites, firebreaks created and managed by shogunal authority became dynamic spaces of urban life and culture.

Like the firebreaks, firefighting too was refashioned through friction between city authorities and residents. At the time of the Meireki fire, samurai and commoners were responsible for battling fires in their respective areas of the city. After 1657, the shogunate organized warriors more formally to protect the castle, especially, from flames. It created a fire guard consisting entirely of samurai who ostensibly served the whole city but were strategically stationed to shore up the vulnerable flanks of the castle. Then came the brigades who oversaw the safety of particular sites such as castle gates, bridges, temples, and granaries. Slightly later, major daimyo won authorization from the shogunate to form their own brigades for battling fires not just on, but also near, their estates. But in 1717, the government began to create a citywide firefighting system that shifted more and more responsibilities onto the shoulders of commoners. No longer comfortable with entrusting merchants and artisans with the safety of their own neighborhoods, the city magistrate ordered each quarter to create a permanent standing force of residents to fight fires. This approach was soon expanded as the city magistrate mandated that a company of commoner men be maintained in each of forty-seven precincts across the city. Eventually, the forty-seven companies merged into eight brigades that served all of the precincts. And these commoner firefighters were increasingly depended on to battle blazes at samurai residences as well; in 1747, they were even called to a fire at one of the central enclosures of the shogun's castle. As the commoner brigades won people's confidence, their composition also shifted from ordinary residents who often had minimal firefighting skills to local roofers and construction laborers who were much more adept at the requisite roof work and demolition. By the late 1700s, these commoner brigades had proven themselves more effective than warrior squads and became the preeminent firefighting organization for Edo.

The gradual transformation of firefighting into a largely commoner institution was met with resistance from various townspeople all along the way. Some had ideas for improvements in organization, logistics, and composition. Others protested the burdens that the system inflicted on them. In the 1720s, when the townspeople's companies consisted mainly of servants and tenants, those property owners for whom the servants worked and to whom the tenants paid rent complained of labor and financial hardships. For their part, tenants and other poorer townspeople who didn't want to shoulder disproportionate responsibility for firefighting just didn't show up for fire duty. And when the commoner brigades came to be composed of hired roofers and construction laborers, neighborhoods bristled at the cost. Even as townspeople came to occupy important roles in the organization and system for fighting fires in the city, they expressed frustration with the terms of their inheritance of an important Edo institution.[12]

• • •

When Ejima and her cohort left Zōjōji temple for the Yamamuraza theater on that fateful day in 1714, they traveled from the southern edge of the city into the heart of its commercial district. Here in the center of Edo were the four theaters licensed by the shogunate as the only authorized venues for Kabuki performances. On approach, the Yamamuraza would have been a striking sight (see Figure 2.2). The building was crowned by an imposing tower like those that adorned the residences of elite samurai, an architectural flourish and symbol of privilege reserved for only the four official theaters. From the tower hung a large cloth banner displaying the theater's crest; mounted just below were huge wooden billboards with the names of the theater's owner and famous actors. More modest billboards on the building advertised the plays. And from the 1720s onward, they were accompanied by colorful life-sized paintings of their scenes. Out in front standing on a low platform were men who tried to draw in passersby by calling out to them, whistling, and mimicking the actors performing lines from the play. The spectacle outside of the theater seamlessly mixed signs of shogunal sanction and regulation, creative energy, celebrity culture, and commercial interest, all of which fashioned the cultural phenomenon of Kabuki. And it was a tantalizing glimpse of the entertainment just inside the theater's doors.

The enticed bought their tickets and stepped through a doorway and under a short curtain into the theater (see Figure 2.3). Many audience members rented a reed mat on which to sit and found a spot on the crowded main floor below stage level. The prime seats were in the front and along the narrow runway extending from the left side of the stage to the back of the theater on which actors made dramatic entrances and exits through the throng of spectators. Those headed to the more expensive box seats came in through a different doorway and climbed stairs to the upper galleries. These choice spots were connected by passageways to the actors'

Figure 2.2 Outside the Nakamuraza theater. Hishikawa Moronobu, *Kabuki zu byōbu*, late seventeenth century. Courtesy of DNP Image Archives and the Tokyo National Museum.

dressing rooms behind the stage. These corridors had been intended as a way for actors to reach the runway, but they also came to be used

Figure 2.3 Inside the Nakamuraza theater. Toyokuni I, *Odori keiyō Edo e no sakae*, no. 118-0023~0025, 1817. Courtesy of the Waseda University Tsubouchi Memorial Theater Museum.

by theatergoers who wanted to visit actors in their dressing rooms and by actors who were invited to join spectators in their boxes. The goings-on in the galleries could also be conveniently hidden from public sight by bamboo blinds hung across the front of the boxes.[13]

In the aftermath of the Ejima-Ikushima incident, the shogunate imposed new regulations on the interior space of the three remaining licensed theaters to discourage illicit socializing between actors and theatergoers. It limited box seats to one tier, prohibited the construction of passageways to the galleries, and banned the use of blinds, curtains, and screens in the boxes. To reduce opportunities for fraternization and dampen the popularity of Kabuki, the shogunate forbid sturdy waterproof roofs that enabled performances on rainy days. And it stipulated that the final curtain must fall by 5 pm, which had the additional benefit of discouraging the use of torches for lighting, a fire hazard. The mandated closing time seems to have stuck. With plays ending before dark, they often began before dawn – the drum in the theater's tower was struck before sunrise to draw people to a full day of performances. Other restrictions, however, were disregarded or renegotiated by theatergoers and owners over time. Blinds and screens in the boxes were regularly depicted in paintings. Although their rendering may have reflected artistic liberties, the repeated prohibition of such visual obstructions by the shogunate suggests that they continued to be used. In more direct protest, theaters objected to the effective prohibition of staging performances on rainy days, arguing that it was hurting not just them but also the various merchants who relied on the theaters for business. Three years after the incident, the city magistrate agreed to let theaters rebuild roofs of wood. But he then added in 1724 that the roofs must be made of fireproof tiles. The theater owners balked at having to purchase the expensive tile but determined that they could handle the cost if the shogunate would allow more than one tier of box seating. The city magistrate acceded, and the theaters – which had kept the more expensive second-floor galleries – reopened the first-floor boxes. Within a decade of the Ejima-Ikushima affair, the three licensed Kabuki theaters left standing had regained their capacity to hold performances regardless of the weather and to sell tickets for box seats on two levels complete with whatever privacy from view might be desired. Teahouses, too, reprised their role of providing a space where spectators and actors could socialize.

Enjoying Kabuki was far from the staid and formal affair it is today. Inside the space of the theater, audiences were festive, uninhibited, and downright rambunctious. The theatergoers on the main floor ordered food and drink from vendors who would make their way through the crowd to deliver lunch boxes, sushi, sweets, tea, and sake. Those in the boxes reserved their refreshments from teahouses that catered Kabuki performances. Spectators also actively responded to what was happening on stage, standing at their seat or stepping onto the runway to express their enthusiasm for a particular actor, shouting or breaking into applause after a moment of impressive acting, and communicating any dissatisfaction by hurling their seating mats onto the stage. Such audience involvement was encouraged by the understanding that a play was an unfolding and malleable event, not a routinized presentation that was rigidly faithful to a set script.

Ejima and her fellow revelers engaged with a production in which all of the roles, including women characters, were performed by adult men. This was an adaptation to a series of shogunate prohibitions in the first half of the 1600s designed to sever the relationship between the Kabuki theater and prostitution, and to discourage fighting and morally questionable behavior among samurai audiences. Women were banned from the Kabuki stage in a series of proscriptions in the 1620s and 1630s, the repeated issuance of such regulations a sign of how slowly and grudgingly the theaters complied. Productions with both male and female actors were also regularly barred through the 1640s. And boy actors were similarly forbidden in the early 1650s. The shogunate's aim was to curtail eroticism on stage as well as samurai patronage of actresses and boy actors, not because it had moral qualms about prostitution or male-male sex, but because it feared that such passions could lead to violence, mixing across status groups, and dereliction of various responsibilities. With casts consisting entirely of men, Kabuki did begin to focus less on a performer's beauty and more on storylines. But this adaptation to shogunate regulations clearly did not extinguish theatergoers' adoration for their favorite actors. Nor did it cleave prostitution from Kabuki. Of the teahouses affiliated with the Kabuki theaters, some provided catering and managed ticket reservations; others specialized in prostitution. In more of a legal gray zone, there were also teahouses with young male prostitutes associated with Kabuki whose clients were not just men, including samurai, but also women, including those from the residences of domain lords and the inner quarters of the shogun's castle.[14]

Despite the shogunate's best efforts, samurai were in the Kabuki audience together with an increasingly broad swath of townspeople. The government's prohibition of samurai frequenting licensed theaters seems to have gone unheeded and unenforced, and although its ban on Kabuki performances at samurai residences discouraged daimyo from hosting major actors at their estates, private stagings continued with actors not affiliated with the licensed theaters. At the Yamamuraza, Ejima and her colleagues surely saw others from samurai households in the audience; after all, it was commonplace for samurai, including the occasional daimyo, to enjoy the experience of going to the Kabuki theater. These warriors were most likely spotted sitting in the boxes rather than squeezing onto the cheaper main floor with the many commoners. On this particular day, one samurai and his wife were sitting in a first-floor box when they were startled by sake raining onto them from above, spilled by someone in Ejima's party. For their part, the theaters were attuned to the desires and expectations of their mixed audience of samurai and townspeople. They staged plays more suited to the female attendants of daimyo estates in the month when they were granted a leave to visit their families. And throughout the year, plays were filled with references to warrior history and culture in a way that spectators from all different status groups could appreciate. Together with the positive sheen put on shogunal lineage so as not to rankle the government, the presence of military characters and themes was particular to Edo Kabuki. Unlike its Kyoto counterpart, which had catered to imperial court nobles as well as wealthy upper-class merchants, Edo Kabuki was colored by its proximity to a disapproving shogunate as well as its early audience consisting primarily of samurai. By the first half of the 1800s, other iconic figures of the city – like the commoner firefighter – appeared in Kabuki plays. In the imagination of theater audiences, the commoner firefighter became a swaggering tough who was prone to fights. Between the familiar characters and narratives on stage to the shared space of the theater, Kabuki helped create an urban popular culture that reflected the uniqueness of Edo and Edoites.[15]

Excitement for Kabuki was fanned not just by the many allures of the theater but also by a vibrant culture of fandom, connoisseurship, and consumption. Kabuki aficionados kept up to date with the latest plays and their favorite actors through a thriving culture of print. Economic growth and increases in literacy rates as well as modest technological innovations in woodblock printing enabled publishers to mass produce text and images about Kabuki which were accessible to many and different Edoites. Posted around the city at bath-houses, barber shops, and street corners at the beginning of every Kabuki season were large advertisements for the theater's planned productions with lists of the actors and pictures of scenes, whetting the appetites of theatergoers. Those who could afford it bought their own copy of the poster from a street vendor making their way through the neighborhood. Reeking of cheap ink, a mix of fermented persimmon juice and soot, these prints exuded "the smell of the new theatrical season."[16] Theaters and teahouses also sold illustrated playbills that audiences could refer to during the performance and keep as a souvenir. And reviews of actors were published regularly in the first month of every year.[17]

The cultural reach of Kabuki was also extended by the marriage of celebrity fandom with things to buy and new styles to adopt. Famous Kabuki actors advertised products, their names appearing on everything from candy and cakes to kimono patterns. Those actors who played women's roles were especially influential in setting trends in hair ornaments and styles, kimono patterns and design, and even fashionable ways of walking and speaking for samurai and merchant women alike. Off stage, star actors didn't lead their lives as the societal outcasts that the shogunate considered them to be, but luxuriated in mansions as lavish as those of daimyo. So intoxicating was the whole culture of Kabuki that samurai adopted the mannerisms of actors, learning how to play the music and putting on their own amateur plays. As one shogunate official bemoaned, high-ranking warriors were "mimicking riverbed beggars (actors), aping female impersonators and stage heroes!"[18] For their part, the less wealthy among the townspeople aspired to participate fully in the culture of Kabuki. Young male clerks who worked at the well-known Shirokiya dry goods store in Nihonbashi, for example, reportedly succumbed to theft for two main reasons – to purchase an expensive courtesan and to enjoy an extravagant day at the Kabuki theater.[19]

• • •

By the time that Ejima and Ikushima became the talk of the town, Kabuki was a vital thread in the rich tapestry of urban society and popular culture in Edo – a lustrous symbol of the amusements that could be enjoyed by the residents of the largest city in the realm. By inhabiting the space of the theater, absorbing characters and storylines, and embracing celebrity actors, both samurai and townspeople participated in the creation of a common experience distinctive to and emblematic of Edo.[20] This flourishing urban culture of the early 1700s extended from the theater to the pleasure quarters, both of which were the primary subjects and inspiration of a new genre of woodblock prints, ukiyo-e, which captured scenes of this ethereal and playful "floating world" with its characteristic joie de vivre. Printing itself had become a mass phenomenon. Publishers and bookshops, many of which were clustered in the commercial district around Nihonbashi, made widely available works of various kinds, from city guides to culinary books which sparked imaginations about different places and different foods. Not all cultural activities and not all spaces were accessible by townspeople and samurai alike; status and class distinctions still very much mattered in people's everyday lives. But as commoners asserted claims to how they built their homes, how they protected their neighborhoods from hazards like fire, what civic responsibilities they should assume, and how they entertained themselves, their interactions with samurai and shogunate authority helped shape a city that pulsed with the energy, initiative, and interests of its many and varied residents.

3

Seismic Shocks

I N midsummer of 1853, the usual hum of news about town turned urgent and tense. Startled Edoites strained to learn about an alarming situation: massive foreign ships, belching black smoke, loomed at the entrance of Edo Bay. The vessels had flouted the convention of conducting business at the faraway port of Nagasaki and were now anchored just outside the political nerve center of Japan. Most Edoites couldn't see the leviathans for themselves. But fishermen, anybody with access to a boat, and anyone along the southern shore could lay their eyes on the commanding ships that dwarfed any they had ever known, including the junks or single-masted wooden sailboats that patrolled the waters of Edo. The four warships (two steam-driven frigates and two three-masted sloops) carried almost a thousand men. Residents of Edo were stunned by the ominous presence of these interlopers, fearing an attack on their city and country and heeding a shogunate warning that there may be war.[1]

Edoites rushed to prepare for the worst, upending the normal rhythms of their daily lives and throwing the city into disorder. Samurai, who hadn't had occasion to take up arms to protect the realm for over 200 years, now scrambled to buy weapons. Smiths busily forged swords and spears as well as armor and helmets, and sellers were even relieved of old second-hand gear, some of which had been pawned by poorer samurai figuring they had no use for instruments of battle. There was soon a shortage of weapons in the city, and whatever could be found was terribly expensive. Samurai and commoners alike also bought up food and supplies to stockpile, creating scarcity and skyrocketing prices for commodities like rice. The price of pickled dried plums doubled. In the streets of Edo, traffic came to a virtual standstill as people fled their homes along the coast for areas further inland, their arms, horses, and carts loaded with clothing, furniture, and other possessions. After some had left the city and others prepared as best they could, an anxious pall fell over Edo. The commercial center of Nihonbashi was eerily quiet, shops along the riverbanks were closed, and the fish market was deserted. The audiences at theaters were small, and the licensed pleasure quarters of Yoshiwara were subdued. Holed up and on heightened alert, people tried to avoid any further calamities by strictly adhering to fire precautions as if it were the dead of winter.[2]

The pervasive sense of insecurity and impending danger was deepened by the events unfolding near the mouth of the bay, where shogunate officials were engaging in diplomatic exchanges with the leaders of the imposing fleet. The foreigners, they learned, had been sent on a mission by the president of the United States to lay the groundwork for a trade relationship with Japan. Head in command of these American warships was Commodore Matthew Calbraith Perry, a seasoned man in his late fifties who had fought in the War of 1812, served in the Mexican-American War, battled pirates, and fathered ten children. This expedition was considered crucial to the projection of American might, a natural extension of westward expansion beyond the new state of California and across the Pacific. But if the United States was going to rival the British in Asia, or even make a transpacific trip all the way to China, its freshly minted steamships would need Japanese coal. So Perry and his crew had set off from Norfolk, Virginia, in late November 1852, traversed the Atlantic, rounded the Cape of Good Hope, crossed the Indian Ocean, and sailed up through the Strait of Singapore. On July 8, 1853, the *Mississippi, Susquehanna, Saratoga,* and *Plymouth* anchored in battle formation at the mouth of Edo Bay. And Perry awaited an audience to receive his demands.[3]

Staring down the barrel of a gun, shogunate officials eventually acquiesced to a formal meeting that was at once carefully respectful and undeniably adversarial. When the American representatives landed at Kurihama near the town of Yokohama on July 14, both the foreign guests and Japanese hosts made a show of their strength. Perry came ashore to the fanfare of his brass band playing the de facto national anthem "Hail Columbia" and was accompanied by several hundred men. The shogunate, for its part, lined the shore with thousands of armed samurai. But despite these dueling displays of power, the Americans clearly had the upper hand. Perry presented to the Japanese officials a letter from President Millard Fillmore bearing the seal of the United States, bound in blue silk velvet, and nestled in a beautiful rosewood case with a golden clasp.[4] Fillmore suggested it would be "wise" for Japan to change its policies and trade with the United States. He asked that shipwrecked Americans be treated well and urged the government to allow American ships to stop in Japan for coal and provisions. His letter struck a few threatening notes, mentioning that American steamships could sail from California to Japan in just eighteen days and referencing Perry's "powerful squadron," but it was clothed in the rhetoric of friendship. Perry was not so temperate. He described the American warships off the coast as "four of the smaller ones" and threatened that "the large ships-of-war destined to visit Japan have not yet arrived in these seas." Having delivered their message, the American delegation announced that they would return in the spring for the shogunate's response with, if necessary, "a much larger force."[5]

• ● •

The sudden appearance of American warships sent shockwaves through Edo that reverberated across Japan. Foreign ships, Russian and British and American, had made overtures and incursions before. But none had been so brazen or so intimidating. Fears spread about the security and future of the realm, which was increasingly thought of as a country or even a nation. The shogunate was already hobbled by financial shortfalls and political strains exacerbated by crop failures, widespread famine, and ineffective government reform efforts in the 1830s. And now, the shogunate found itself facing the difficult question of how to respond to American demands. All the while, doubts mounted about its ability to govern.

Before American guns delivered this jolt to the established order, certain foreign ideas had already created tremors in the way some Edoites understood their world. In March 1771, a physician in Edo named Sugita Genpaku excitedly accepted an invitation to attend the dissection of a corpse, a rather recent practice and highly unusual event. As a scholar of so-called Dutch Studies, Genpaku was curious to see for himself whether the inside of a human body more closely resembled the established Chinese understandings of anatomy or the European representations that he had been scrutinizing. So on the morning of March 4, he headed out toward the northern outskirts of the city where, at the execution grounds in Kotsugahara, a condemned criminal would soon meet her end and become the subject of this postmortem examination. Genpaku rendezvoused with two fellow students of European scientific knowledge at a teahouse in Asakusa near the execution site and was delighted to find that one of his friends, the Edo physician Maeno Ryōtaku, had with him one of the very same books that Genpaku had recently acquired – *Ontleedkundige Tafelen*, the Dutch translation of the illustrated anatomy textbook *Anatomische Tabellen* penned in German by professor of medicine Johann Adam Kulmus. Together with doctor and botanist Nakagawa Jun'an, the men made their way to Kotsugahara. Here, the dissection was carried out by a member of an outcaste group called *eta*, literally meaning "much filth," who were tasked with jobs considered unclean.[6]

As the skilled outcaste did his work, the three physicians were stunned to discover the accuracy of the European illustrations. The heart, liver, gallbladder, stomach, main arteries and veins, and suprarenal glands of the cadaver could all be matched up with the pictures in *Ontleedkundige Tafelen*. "We were amazed," wrote Genpaku, "at their perfect agreement."[7] The bones, too, were represented exactly in the Dutch book. The dissection had demonstrated not just the veracity of European knowledge of the human body but also the inaccuracy of Chinese understandings. There were no six lobes and two auricles of the lungs, the intestines and the stomach were not in the expected places, and the bones were not anything like they were described in conventional books. The Chinese ideas, it turned out, were wrong.

The physicians' "startling revelation[s]" inspired them to become trailblazers in the dissemination of European scientific knowledge. This was not the first dissection conducted in Japan; that had occurred almost twenty years earlier. But the autopsy at Kotsugahara moved Genpaku, Ryōtaku, and Nakagawa to share much more widely than their predecessors what they now considered the truth about the human body. They resolved to translate *Ontleedkundige Tafelen* into Japanese. The publication of the five-volume *Kaitai shinsho* in 1774 was groundbreaking. It made available to a Japanese readership valuable information about

European anatomical concepts and scientific ideas straight from the source. To commemorate this landmark achievement, a large plaque at Ekōin temple near Kotsugahara now memorializes the dissection, and a monument now stands in Tsukiji near the location of Maeno Ryōtaku's former residence on a daimyo estate where the three men had labored over the translation.

Kaitai shinsho sparked an interest in European medical knowledge among physicians in Edo, who became the leading figures of a growing national community of scholars committed to the study of European ideas. The center of gravity of Dutch Studies shifted from Nagasaki, with its cadre of official interpreters, to Edo, where a modest but dedicated group of intellectuals explored and spread information on anatomy, and also medicine, pharmacology, chemistry, physics, astronomy, geography, cartography, military science, and art.[8] This broadening of Dutch Studies didn't just spread information, it also forwarded a certain way of viewing and approaching the world – it established fundamental principles about the importance of evidence, the need for observation and investigation, and the intrinsic value in the rigorous pursuit of truth.

Such shifts in scientific thinking had ramifications for understanding other aspects of human experience, from morality and religion to politics. Scholars like Sugita Genpaku and Maeno Ryōtaku were steeped in Confucian thought, moral and political ideas of Chinese origin that undergirded the Tokugawa political and social order. But their engagement with European ideas provoked them to reconsider previous assumptions – often in complicated ways, and sometimes with subversive implications. Genpaku, for one, didn't completely reject Confucianism, but his embrace of European scientific concepts did lead him to challenge Chinese claims about its moral and cultural excellence. In Genpaku's assessment, China – the country that was the source of so many foundational principles of Japanese politics and society – might not be the center of the world. Ryōtaku went much further, arguing that the superiority of Western science reflected the superiority of Western morality. The embrace of Western science in Japan might then require renunciation of the existing political order. Explicitly critical of the shogunate, Ryōtaku determined that Tokugawa institutions simply did not measure up to those in the West.[9] By the early 1800s, even Genpaku was offering an unvarnished take on those at the top of Tokugawa society; samurai, he said, were lacking a warrior spirit because they had "grown up in extreme luxury for the last 200 years and ha[d] not known the word 'fight'."[10] And though he was quite concerned about Japan preserving its strength and autonomy, he acknowledged that more foreign trade might be desirable. As the specter of an aggressive West encroached on the shogunate, many Dutch Studies scholars were more inclined to turn a critical eye on domestic politics and to consider greater engagement with Europe and the United States. By the 1850s, scholars of Dutch Studies were prominent advocates of openness to the West in the political debates that roiled the country about how to respond to Perry.[11]

• ● •

Perry's fleet, his so-called "black ships" with their dark hulls and thick smoke, were frightening apparitions in the imagination of many Edoites (see Figure 3.1). In the thousands of newssheets that circulated around the city in 1853 and 1854, prints about the American menace eclipsed the typical fare about fires, earthquakes, and actors. The warships appeared as monsters with sinister faces and demonic eyes, spewing smoke and the fires of hell. Perry himself sometimes had the same devilish eyes as his ships and was variously a "hairy barbarian," a droopy-faced man in uniform, and a long-nosed goblin with supernatural powers.

49

Figure 3.1 Imaginative rendering of a "black ship." *Kurofune no zu*, 1854. Courtesy of the Kanagawa Prefectural Museum of Cultural History.

The fear expressed by these images resonated with readers and helped sell newssheets. And it fed a growing sense of identification among Edoites not just with their city but also with their country. It was increasingly clear that what happened in and around Edo and what the shogunate decided to do was about more than the shogun's capital. At stake was the future of the country as a whole. And in the face of threats to the country there developed an incipient nationalism – a pride, sometimes defensive and indignant, in Japan and its place in the world.

Stoking this feeling, newssheets conveyed to readers the supposed superiority of Japan's strength. One depicted husky sumo wrestlers helping Perry's scrawny crew load their ship with large bales of rice, an official gift from the shogunate and a symbol of Japanese prosperity and generosity (see Figure 3.2). The sumo

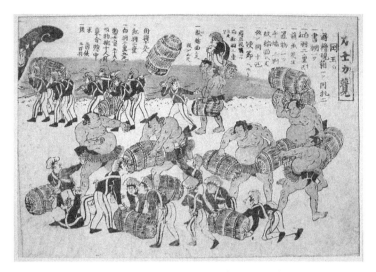

Figure 3.2 Demonstrating strength greater than Commodore Perry's crew. *Rikishi chikara kurabe*, 1854. Courtesy of Kurofunekan, Ippan Zaidan Hōjin.

wrestlers lifted the rice effortlessly, while the weak Americans fell to their knees, multiple men struggling to get a single bale off the ground. It took four of Perry's men to manage what came easily to one Japanese behemoth.[12] Another newssheet regaled readers with a completely fabricated account of powerful Japanese forces crushing an attack by marauding Americans. As the story went, an American steamship pulled into a harbor under the cover of night and unleashed its crew to ransack a nearby village. Having anticipated the incursion, local Japanese authorities had mobilized 1,500 men. When the Americans landed, the Japanese unit destroyed the steamship with cannons, killed 3,700 foreigners, and captured the fifty-three men who had raided the village, five of whom were sent to Edo for punishment. A caption summarized the message of the newssheet: "Our country is a land of military prowess and a land of righteousness, beyond compare with the foreign 'red hairs'."[13]

Conceptions of Japan as a country that compared favorably to others in the larger world were also rendered in maps. Japan was placed squarely in the middle of cartographic representations of the world, departing from Confucian versions fixed on China, Buddhist depictions focused on both China and India, and some centered on the Pacific with Japan slightly off to the left. Other pictorial representations were more brash, such as a print featuring "Great Japan" personified by the heroic Kabuki character Kamakura Gongorō Kagemasa who was modeled after a historical samurai famed for his bravery in battle. Positioned around the map were other countries of the world, their distance from Japan determined by their relative level of "civilization."[14]

This burgeoning sense of national community, shared by commoners and samurai alike, upped the stakes on the shogunate's handling of the American demands. Already the object of satirical humor and criticism in newssheets, the shogunate was now expected to formulate a national response before Perry's impending return.[15] But views in the country were disparate and impossibly divided. Some objected to reaching any agreement with the Americans and called on the shogunate to repel foreign overtures with prejudice and force. Some acknowledged that the shogunate had no choice but to negotiate with Perry and suggested some openness to engagement, if only to learn from the Americans so as to ultimately expel them from Japan. Some supported accepting the American terms so as to avoid a military confrontation that Japan would surely lose. Some were open not just to Fillmore's immediate requests but also to trade with the United States. At a loss about what to do, the shogunate took the unprecedented step of asking the roughly 250 daimyo for their advice. If this was an attempt to build consensus, it didn't work. There was no agreement on how to handle the situation, and the shogunate looked ever more indecisive and weak in the eyes of its critics.

In February 1854, as threatened, Perry returned with a squadron larger than the first – nine ships with over a hundred mounted guns and cannons, and almost 1,800 men. This time, the fleet advanced further into Edo Bay and dropped anchor closer to Edo at Kanagawa. During the Americans' lengthy stay, the shogunate entered into negotiations with Perry and engaged in the more social aspects of diplomatic relations. There were banquets and entertainments like a minstrel show and sumo wrestling. However civil, even cordial, these interactions may have been, they were punctuated by reminders of American military and technological superiority. In an exchange of gifts (see Figure 3.3), the Japanese officials offered lacquerware, porcelain, and silk as well as brooms, umbrellas, rice, and chickens. The Americans presented whiskey, books, and perfume as well as rifles, muskets, pistols, two telegraphs, a telescope, a daguerreotype camera, and, most impressively, a quarter-size steam locomotive, tender, and passenger car with 338 meters of track.[16]

Acknowledging these uneven dynamics, the shogunate took a pragmatic tack to the negotiations and eventually reached a relatively modest agreement that left Japanese dignity and sovereignty intact, even as it presaged a coming humiliation. By the terms of the Treaty of Kanagawa, signed in late March 1854, Japan did not agree to trade with the United States and did not open the port of Edo to American ships. But it allowed American vessels to put in at two other ports, granted those ships coal and provisions, promised good treatment of shipwrecked sailors, and consented to the stationing of an American consul at Shimoda, south of Edo. The first American consul would conclude with the shogunate in 1858 the Treaty of Amity and Commerce, or Harris Treaty, which

Figure 3.3 Gifts from the United States government presented at Yokohama. *Delivering of the American Presents at Yokohama*, c. 1853–1854, lithograph, in Matthew Calbraith Perry, *Narrative of the Expedition of an American Squadron to the China Seas and Japan: Performed in the Years 1852, 1853, and 1854, under the Command of Commodore M. C. Perry, United States Navy, By Order of the Government of the United States* (Washington: A.O. P. Nicholson, 1856). Courtesy of SSPL/Getty Images.

was considered a disgrace by many in Japan. Five cities opened their ports to trade with the United States. And not only did the shogunate agree to trade relations, but it also accepted disadvantageous tariffs and surrendered Japan's autonomy to set its own duties. The treaty also acceded to greater American presence on Japanese soil, permitting Americans to live in the opened port cities, where they were explicitly granted the free exercise of their (Christian) religion. Americans could also now reside in Edo for the purposes of trade. In an additional insult, Americans accused of committing crimes in Japan would be tried not in Japanese courts but in American consular courts under American law. Once the Harris Treaty had been concluded, similar agreements followed with the Russians, British, Dutch, and French. Taken together, these "unequal treaties" helped set the terms of Japan's engagement with the United States and Europe for the foreseeable future. For Japan, overcoming the affront on its sovereignty and overturning its legal subordination would become the prime motivations of foreign policy for decades to come. More immediately, for Edoites, the crises precipitated by the "black ships" and "unequal treaties" fueled political instability, a deepening economic recession, doubts about the shogunate's ability to govern the country, and an uneasy sense that all was not right with the world.

• ● •

About eighteen months after Perry's departure, the ground under Edo shook with unusual violence. An estimated 7.0 magnitude earthquake struck at around 10 pm on November 11, 1855, as many Edoites were winding down their day or falling into sleep. The initial jolt set off a thunderous bang as thousands upon thousands of buildings collapsed. At least twenty aftershocks roiled the city throughout the night, and for more than a week hundreds of tremors continued to shake the city. Several dozen fires erupted. While mercifully calm winds prevented their spread, the flames claimed the lives of many people in crowded quarters, including hundreds of women in the brothels of Yoshiwara. When its grim toll could be assessed, the Ansei earthquake was found to have killed 5,000 to 7,000 residents and injured close to 3,000 people. About 15,000 buildings were reduced to rubble. Edoites were left homeless, taking refuge in temporary shelters and scrounging for food.

The earthquake didn't strike the city evenly, convulsing most severely those areas in the lowlands originally built on landfill. It laid bare the early history of Edo, revealing where wetlands had been turned into buildable soil for daimyo estates, government buildings, and crowded commoner neighborhoods. Astonishingly, waters of the Hibiya Inlet reappeared, a reminder from around 250 years ago of the city's fragile foundations. The very selectivity of the earthquake also seemed to be conveying messages. That residences of elite daimyo and buildings of important government bodies like the highest judicial court, treasury, and city magistrate were destroyed was taken as a bad cosmic sign for the shogunate. Another ill omen was the destruction of around 1,400 storehouses around the city. The storehouses were associated with the shogunate, constructed as they were to government specifications. But their heavy, mud plaster walls and tiled roofs intended to improve fire resistance made them more vulnerable to earthquakes. Their collapse was deemed responsible for as many as half of the injuries and many of the deaths in the city. The especially extensive felling of storehouses, a symbol of wealth as well as an exemplification of shogunate regulation, was considered yet another cosmic indictment of the rich and powerful.[17]

To many townspeople, the Ansei earthquake did more than highlight the city's political and social inequities; it presented a chance to "renew the world" through the circulation and redistribution of wealth. As shogunate officials, daimyo, and rich merchants embarked on the reconstruction of their offices, residences, and storehouses, they required the work of skilled and unskilled laborers who were now in very high demand. Able-bodied men could find such jobs easily, and laborers from across the country migrated to Edo for work. Because they were in short supply, carpenters could draw five times their usual wages, plasterers and roofers up to seven times; dirt haulers earned as much as ten times their normal rate. The shogunate attempted to rein in wage increases, but to no avail. So high were the costs of rebuilding that some domain officials began summoning construction workers from their home regions to Edo. While the earthquake exacted a financial toll on many a daimyo and property owner, for the laborers it provided an opportunity to reap unprecedented earnings.

This flow of money into the pockets of commoners was celebrated and satirized in vivid woodblock prints now known as "catfish prints." Appearing just days after the Ansei earthquake, the large, colorful illustrations depicted the catfish as a familiar symbol of earthquakes and a divine agent of world renewal. As a medium for social commentary, the catfish prints highlighted a theme: the earthquake was revitalizing Edo by fixing the gap between rich and poor.[18] In one print, titled *Prosperity Treasure Ship*, the conventional image of the treasure ship was changed to witty effect (see Figure 3.4). A large catfish formed the body of a boat whose sail was the cracked plaster wall of a storehouse. And the seven gods of good fortune who typically rode in the treasure ship were instead seven skilled laborers: a carpenter, general construction laborer, high-beam construction worker, courtesan, roofer, tile vendor, and plasterer. These seven lucky souls sailed with bundles of copper coins in the shape of the iconic pine tree, atop waters made of blue roof tiles. Above their heads, the short text exclaimed: "With plans to make big money, we bravely rise up from the waves."[19] Other catfish prints captured not just the exuberance of those who benefited from the earthquake but also the hardship of townspeople who suffered, be it teahouse proprietors, musicians, comedians, or sellers of imported goods. Absent from the group deserving sympathy were wealthy merchants who were regularly derided in the catfish prints, an echo of historical resentments harbored by ordinary townspeople against greedy and well-heeled merchants with flush storehouses.[20]

Figure 3.4 A satiric catfish woodblock print, *Prosperity Treasure Ship. Hanjō takarabune*, 1855. National Diet Library Digital Collection, accessed August 2, 2023, https://dl.ndl.go.jp/pid/1302079.

Ideas about renewing the world, about imagining a future somehow better than the present, appealed to Edoites as they were beset by problems of national proportions. The Ansei earthquake, like Perry's arrival, was understood as a calamity with countrywide reverberations. Given their sheer magnitude and proximity in time, it's not surprising that the residents of Edo considered the "black ships" and the earthquake as related national catastrophes. Even shogunate officials, like the popular press, linked together the coming of Perry and the Ansei earthquake. In 1855, one high-ranking official concluded in a memo that these events "definitely constitute a heavenly warning."[21]

The frustration and impatience of Edo commoners with the twin calamities was expressed in a print titled *Dialogue between*

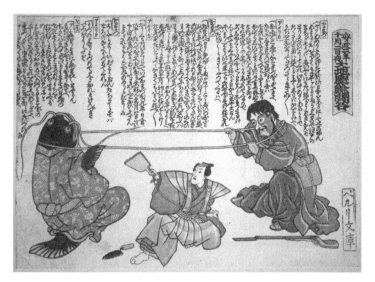

Figure 3.5 Tug of war between a catfish and Perry, *Dialogue between the Catfish and the American. Daijishin namazu mondō*, 1855. Courtesy of Kurofunekan, Ippan Zaidan Hōjin.

the Catfish and the American, in which a large catfish and Perry engage in a physical and verbal tug of war (see Figure 3.5). After several rounds of the catfish insisting that the Americans leave Japan alone and Perry refusing, the plasterer who stood between the two adversaries delivered the last word as the voice of an ordinary townsperson. "Both of you be quiet," he began, then went on to suggest that it was commoners like himself who fixed problems, the cracks and holes and broken walls. The plasterer expressed appreciation for the opportunities created for him by the earthquake but ended with a pleading admonition: "Both of you should try to resolve your differences without causing us any trouble. We don't want to see it; stop it!"[22] The print not only equated the earthquake and Perry as problems for townspeople, it also made no mention of the shogunate. While the United States was represented by Perry, Japan was portrayed not by a samurai official but by the catfish, who called upon deities and divine intervention rather than military might or any other governmental action to protect and defend the country.

By late 1855, the government was, in fact, weakened. The earthquake had struck with particular ferocity the compounds of *fudai* daimyo, those domain lords who had been most loyal to the Tokugawa even before the founding of the shogunate. The destruction of their estates was not just seen as a cosmic sign, it also drained their coffers, putting them in an unfavorable financial position compared to some of the less trustworthy daimyo. And it handicapped those on whom the Tokugawa most relied for defense. The shogunate's own finances were also strained by the earthquake as it hemorrhaged funds to pay for relief efforts, including the extension of generous loans and grants to its daimyo and retainers.

Even though many Edoites appreciated the shogunate's prompt and effective response to the disaster, the Ansei earthquake deepened the general sense that the power of the shogunate was limited. It didn't help that samurai attempts to secure the city had backfired; the firearms and gunpowder that warriors had amassed in response to the "black ships" exploded in the earthquake, fueling destructive flames. In an even more visible blow to the shogunate's image, the earthquake destroyed the artillery batteries or *odaiba* that had been built on manmade islands to guard Edo Castle. The devastation of these instruments and symbols of military defense was seen as yet another cosmic indication of the shogunate's weakness. Some Edo commoners went further, suspecting that the Tokugawa family had lost the mandate of heaven to rule.[23] One Kabuki actor observed in his firsthand account of the quake, "People are gossiping that possibly the government will fall."[24]

• • •

The Ansei earthquake was followed by a string of calamities that heightened doubts about the shogunate's ability to govern and deepened unease about the state of the country. In the five years after the earthquake, Edo was struck by a typhoon, an influenza epidemic, a cholera outbreak that took the lives of around 30,000 people, and a destructive fire at Edo Castle; that was followed by a measles epidemic and another cholera outbreak. The shogunate, aware of its deepening infirmity and a growing tilt in the balance of power toward the imperial court, attempted to forestall an outright rift with the emperor by brokering a marriage between the shogun Tokugawa Iemochi and the emperor's half sister Kazunomiya. Kazunomiya had no desire to leave behind her family in Kyoto and move to Edo, which she feared was overrun with foreigners because of the shogunate's capitulation toward Western nations. The emperor himself opposed the shogunate's signing of the "unequal treaties," but thought he could leverage the marriage for their abrogation. So in late 1861, Kazunomiya grudgingly stepped into her palanquin and departed her palace, embarking on a spectacular procession to the shogun's capital complete with an entourage of around 10,000 armed men and the pieces of a Kyoto-style home to be erected for her in Edo, all in an attempt to salvage the appearance of some solidarity between the imperial court and the shogunate.[25]

Around the same time, the shogunate and Edoites came to feel acutely the economic fallout from the signing of the "unequal treaties." The government struggled with various financial challenges as newly established trade relationships with the United States, Russia, Britain, and France drained the country of gold and pushed prices upward. Loans were provided to retainers and relief rice to day laborers, peddlers, and unemployed artisans. Recognizing the financial hardships afflicting domains, the shogunate significantly relaxed the expectations of alternate attendance in 1862, virtually undoing the system that had endowed it with control over daimyo and brought so many people to the shogun's capital. The ensuing exodus of domain personnel precipitated a dramatic drop in the city's population; over the next six or so years, the number of Edoites was cut in half. Those townspeople who had worked in or catered to the many needs of daimyo estates suffered an especially hard blow, and the commercial economy of Edo shrank, condemning the city to an economic depression and continued inflation.

Seeing little sign that their lives might soon improve, the less powerful and wealthy fused their economic, social, and political resentments into anger directed at the shogunate for its incompetence and at rich merchants for their enviable fortune. Low-ranking samurai who were denied government positions or who eked by on relatively small government stipends harbored anti-shogunate and anti-foreign animosities that turned increasingly and alarmingly violent. In 1860, such men attacked the shogunate official who had signed the Harris Treaty, assassinating him in front of the Sakuradamon gate of Edo Castle. About a year later, the Dutch American interpreter who had participated in the negotiations of the treaty was mortally injured near the Nakanohashi bridge. And in 1862, an attempt was made on the life of the shogunate's chief senior councilor outside the Sakashitamon gate of Edo Castle. Many of these low-ranking samurai assailants were from distant domains increasingly hostile to the Tokugawa. But Edoites too brought violence to the streets of their city. In 1866, residents were feeling squeezed by prices for food and other staples so high that only the humble sweet potato was affordable. Posters began to appear criticizing wealthy merchants and samurai of various stripes. Frustrated and upset, rioters smashed over 200 buildings around Edo, targeting rice stores, pawnshops, sake shops, and the establishments of merchants who had benefited from foreign trade.[26]

At a moment when the Tokugawa shogunate was as weak and vulnerable as it had ever been, townspeople reported that pieces of paper and tablets of wood bearing the names of deities were falling from the skies over the city. In celebration of these sacred talismans, they took to the streets, dancing wildly, drinking, parading, cross-dressing, and singing. If Edoites were like fellow merrymakers in other parts of the country, they exuberantly chanted the refrain *"ee ja nai ka, ee ja nai ka"* or "What the hell! What the hell!" This carnivalesque revelry was a remarkable expression of desires, hopes, and expectations for world renewal. For some, renewal was economic betterment; for others, it was political transformation through open defiance of the shogunate. The act of partying in the streets wasn't necessarily or explicitly political, but this extraordinary departure from everyday life was charged through with political meaning and portent. So faint was the presence of the shogunate and so loose its hold on power that people all across the country, from villages in western Japan to Edo, rejoiced in the possibility of change.[27]

As villagers and townspeople cried out for change, the most consequential renewal of the world – the toppling of the Tokugawa shogunate – was carried out by military forces. These men hailed from a handful of insurgent domains, almost all of which hadn't declared their fealty to the Tokugawa until after the Battle of Sekigahara in 1600, were thus located on the geographic peripheries far from Edo, had seen menacing foreign naval power firsthand, and felt aggrieved by the shogunate's decisions to accommodate Perry and sign the Harris Treaty. With a xenophobic streak and no historical loyalty to the Tokugawa, these domains coalesced around the aim of overthrowing the shogunate and replacing it with a national government centered on the emperor, who was to emerge from under the shadow of the shogunate and samurai rule as an empowered political figure.

In December 1867, armies from the southwestern domains of Satsuma and Chōshū seized control of the imperial court in Kyoto, and in early January 1868 the emperor officially proclaimed that the shogun had relinquished his authority and that imperial rule had been "restored," harking back to the era of sole governance by the imperial court before the establishment of the first shogunate in the late 1100s. The emperor was formally crowned many eventful months later, in the fall of 1868, in an elaborate ceremony at the Imperial Palace in Kyoto. Donning a coronation robe, the emperor entered the Hall for State Ceremonies, received the imperial regalia, and was proclaimed the emperor. Over a month later, the era over which he would preside was bestowed with a name meaning "enlightened rule," or Meiji, and he became known as the Emperor Meiji.

While the emperor's star rose, the shogun's capital fell into chaos as imperial forces pursued shogunate troops retreating from Kyoto to Edo in early 1868. One of the Tokugawa's chief negotiators observed that, "Edo is in great confusion ... the people are angry and upset ... the situation is like a boiling cauldron."[28] Advance men from Satsuma, mostly masterless samurai, set fires, destroyed property, and incited riots; some Edoites looted, and thieves stole valuable items. Women were assaulted. To escape the disorder and feared imperial onslaught, thousands of residents fled to the countryside.

In April 1868, overwhelmed by imperial forces, the enfeebled Tokugawa shogunate relinquished Edo Castle, surrendering the city that had been its capital for over two and a half centuries. In northeastern Japan, a civil war between imperial forces and Tokugawa allies was waged for over a year until the last of the Tokugawa holdouts was defeated. In Edo, pro-Tokugawa troops resisted the new regime until they were dealt a final blow in a devastating battle on Ueno Hill in July 1868, which reduced the

temple of Kan'eiji to ashes and left the northeastern neighborhoods of the city in flames. No longer could Edoites deny that the
Tokugawa regime and the Tokugawa era had ended. Having
carried out their coup d'état, its leaders expelled the Tokugawa
family and retainers, emptying the city of over a hundred thousand residents.[29] Edo, the once vibrant capital of the shogun's
realm, felt enervated and desolate.

• • •

One of the first questions taken up by the new, nascent government was where to put its capital. Osaka and Kyoto were obvious
and logical options. But key figures, men who had spearheaded the
imperial "restoration," made a compelling case for Edo. It was
centrally located, allowing for easier management of the northern
reaches of the country. Edo Bay was valuable for military and
economic purposes. And the city itself had many former daimyo
estates that could be used as government offices, as well as an
already large urban footprint and considerable room for further
growth and expansion.[30] In mid-1868, it was decided that Edo was
to be renamed "eastern capital," or Tokyo.

Later that year, the young Meiji emperor was escorted by
a procession of thousands of courtiers and samurai on a three-
week journey over the Tōkaidō road from Kyoto to Tokyo for an
imperial visit to the "eastern capital." He rode in an enclosed
palanquin, hidden from the view of curious onlookers who must
have wondered what he looked like and what kind of person he
might be. For most villagers and townspeople outside of Kyoto,
the emperor had never been an important presence in their lives.
The Tokugawa shogunate had been overthrown in his name, but
commoners across the country cared little about the imperial
institution. So when he arrived in Tokyo, where no emperor had
ever stepped foot before the fall of the Tokugawa, the Meiji

emperor was seen as a stranger. If anything, he was an interloper, the figurehead of an incipient Meiji government consisting of men who were not Edoites but had come from distant, unknown, and hostile domains to seize control of their city. Seemingly aware of his chilly reception, the emperor made a brilliant political move. He decided to throw a citywide party. A two-day holiday was declared, the streets were adorned with fresh-cut bamboo and pine, and almost 3,000 barrels of sake along with dried squid were distributed from the castle to wards across the city. The imperial sake was carried on sacred floats that were decorated with banners and accompanied by the music of drums and bells, and in some neighborhoods, by geisha. As residents imbibed their gift from the emperor, they listened to music, danced in the streets, and enjoyed mochi as if they were celebrating the ringing in of a new year.

In the spring of 1869, the emperor made his last trip from Kyoto to Tokyo. It was now clear that the imperial court would no longer be in Kyoto as it had been for almost 1,100 years. The emperor was to reside in what had been Edo Castle, reigning from Tokyo.[31]

Although the recently renamed Tokyoites must have sensed that they were living through a momentous transition, they couldn't imagine in these inaugural years of the Meiji era how their city would be transformed and how their world would be renewed. Some things were clear. The imperial institution would be more politically prominent than it had been in many centuries, and the castle in the center of the city would be remade into an imperial palace. And though the Tokugawa family would no longer rule and government in the form of a shogunate would no longer be, the city would continue to be the political center of gravity. But much was yet to be determined. Questions of who could participate in politics, how the country would define its identity and its aspirations, and how it would relate to the wider world were very much open. Tokyoites haunted by the many shocks of the recent past might have wondered if the new political rulers would be able to prevent the hardships they had experienced and to protect their city from another Perry. Over the next several decades, the debates and decisions about these formative questions would fundamentally reshape what it meant to live in Tokyo – to move through, work in, and find pleasure in the national capital.

4

Modernizing the Nation's Capital

ON a crisp fall morning in October 1872, curiosity drew a large crowd of Tokyoites to the Shinbashi railroad station. The new terminal building, constructed at the behest of the nascent Meiji government, was unlike anything they had ever seen in their city made of wood. Distinctively French in architectural style, it was the Gare de l'Est of Paris reimagined by an American architect, with a central one-story pavilion embellished by a decorative glass window, covered by a metal roof, and flanked on both sides by taller rectangular structures, two stories high and clad in stone (see Figure 4.1). The station was festooned with garlands and streamers of flowers for the occasion. Just before 10 am, the assembled Japanese government ministers, European and American foreign dignitaries, and expectant Tokyoites heard trumpets announce the arrival of the imperial procession. The Meiji emperor, young and still relatively unknown, stepped out of his carriage and strode over a carpet into the station's main hall and then into the waiting train that whisked him and his retinue across the twenty-nine kilometers to Yokohama. At Yokohama Station, identical in design to its Shinbashi twin, the emperor conducted formalities and then reboarded the train, making the return trip to Tokyo in just less than an hour. The crowd at Shinbashi, having explored every corner of the station, reassembled to welcome the emperor's return and partake in more inaugural ceremonies and festivities. From

68

Figure 4.1 Ginza Bricktown and a train departing the Shinbashi railroad station. Utagawa Kunimasa IV, *Shinbashi tetsudō jōkisha no zu*, 1873. Courtesy of the Tokyo Metropolitan Library.

a specially built dais, the emperor officially proclaimed the opening of the Shinbashi–Yokohama railroad line and deemed it a foundational step toward creating a nation crisscrossed by railways. At a shiny new train station in the nation's capital, on a day capped off with fireworks, the youthful emperor heralded the age of rail in a modernizing Japan.[1]

For the many Tokyoites accustomed to moving about the city on foot, the sheer power and speed of the steam locomotive inspired awe. One man who attended the festivities at Shinbashi was astounded to see the engine pulling a veritable small town behind it, with each train car as big as a house. Some curious onlookers had snagged a little space along the railway between Shinbashi and Yokohama, camping out with their bento lunches overnight or squeezing into the crowd in the morning, but were scared when the imposing locomotive roared past, rumbling like thunder and billowing thick smoke. One spectator described those around her putting their hands over their ears, shutting their eyes, and facing the ground. But fear and apprehension were eclipsed by astonishment, especially by the speed of rail travel. The train, moving at an average of thirty-two kilometers an hour, reduced the eight-to-ten hour walk from Shinbashi to Yokohama down to a fifty-four minute journey. Journalists and writers marveled at how the railroad had bestowed to people the power of flight. As one popular book exclaimed of the train ride between the two cities, "truly this is a wonderful means of putting wings on people!"[2] Attraction to the railroad grew as more and more people experienced the magical speed of the train, read guidebooks about railway travel, and hummed along to ditties about the locomotive. By 1900, people across the country were listening to the popular hit "Railway Song" (whose catchy melody still plays in train stations) and could belt out its famous first line: "With one sound of the whistle, our train swiftly departs from Shinbashi."[3]

In the years after the carefully orchestrated inauguration of the Shinbashi–Yokohama line, three of the ceremony's most striking elements – the railroad, the emperor, and the capital city – became resonant emblems of the "civilization" and "progress" that were the watchwords of a modernizing era. For the Meiji government, civilization and progress entailed the adoption and adaptation of Western institutions, technologies, and culture; from building factories, writing a constitution, and establishing a parliament, to changing hairstyles and ways of dress. Only in this way could Japan become a strong and prosperous nation capable of commanding respect from the major powers of the Western world. And only by displaying familiar symbols of Western civilization, by demonstrating that it did not need civilizing, could Japan protect its sovereignty from those very powers. Though initially propounded by political and intellectual leaders, the desirability of civilization and progress became so widely assumed and so ingrained that while critics of the Meiji government offered their own definitions, they didn't reject the ideals outright. Clothed in this conception of modernity pegged to Western nations, the government-led project of railway construction sought to transport goods and people more efficiently, promote technological advancement, and create a sense of national cohesion. As important, the railroad was a clear and recognizable symbol of Western-style civilization. The completion of the Shinbashi–Yokohama line was an irrefutable sign that Japan was no longer the "backward" country that had gaped at the gift of a miniature locomotive from Perry but had transformed, in less than two decades, into a nation capable of building its own railway. Unveiling this achievement for the world to see, the emperor was both presenting, and presenting himself with, an icon of modernity in an early effort to associate the imperial institution with markers of civilization and progress. Over the following decades, much more work would be done to remake a marginal political figure into a modern monarch who embodied national integration and accomplishment.[4]

Like the railroad and the emperor, the recently renamed capital was envisioned by the Meiji government as a showcase of modernity. Innovations in urban planning and design were focused on the capital, spreading only later to other cities across the nation. Civilization and progress were to be seen first and foremost in Tokyo, the city at the very heart of an emergent modern Japan.

• ● •

Despite the government-inspired ambition to dress the nation in the trappings of Western-style civilization, Tokyo did not and would not ever look like a European capital. Unlike the technology of the railroad or the recently enthroned emperor, the city was not new. The considerable size and infrastructure of Edo, coupled with the exodus of domainal lords and staff, rendered planning for urban growth and expansion unnecessary. And the strained coffers of the fledgling government snuffed out any visions for extensive reconstruction projects of the sort carried out in European cities of the time, like Georges-Eugène Haussmann's famous renovation of Paris.[5] Instead, Tokyo was remade in bits and pieces, fits and starts. The capital retained the scaffolding of Edo and its character as a pastiche of neighborhoods, as certain areas of the city adapted in particular ways to the aspirations of a modernizing nation.

An early opportunity to reimagine one such neighborhood was created out of a disaster all too familiar to the city's residents. In April 1872, six months before the celebration at Shinbashi Station, fire laid claim to about ninety-five hectares of the capital, an area roughly equivalent to forty-five of today's Manhattan city blocks, from just outside the Imperial Palace through the Ginza area to Tsukiji, destroying over 5,000 buildings and leaving over 20,000 people homeless. In the eyes of some determined and opportunistic government leaders, the razed land was a fresh canvas primed for the design of a Western-style district with fire-resistant brick buildings and wide streets. Their great project – Ginza Bricktown – was to be, in the words of statesman Inoue Kaoru, a "shortcut to civilization."[6]

Ginza Bricktown was strategically situated to encourage people moving around the middle of the city to relate the neighborhood with two other consummate modern spaces. To its west was the residence of the emperor, a reminder that Tokyo was both a national and an imperial capital: the center of an emerging nation and new home of the imperial institution. Just to its south was Shinbashi Station, increasingly representative of a national connectedness emanating from Tokyo as the railway network expanded well beyond the Shinbashi–Yokohama line.

Ginza Bricktown's proximity to the railroad station also enhanced its importance as a showpiece of civilization for Western eyes. Foreign visitors coming from the port of Yokohama by train would disembark at Shinbashi and walk westward through Bricktown to government buildings near the imperial palace grounds; or they might make their way through Bricktown eastward to their lodgings in the foreign settlement at Tsukiji. The recently established foreign settlement was on about nine hectares of reclaimed land along today's Sumida River, located such that any of its foreign residents (mainly from various European countries, the United States, and China) or any guests at its Western-style hotel would almost surely pass through Ginza Bricktown on their way into the rest of the city.[7]

What city dwellers and visitors saw and experienced in Ginza Bricktown was largely designed by the Irish civil engineer and architect Thomas Waters, hired by the government to create in Tokyo its own Regent Street or Rue de Rivoli. To evoke the feel of London or Paris, the buildings were made of red brick and stuccoed with plaster. The nonflammable brick had the added benefit of withstanding fires more effectively than wood, serving as both a sound economic decision and a representation of prosperity and permanence. Running between the European-style buildings were widened streets that were visually arresting and practical as firebreaks. Straightened and paved, the roads were also intended to make the transport of people and goods more efficient. To help ensure the smooth flow of street traffic and improve the experience of pedestrians, the capital's first sidewalks were laid, paved with brick, and separated from the road by gutters. Maple and cherry trees lined the roads, and pines were planted at intersections. Gas lamps were introduced to the main street in 1879, lighting up the neighborhood so that it could be enjoyed at night.[8]

The idea of Ginza Bricktown as an embodiment of modernity captured the imaginations of prominent artists, who rendered the neighborhood in all of its civilized glory. In one colorful woodblock print of 1874, Utagawa Kinuteru II depicted the hustle and bustle of the district.[9] Down the middle of the center triptych was a wide, paved street filled with just the right amount of traffic, the carriages and rickshaws moving far into the distance. The main thoroughfare was lined on both sides by a dense row of trees, spacious sidewalks for the many pedestrians, and fairly uniform, two-story, Western-style buildings. Utagawa Hiroshige III gave a similar impression of a lively and exciting Ginza in his print of the same year, foregrounding horse-drawn carriages and rickshaws against a backdrop of blossoming cherry trees, elegant pines, and two-story, Western-style buildings (see Figure 4.2).[10]

But the completed Ginza Bricktown didn't quite look as artists had fancied and government leaders had hoped (see Figure 4.3). Japanese craftsmen and laborers altered planned designs, adapting them to their knowledge and expertise. So the

Figure 4.2 Woodblock print of main street in Ginza. Utagawa Hiroshige III, *Tokyo meishō Ginza no tōri rengaishi shōka no zu*, c. 1874. Courtesy of the University of British Columbia Library.

Figure 4.3 Photograph of main street in Ginza. Kenchiku Gakkai, ed., *Meiji Taishō kenchiku shashin shūran* (Tokyo: Kenchiku Gakkai, 1936), 16. National Diet Library Digital Collection, accessed August 8, 2023, https://dl.ndl.go.jp/info: ndljp/pid/1223059/28.

same tile was used to roof brick buildings as wooden ones and the stuccoed exterior could look more like conventional plastering. Unfamiliar with sidewalks, some engineers placed trees and even some lampposts in the road so they wouldn't get in the way of pedestrians. For buildings not facing the main street, landowners could make their own decisions about whether to use stucco plaster or traditional warehouse-style plastering, or to leave the brick exposed.

Other deviations from the original plans resulted from deliberate challenges to the dictates of an overbearing central government by local residents of this neighborhood historically home to Edo's townspeople. The decision by Meiji officials to prioritize the construction of brick structures over relief funds for fire victims was opposed by the governor of Tokyo, who had himself lost his home to the flames. To build Ginza Bricktown, the central government expropriated land to widen the streets, took down makeshift shelters that people had built on their charred land, razed or moved traditional-style houses that had survived the fire, and relocated residents. Those who were evicted included poor artisans and small merchants who didn't receive any provisions from the government. In response, neighborhood residents built temporary homes in defiance of the authorities, publicly voiced their criticisms of the new buildings, and spread pernicious rumors about the project. They also refused to move into the brick structures. About a third of the over 100 buildings constructed sat vacant in the early years of Ginza Bricktown, with some remaining empty for quite a long time. Those who did take up residence in the new brick buildings found the construction shoddy and the interiors too damp in the humid summers; some demanded rent deferral. Faced with resistance, the Meiji government decided just a year into the reconstruction to abort their plans for brick construction beyond Ginza. Between its unpopularity and financial shortfalls, the Ginza Bricktown project was brought to a close in 1877. At that time, only about a third of the nearly 1,000 planned buildings was complete and there were fewer than twenty brick buildings in the rest of the city.

The shortcomings of the effort to thoroughly transform Ginza influenced how the city would be modernized in the ensuing decades. Planners learned that top-down imposition of a fixed architectural vision would generate so much friction with local communities that it would be impossible to realize. For its part, the Meiji government didn't attempt another wholesale reconstruction of urban space in Tokyo after Ginza Bricktown. Instead, when a certain neighborhood could be renovated, as after a fire, residents would be allowed to choose what their buildings looked like. The government would pay more attention to infrastructure improvement, from better streets and water systems to enclosed sewers, then encourage private sector initiatives as it ultimately did in Ginza. Over the decade or so after the end of the Ginza Bricktown project, the area became a commercial and intellectual hub of the city, home to modern shops selling imported goods and the headquarters of major daily newspapers – the precursor to today's upscale Ginza neighborhood.[11]

Government and city visionaries next focused their planning efforts on the core of the capital: the Imperial Palace and the surrounding areas to its immediate south and east. In the 1880s and 1890s, different ideas for urban reform coalesced around the principle that a civilized nation's power, and the Meiji regime's power, should be made visible through political symbolism and spectacle as well as commercial prosperity. Concentrating on the central spots of the city where it already had a presence, the government turned its attention to remaking the Imperial Palace on the site where Edo Castle once stood. It migrated many of the government offices housed in former daimyo estates to a cluster of new buildings immediately south of the Imperial Palace, in the Kasumigaseki district. Just to the east of the Imperial Palace, in Marunouchi, industrialists and entrepreneurs took the lead in transforming a forlorn piece of land into a prominent district of business and commerce.

When fire consumed the Imperial Palace in 1873, laying waste to everything from the emperor's quarters to the offices of the Imperial Household Ministry, the imperial couple took up residence in what was supposed to be a short-term home – a former daimyo estate, dubbed a temporary palace, located outside of the old outer moat. As it turned out, the emperor and empress would not return to living on the palace grounds for almost sixteen years.

Eleven years would pass before ground was even broken for a new palace. The delay was due in part to the emperor's repeated insistence that reconstruction would put too great a strain on the Meiji government's insecure finances. There were also disagreements about whether the palace should be built in a Japanese style with wood or a Western style with stone, as engineers debated the relative earthquake resistance of wood versus European masonry. But the postponement also reflected friction over a gradual shift in the meaning and significance of the palace as a political space. By the early 1880s, the Imperial Palace was no longer seen as just the residence of the emperor; a newly constructed complex had the potential to be a physical manifestation of modern imperial authority and national eminence. As government leaders came to agree that the palace would be the site for national ceremonies and diplomatic rituals, the importance of the reconstruction project came to trump concerns about its price tag.

In April 1884, construction crews swept aside the charred ruins of the first imperial palace (the lightly renovated Edo Castle) and began to erect its modern incarnation, a complex of thirty-six connected buildings. The private residence of the imperial couple was constructed of wood in thoroughly Japanese style, the Imperial Ministry offices were built of brick, and the public spaces intended for hosting ceremonies and welcoming foreign guests were more mixed in style, with much of the interior décor and furniture imported from Germany. Intended to project national power and civilization, the adaptation of German interior design in spaces like the famous throne room reflected a respect not so much for its aesthetics but for the ascendance of German might, and military might in particular.[12] When it was completed in October 1888, the new Imperial Palace was a regal site of civilization and pageantry at the very core of the national capital (see Figure 4.4).

Figure 4.4 The Meiji emperor and empress on their way from the Imperial Palace to a military review in Aoyama. Yōsai Nobukazu and Nagamatsu Sakugorō, *Nishonomaru kōkyo yori Aoyama kanpeishiki hōōsha miyuki no zu*, 1892, woodblock print, ink and color on paper. Courtesy of the Museum of Fine Arts, Boston.

The economic counterpart to the modern Imperial Palace developed just to its east in Marunouchi, spurred by an investment decision made by the industrialist Iwasaki Yanosuke. Iwasaki was the president of the Mitsubishi conglomerate, and later governor of the Bank of Japan, who in 1890 purchased from the Meiji government a derelict military parade ground overrun with weeds. Some thought Iwasaki a fool for spending 1.5 million yen on abandoned land in a sleepy area, but Iwasaki set about constructing a company town out of red brick. The first building was completed in 1894 and was quickly followed by a second and a third; after an inconveniently situated prison was moved out of Marunouchi in 1902, nine more structures would be erected by 1910. Following Mitsubishi's lead, other enterprises such as the Meiji Life and Fire Insurance Company, Mitsui conglomerate, and Tokyo Chamber of Commerce and Industry followed suit. As this central business district took shape, it came to be known as "One Block London" for Mitsubishi's Victorian-style buildings of brick and stone.[13]

As government officials and business leaders homed their renovation efforts on strategic areas of the city, a cluster of districts epitomizing the civilization and progress of the modern nation emerged in the center of the modern capital. The higher-end commerce of Ginza, government ministry buildings in Kasumigaseki, big businesses in Marunouchi, and the Imperial Palace at the nucleus together served as the engine and jewel of modernity – of Western-influenced aesthetics and architecture, administrative centralization, economic prosperity, and political power. Outside of this urban core, however, the piecemeal approach to urban reform amplified the existing patchwork quality of the city. Shaped by its Edo inheritance, modernizing Tokyo was a mélange of several renovated districts and many older neighborhoods, each with its own historically distinct character.

• ● •

Woven into the landscape of the modernizing city were the homes of poor Tokyoites, many of whom were lower-wage townspeople from the city's Edo days who plied their trade as peddlers, street entertainers, prostitutes, porters, craftspeople, day laborers, and ragpickers and in newly created jobs as rickshaw pullers and, in smaller numbers, factory workers. As in the later years of the Tokugawa era, they lived in ramshackle housing that was both scattered across the city and clustered in certain areas like the "low city," or Shitamachi, that encompassed Nihonbashi, reached further north to Asakusa, and extended across the Sumida River to Honjo and Fukagawa. As the city and the nation modernized, slums were squeezed out of some planned districts and concentrated in historically lower-status areas of the low city along the northeast margins of the capital.[14]

Urban renewal efforts magnified the income distinctions between city residents. To support the creation of the central business district, the Tokyo government had cleared slums and imposed regulations that pushed some property owners from the core areas of the city. Government fireproofing initiatives, for instance, required owners of lots facing major streets to rebuild structures in fireproof clay and plaster, stone, or brick; those to the rear were obligated to reroof their buildings with tile or other fire-resistant material. By the late 1880s, the ownership of a good many lots in such planned areas had changed, suggesting that those who couldn't afford to renovate their property decided to sell. And small shopkeepers and residents didn't receive the government support they requested to help fund fireproofing.[15]

As lower-income residents were displaced from certain renovated areas of the capital, the geographic marginalization of the city's poor was aggravated by a tremendous influx of rural migrants into the city. Struck by an economic depression caused by the Meiji government's deflationary policies of the 1880s, farm-ers not only emigrated abroad to places like Hawai'i but also poured into Tokyo in the 1890s and early 1900s. Settling mostly in the existing slums of the low city, the migrants swelled the areas of concentrated poverty in Asakusa, Shitaya, Honjo, and Fukagawa. As homes to the new urban poor, pockets of the low city grew far faster than the rest of the capital, and the population of the city as a whole catapulted from about 1.3 million people in 1897 to 3.4 million by 1920.

Along with the expansion of slum areas, the siting of most factories in the northeast of the city marked neighborhoods along the Sumida River as peripheral spaces. While factories of this era were not as large as might be imagined, with most employing no more than forty people, the disproportionate number in Fukagawa and adjacent areas inflicted environmental harm on these communities. On the east side of the Sumida River in Fukagawa, the Meiji government had built a cement factory, later purchased by the Asano Cement Company, whose black smokestacks spewed a white powder created by the burning of limestone. Nearby was the Tokyo Spinning Company and Tokyo Gas as well as the company that would become Kaō Soap. And on an island at the mouth of the Sumida sat the Ishikawajima Shipyard that had been acquired by an entrepreneur from the Meiji government. This concentration of factories began to redefine the eastern rim of the city as an industrial zone, polluting the waters of the Sumida River and the shores of Tokyo Bay.[16]

Further up the Sumida, just north of Fukagawa and Honjo, the Mukōjima area that had been a haven for recreation in the Tokugawa years with its temples, shrines, and gardens was increasingly populated by industries attracted by the relatively inexpensive land and readily accessible water. In the late 1880s, the Kanegafuchi Spinning Company opened the first of several large textile mills that would be built on this edge of the city, recruiting over 2,000 workers in its first several years of operation. Unlike the majority of rural migrants, and very much like textile laborers across the country, three-quarters of the Kanegafuchi employees were women. (Among lower-wage occupations, only ragpicking and prostitution were similarly dominated by women.) Most of these women were young and single, likely the daughters of tenant farmers, and lived in one of the company dormitories on site. The several dozen dorms were part of a comprehensive facility that included a bathhouse, two cafeterias, classrooms, a sick bay, and a quarantine room in addition to the factory buildings themselves. Other textile mills would follow Kanegafuchi's lead in housing young female workers, confining them inside their walled-off complexes in an attempt to discourage flight from their harsh working and living conditions.[17]

Although certain areas of the city came to house an especially large number of the workplaces and residences of the working poor, many of these neighborhoods were not enclaves of the lower classes but a mixed space composed of people from different classes and buildings of different types. The poor, almost all of whom were low-wage workers and not unemployed, occupied various kinds of cramped lodgings, with the poorest and most transient among them taking refuge in inexpensive flophouses. Paying by the day, most of the residents were single men who made money as rickshaw pullers, cart drawers, day laborers, street musicians, or itinerant priests. Others, including various craftsmen and small merchants, lived in flimsy wooden tenement row houses with thatched or wood-shingled roofs prone to fire and rot. Families squeezed into these one-room spaces with no running water, no toilet, and, in some cases, no kitchen. Water was drawn from a well, a communal toilet was shared with other families, and cooking was done and laundry was hung in the back alley. Interlaced with such residences were more comfortable homes; in neighborhoods like Nihonbashi, it wasn't unusual to see an intermixing of thatched-roof and Western-style houses. In Fukagawa, tenement row houses abutted the picturesque Kiyosumi Garden, owned by the family who founded Mitsubishi. In Honjo, there were slums, some factories, temples, and buildings that hosted national sumo tournaments. In various parts of the city, temples, shrines, warehouses, restaurants, tourist attractions, and fancy villas dotted the landscape; so too did meadows, ponds, swamps, paddies, and fields, especially in the low city. Within neighborhoods, residents of various backgrounds enjoyed going to public baths, or *sentō*, to soak in piping hot water and swap the latest news and gossip. And children would follow the singsong calls of itinerant peddlers offering cheap and comforting roasted sweet potatoes.[18]

• ● •

As the emperor had portended and the Meiji government had planned, the Shinbashi–Yokohama railroad line was the cornerstone for the construction of a countrywide railway network that bound the nation more tightly to its capital. In 1889, almost two decades after the opening of the Shinbashi–Yokohama route, the government unveiled its Tōkaidō line which stretched from Shinbashi Station westward across 605 kilometers to the city of Kobe. This trip from the Kanto to the Kansai region, which had taken twelve to fourteen days over the Tōkaidō road by foot or palanquin, turned into a twenty-hour train ride and was much less expensive than overland alternatives like the rickshaw. As one newspaper exclaimed, "How convenient! From Shinbashi to Kobe within a day!"[19] Over the next decade, private companies spearheaded railroad development, laying track in the country's largest islands of Hokkaido in the north, Honshu, and Kyushu in the south, mainly to support the mining industry. In these ten years, the distance covered by the railway system almost tripled; by the end of 1900, you could get on a train in Aomori at the northern tip of Honshu and travel all the way to Asa at the southern end of the main island.

At the center of the national railway network was the capital city, the reference point for all routes that were described as either going toward (*nobori*) or away from (*kudari*) Tokyo. With more efficient transport to a major urban market, prefectures in the interior and along the western coast of Honshu set their sights beyond regional trade, redirecting and strengthening their commercial ties to the capital. Goods from Tokyo also traveled outward more quickly and spread more widely along the rail lines, enhancing the city's standing as a trendsetter in fashions and tastes, and helping to standardize styles across the country. Through the accelerated movement of cargo and passengers, the train compressed time and space, bringing people closer and making them feel more connected to the nation's capital city.[20]

As fares came down and more people could take to the rails, the temporal conventions of train travel cultivated a new, more standardized sense of time. The railroad schedule – the idea that a train would arrive at and depart from a particular station at a particular hour – required a conception of time as precise, measured by the clock down to the minute. In the early days of the Shinbashi–Yokohama line, trains left the station on the hour between eight and eleven in the morning and two and six in the afternoon, with the gates to the platform closed three minutes prior to departure. At intermediate stations, trains came and went at a certain fraction of the hour. Unlike the river ferries of the Tokugawa era that set off whenever they had enough passengers, the railroad system required riders to learn the virtues of punctuality and to have access to a timepiece which, in the early Meiji years, most people didn't own. There was also no town clock. Railroad stations, along with government offices, schools, and military barracks, were among the first buildings to have public clocks or clock towers, promoting adherence to a fixed timetable. But even as the railroads were attempting to instill promptness in its customers, the trains themselves didn't always run on time. It wasn't until railroad employees, from station managers and conductors to ticket sellers and porters, gained experience with clock time, and after the railroads were nationalized in the early twentieth century, that the punctuality of trains improved.[21]

Along with inculcating modern conceptions of time, the railroad enabled ordinary people to consider new opportunities for leisure. A train trip itself could be a kind of recreation, especially with the addition of amenities from the more modest – such as bento sold at stations (the earliest of which was rice balls sprinkled with black sesame seeds and stuffed with pickled dried plums, with a side of pickles) – to the more extravagant – such as sleeper and dining cars. Recreational travel also became a possibility, first for wealthier Tokyoites in the late 1890s who could spend summer weekends at resorts to the south in places like Kamakura, Hakone, and Atami. Over the next decade, such leisure pursuits became conceivable for more ordinary Tokyoites thanks to discounts for third-class passengers, special excursion trains, and group rates. In July 1905, the Sōbu Railway Company introduced a special excursion train which filled with hundreds of passengers – tradespeople of various stripes, prostitutes, young, and old – donning straw bonnets and sandals, excited about getting out of Tokyo and enjoying the coastal resort town of Chōshi.[22]

The railroad not only fostered a sense of national connectedness by whisking people into and out of the capital but also created intracity networks by opening up different ways of moving within Tokyo. The east and west, north and south would come to be linked by the piecemeal construction of a loop line around the Imperial Palace, circling the city. The links of what would eventually comprise the Yamanote line – named after the "high city," or Yamanote, that encompassed neighborhoods in the city's west – were first laid between terminal stations. Initially stemming from a desire to move farm goods and other cargo more efficiently, a line was developed in the 1880s between Akabane in the north to Shinagawa in the south; in the early 1900s, the first east–west section was formed by a route between Ueno in the east and the newly constructed station of Ikebukuro in the northwest. When the loop was completed in the mid-1920s, it enabled passengers to move in a full circle around the city and drew the west closer to the core of the capital.[23]

Swift movement around the city was also made possible by other methods of transportation new to Meiji-era Tokyo. In the same year as the opening of the Shinbashi–Yokohama railroad line, the capital saw the introduction of horse-drawn minibuses, a kind of enclosed carriage accommodating a fair number of passengers and typically pulled by a pair of horses. By the time Ginza Bricktown was completed, Western-style, two-story mini-buses were traveling down its wide streets. While the minibuses were a Western import, the rickshaw was allegedly birthed in Tokyo around the early 1870s. Appearing first in Nihonbashi, the rickshaw quickly became ubiquitous. At their peak, there were more than 40,000 rickshaws on the city streets, quickly moving hundreds of thousands of Tokyoites, rich and poor, around the capital at inexpensive rates. The vehicles were initially quite simple, a platform on two iron wheels with a seat and an overhead cloth covering; over time, they evolved into black cabs with steps, a cushioned seat, and canopies. Rubber tires became standard in the early 1900s, improving speed and muting the clickety-clack of the wheels. But the streets still echoed with voices of rickshaw pullers dressed in trousers, shirt, and cap, shouting out greetings as they darted through the city streets.[24]

• ● •

Over forty transformative years after the opening of Shinbashi Station, in December 1914, the splendor of national pomp and circumstance drew a large crowd of well over a thousand people to the recently completed Tokyo Station, a culmination of the Meiji-era promotion of civilization and progress. The new station was a symbol not of fledgling national aspirations, as Shinbashi had been over four decades earlier, but of national achievement. Replacing Shinbashi as the central node from which all national railway distances were measured, Tokyo Station displayed its brick architecture with great flourish, standing confidently as a testament to Japan's arrival among the modern and civilized nations of the world. Designed by the prominent, British-educated architect Tatsuno Kingo, the three-story building of signature red brick and white ornamentation was his take on Queen Anne Revival style. The grand terminal was a strikingly long rectangle with a regal main entrance and domed octagonal pavilions on the north and south wings; accenting the building were turrets and rows of innumerable windows. For its ceremonial opening, the station's platforms were adorned with red and blue lace braids and flags of all the world's nations except Japan's World War I adversaries of Germany, Austria, and the Ottoman Empire.

The capital's new central terminal was also situated to project the nation's strength. The British-inspired architectural style visually linked the station to One Block London immediately to its west, spotlighting the hub of commercial and business activity in Marunouchi. Even more visible were the connections drawn to the figure of the emperor. That the recently enthroned Taishō emperor himself was not familiar to many was of no matter, because Meiji-era efforts had turned the monarch into a transcendent symbol of modernity. From the Imperial Palace, the modern monarch would only have to travel down a short, wide boulevard to arrive at Tokyo Station, where he would use the central entrance reserved for the imperial family and step into a magnificent rotunda embellished with marble and wood parquet floors, murals on the walls, and stained glass ceilings. Located in the heart of the city, Tokyo Station was an affirmation of Tokyo as both a national and an imperial capital.

That Tokyo was an imperial capital in two senses – the home of the emperor and the nucleus of an expanding empire – was starkly demonstrated by the political spectacle arranged for the station's dedication. While the first train out of Shinbashi had been reserved for the emperor, the honor of the inaugural trip into Tokyo Station went to a military commander: Kamio Mitsuomi. At the time, Lieutenant General Kamio was heading the Japanese forces that were occupying areas of the Shandong Peninsula recently seized from Germany. Traveling from China to the capital, Kamio arrived on the first train into Tokyo Station at 10:30 am to fireworks and an exuberant crowd cheering and waving flags. He then strode through an arch and towers specially built for the occasion, and paraded down the street named Triumphal Return Boulevard (today's Tokyo Metropolitan Road 404, known as Imperial Visit Boulevard) to the Imperial Palace for a meeting with the emperor.[25]

Every aspect of the design and presentation of Tokyo Station exuded national power. The "entranceway to the imperial capital" was a monument to the importance of the railroad, now a given in the daily life of the country. Its Western-style building with a large plaza and wide boulevard was a beacon of civilization and its integration with the emperor a reverberating emblem of the political, economic, and military strength of the modern nation state. But Tokyo Station was also a public space, a space for the public, which could be redefined and redeployed by any and all residents of the nation's capital.

5

The Politics of Public Space

WHEN Hibiya Park opened in 1903, the Meiji regime hailed the creation of a European-style urban park in the heart of the capital. Built on land just south of the Imperial Palace and nestled among government buildings, Hibiya was the country's first planned, public park – a space designed from the ground up with the distinctly political aims of promoting cultured amusements and holding large gatherings to celebrate the nation, the emperor, the expanding empire, and by extension, the Meiji government. But before long, the government's hopes for this public space were challenged by tens of thousands of people who assembled in Hibiya Park not to laud but to excoriate the regime.

On the morning of September 5, 1905, demonstrators began arriving at the park for a rally against the terms of the treaty ending the Russo-Japanese War. The war had been a bruising conflict between Russia and Japan, both aggressive empires with ambitions for supremacy in Korea and Manchuria, in northeastern China. For Japan, the war stemmed from impulses to protect the nation's sovereignty from foreign domination, spread Meiji-era notions of civilization and progress, and emulate the expansionism of Western powers. What began with a Japanese naval attack and subsequent declaration of war in February 1904 ultimately ended with a narrow, hard-won victory over the formidable Russian Empire. The concluding Treaty of Portsmouth gave Japan

international assent for control of Korea, over which it established
a protectorate; rights to railways and ports in Manchuria; and
territorial claims to the southern half of Sakhalin Island. But the
strategic footholds in Korea and Manchuria were disappointing to
a Japanese public that had come to expect far greater spoils of war
from a government championing the causes and strength of an
imperialist Japan. Hopes had also been raised by the nation's
recent experience in the Sino-Japanese War of 1894–1895, modern
Japan's first major war, which had been waged against China over
influence in Korea. This war had delivered to Japan a stunning
victory, a financial windfall in the form of a sizable indemnity, and
the acquisition of Taiwan as a colony. In contrast, at the peace
negotiations for the Russo-Japanese War, Japanese officials recognized how different this war was, how costly in lives and yen, and
how slender the nation's margin of victory. Bitterly disappointed
by their government and the terms of the war's end, protesters
gathered in Hibiya on the day the Treaty of Portsmouth was to be
signed, only to find themselves barred from the public park and
facing police at the barricaded entrances. One protester,
a newspaper reporter, stood on a box near a park gate and
moved the crowd with his words: "The government has taken
unconstitutional actions and caused the police to close off this
park, which is a place for us to enjoy freely. By what means can we
guarantee our freedom? In order to make our demands prevail we
must carry out a great movement . . . A treaty that could do honor
to the lives of 100,000 people and the expense of two billion yen
has been lost because of the present government."[1] At the park's
main gate, a few hundred policemen started to sweat under the
unseasonably hot afternoon sun as the crowd swelled to around
30,000 people – merchants, construction workers, students, craftsmen, factory hands, and rickshaw pullers who threw stones at
them, pushed down and struck the log fence barriers, and rushed

onto the grounds (see Figure 5.1). Standing in what they considered their park, protesters unleashed a torrent of frustration and anger with a government they felt had betrayed them, their nation, their emperor, and their empire.

After the planned rally, demonstrators poured into the streets in three torrential streams: about 2,000 people headed toward the Nijūbashi bridge of the Imperial Palace where they clashed with police; around 4,000 people attacked the offices of the pro-government Kokumin Newspaper Company, throwing stones and bricks and breaking down the door with logs; and almost 10,000 people descended on the home minister's official residence and set it ablaze. In the evening and well into the night, as the government instituted martial law, groups of several hundred to a thousand rioters spread across the city, razing police boxes. These small police stations, typically staffed by a couple of officers and embedded in local neighborhoods, were targeted by rioters who pelted their windows with stones, destroyed much of their contents, and set the buildings on fire. The burning of police boxes continued through the following day and into dawn of the next, as did the destruction of streetcars in the main streets of the capital. By the time the riot subsided on September 7, dampened by heavy rain, almost three-quarters of the police boxes in the capital lay in ruins. Some 500 rioters were injured and well over a dozen were dead; more than 500 policemen and about fifty firemen sustained casualties.[2] What had begun as an anti-government demonstration in Hibiya Park had intensified into a destructive riot that left few areas of the capital untouched.

In 1905, the demonstrators who made their way past the barricades and voiced their political views were asserting that Hibiya Park was not for the government but for the people. And those who followed in their footsteps reinforced popular claims on public parks and streets. Throughout the early decades of the

The Great Disturbances in Tokyo: The upper picture—Mr. Kōno, ex-president of the House of Representatives, speaking at the anti-peace mass meeting of Tokyo citizens. The lower picture—riotous scene which followed in consequence of the attempt of the police to prevent the ingress of the crowd into Hibiya Park.

Figure 5.1 Politician and activist Kōno Hironaka speaking to an assembled crowd at Hibiya Park in September 1905 (above). Conflict between citizens and police at the entrance to Hibiya Park (below). *Kinji gahō* no. 66 (September 18, 1905). Courtesy of Andrew Gordon and Visualizing Cultures, Massachusetts Institute of Technology.

twentieth century, confrontations between the state and Tokyoites accentuated the question of who government was for and who could be political, laying bare competing visions of how to define the meanings of public space in the national and imperial capital.

Tokyo had seen protest and political violence before. Large political meetings were a staple of the democratization movement of the 1870s and 1880s, and ruffianism was endemic to the electoral and parliamentary politics of the 1890s. But a mass rally followed by widespread physical destruction was new with the so-called Hibiya riot, which ushered in an era of popular political expression through violence that extended through the 1900s and 1910s.[3] In the early decades of the twentieth century, a wider range of Tokyoites politicized spaces in a city that was ever more imperial, colored in dissonant shades by the capital's deepening identification with the emperor and the expanding empire.

• • •

In its early years, the Meiji government cared little about creating public spaces in Tokyo. With more pressing items on their agenda for modernizing the capital, government leaders gave scant attention to cultivating anything like the plazas, squares, and parks of many a European city. Aside from the unbuilt area in front of train stations which might be kept clear for traffic, many of the city's open spaces were holdovers from early modern Edo, be it the firebreaks around major bridges or temple and shrine grounds with room for leisure as well as worship. When the government designated certain sites as public parks in 1873, all five in Tokyo were on temple or shrine lands that had historically been places for popular amusements.[4] None of them were modern public spaces. They weren't designed to encourage "civilized" behavior or promote state-defined modernization, in line with the government's ambitions. Nor did they have a democratic ethos, owned by the people and intended for the citizenry, in line with views later expressed by the Hibiya demonstrators.

There are a few instances of the Meiji government constructing modern public spaces before the opening of Hibiya Park. One was the Imperial Palace Plaza, built in 1888, which would come to showcase not just the emperor but also the empire as a grand stage for national ceremonies. Known today as the Imperial Palace Outer Garden, the area in front of the palace's main entrance had been occupied by sundry government and military facilities, from the library of the Home Ministry to grounds for horse training. Almost all of these structures were cleared to create a sweeping plaza with the recently reconstructed palace as a striking backdrop. Here, the emperor could gaze upon a crowd of his assembled subjects and they, in turn, could behold with their own eyes the emergent symbol of the modern nation.[5]

Imperial power was displayed on the plaza on numerous occasions, including the promulgation of the Meiji Constitution in 1889. After private rites were conducted in the palace sanctuary, the emperor donned his Western-style military uniform for the formal conferral of the document in the stately throne room. Then, in the afternoon, to demonstrate that the emperor was bestowing a constitutional monarchy upon his people, a procession of imperial household aristocrats, high-ranking government officials, and the imperial couple slowly made its way out of the palace and into the streets of the city. Along the way, the imperial cortege paraded through the plaza, which was filled with onlookers, including 5,000 schoolchildren who had been instructed to greet the glittering carriages with song and jubilant cheers.

The theatrical grandeur of the plaza and its association with the growing empire was enhanced in 1906 with the so-called Triumphal Military Review, an imperial review of military personnel that was to be the capstone of national festivities celebrating Japan's victory in the Russo-Japanese War. The plaza was prepared as an exhibition site for the nation's achievements and a majestic corridor for imperial passage. Grander entrances were constructed, and two wide, intersecting avenues were cut across the square. Just for the military review, monumental arches were erected at the two remodeled entryways and an extraordinary display of captured weapons was put on view, with about 70,000 rifles, 2,000 wagons, hundreds of pieces of artillery, and a massive stockpile of ammunition extending across the square.[6]

Like the Imperial Palace Plaza, Ueno Park was among the few modern public spaces forged by the Meiji government. In general, government leaders were as uninterested in creating parks as plazas. It's not surprising that, even by the 1910s, less than 2 percent of Tokyo was dedicated to parks and other green spaces, measuring unfavorably against its American and European counterparts. The capital offered less than thirty parks, most of them small, for well over two million Tokyoites. Ueno was a notable exception – the large space in the northeast of the city was singled out as a promising site for advancing the goals of state-sponsored modernization and nation building.

Transforming Ueno required sustained effort, given its strong associations with the Tokugawa-era past. When Ueno Park opened in 1876, the area had long been known as a spot for popular recreation. Famed for its cherry trees, planted in the mid-1600s, Ueno Hill was an ideal place for viewing their ethereal pink and white blossoms (a springtime diversion that present-day revelers in the park enjoy with food and much drink). The area was also deeply etched with symbolic reminders of the shogunate, including a shrine for Tokugawa Ieyasu and the graves of six Tokugawa shoguns. And in July 1868, Tokugawa holdouts had established their base at Ueno Hill, fighting to fend off imperial forces in the famous Battle of Ueno.

The Meiji government set about loosening these historical ties between Ueno and the previous regime, layering onto the early modern landscape its particular vision of modernity. A couple of months after the park opened, the government decreed it the site for national exhibitions, thought important for increasing the country's productivity, wealth, and standing in the world (see Figure 5.2). The first National Industrial Exhibition, held from August to November 1877, presented over 80,000 exhibits in such areas as agriculture, horticulture, and art in addition to manufacturing, machinery, metallurgy, and mining. The exposition was a truly national affair. Exhibitors hailed from all of the country's prefectures, and over 450,000 visitors made the trip to Ueno to peruse the displays in the Western-style pavilion, enjoy the outdoor stalls selling everything from lacquerware to candy, and just take in the fair that spread across ten hectares of the park.[7]

Figure 5.2 The museum and fountain in Ueno Park at the time of the second National Industrial Exhibition in 1881. Utagawa Hiroshige III, *Ueno kōen naikoku kangyō daini hakurankai bijutsukan oyobi shōjō funsuiki no zu*, 1881, woodblock print, ink and color on paper. Courtesy of the Museum of Fine Arts, Boston.

The emperor, as the emergent symbol of the modern nation, was cast in the lead role for the national pomp and circumstance staged in Ueno Park. It was the emperor who officially opened the park and graced the first national exhibition, as well as the second and the third. In 1879, he served as ceremonial head of state, hosting the American general and former president Ulysses S. Grant at an exuberant festival where they and the assembled crowd were treated to musical performances by military bands, impressive shows of mounted archery and swordsmanship, and fireworks. A decade later, Ueno was chosen as the site for the emperor's presentation of the constitution to the public. On the day after the document's promulgation, the imperial procession made its way through festooned streets packed with onlookers from Shinbashi, down the central avenue of Ginza, to Ueno for the formal announcement.

As Japan pursued its imperial ambitions, Ueno Park also became a site for public festivities championing the country's soldiers, the war cause, and empire. In December 1894, a large crowd came together to rally for troops fighting in the Sino-Japanese War. They listened to speeches, looked at exhibits of objects from the front, and hoped for a military triumph. Many Tokyoites attended similar events held for the Russo-Japanese War, and around 250,000 people gathered here in October 1905 to rejoice in their nation's victory.[8]

Over time, Meiji government officials, particularly those who had traveled to European capitals, came to see modern parks as sites not just for shared national and imperial rituals but also for cultural institutions that civilized and enlightened the public. At Ueno, this meant the addition of facilities with educational purposes, or at least didactic overtones. For artistic and aesthetic edification, the park welcomed a concert hall, the Tokyo School of Fine Arts, the Tokyo School of Music, and an art museum. To promote knowledge and learning, it came to house the Japan

Academy (modeled after the British Royal Society), a national museum (modeled after the South Kensington Museum), and a national library. The recreational activities encouraged of parkgoers were also a lesson in Western-style civilization. Visitors of means could dine at the French restaurant, Seiyōken. And those with a thirst for some excitement could watch horses race at a track encircling Shinobazu Pond. Adults and children alike could enjoy the Ueno Zoological Garden, the country's first modern zoo, where they could learn about kangaroos and leopards and bison, and also see animals enclosed, ordered, and displayed as specimens of the natural world. To underscore the sophistication of these pastimes, the emperor attended the opening ceremonies for the zoo and the national museum, and the first horse race.[9]

As people experienced Ueno Park, pausing before an especially striking piece of art in the museum or petting a camel brought to the zoo from China or celebrating a military triumph with compatriots, they were not just looking at a public display of modernity. True to the government's intent, parkgoers were also actively consuming and participating in a state-driven vision of imperial modernity.

• ● •

The modernizing impulse that transformed Ueno into the nation's first public park was amplified with Hibiya, planned from the very start as an urban park along European lines. Even before ground was broken in 1901, the Meiji government had impressed itself upon the sixteen hectares that would become Hibiya Park. For sixteen years, the land was under the jurisdiction of the Army Ministry, which used it for drills, parades, and troops guarding the Imperial Palace and nearby government buildings. After the army moved elsewhere, the field was reenvisioned as a modern urban park.[10]

To project and encourage civilized activities, its design and facilities were informed by Western models. Working with a space that was about 4 percent the size of New York City's Central Park and one-third of Ueno Park, the German-educated landscape architect and forestry expert Honda Seiroku applied German and French principles to about three-quarters of the area, creating an open lawn, decorative fountains, formal gardens, and thickets of trees. The rest was dedicated to a Japanese garden. Paths snaked around the park for pedestrians, wider lanes accommodated horse-drawn carriages, benches offered a place to rest and take in the scenery, and gas and electric lights dotted the landscape. The park was also equipped with sewers, bathrooms, and drinking fountains. In keeping with the idea that modern parks should better the public, the opportunities for physical rest and relaxation were supplemented with a large athletic field encircled by a running track to build strong and healthy bodies. Parkgoers could also enjoy a meal at the Western-style restaurant, Matsumotorō. Diners might lounge at Matsumotorō well into the night, sipping sake, beer, whiskey, or cognac. An octagonal bandstand was a later addition, inaugurated by a concert that included performances of a Strauss waltz, a Sousa march, Wagnerian opera, and Japanese military music. Lest parkgoers not know what was improper in a modern public space, signs were posted at all six of the entrances forbidding street performers, unlicensed merchants, unoccupied rickshaws and carriages, freight trucks, advertisements, inappropriate dress, and civil unrest.

Like Ueno Park, the government used Hibiya Park for large political gatherings to cultivate support for national endeavors, including the construction of an empire (see Figure 5.3). It sponsored almost two dozen events in the park's first few years, many of which drew so many people that the crowd overflowed into the Imperial Palace Plaza just to the north. The

Figure 5.3 Citizens gathered at the Triumphal Arch in Hibiya to welcome the emperor after the end of the Russo-Japanese War. Photograph, 1905. Courtesy of Buyenlarge, Archive Photos and Getty Images.

most well attended of the rallies, in support of the Russo-Japanese War, drew over 100,000 people. The government also held more somber official ceremonies here, including public funerals for statesmen such as the resident-general of Korea and former prime minister Itō Hirobumi, and the army general and former prime minister Yamagata Aritomo.[11]

At the same time, and contrary to the government's intent, Hibiya Park became the capital's preeminent site for unofficial mass political gatherings. In stark contrast to the government's view of modern urban parks as spaces that disciplined the public and promoted allegiance to the state, the protesters who laid claim to Hibiya in September 1905 insisted that it was a place where citizens could exercise their freedom to assemble and their right to express criticisms of government wrongdoing and state oppression. Using the language of democratic freedoms and constitutional rights, one demonstrator declared that, "The police actions at Hibiya Park were extraordinarily unconstitutional. They closed off the park which should be free to all of us. They prevented us from voicing our demands and violated our rights."[12] From the assembled crowd of 30,000 people arose impassioned shouts of, "It's illegal to close the park!"[13]

As the rioters moved out of the park and into the streets of the city, they expanded their demands on public space and strategically attacked government institutions they saw as curtailing their rights. The official residence of the home minister was a ready target, not simply because of its proximity to Hibiya Park but also because the Home Ministry was the state apparatus most responsible for restricting the political activities of the people; out of the many government buildings around the park, the rioters chose to torch the one representing the ministry that censored the press and managed the police. The web of police boxes in neighborhoods across the city also came to be seen not as approachable and trustworthy components of community policing but as agents of state power that reached down into people's everyday lives.

Trams were besieged by rioters out of a mix of economic insecurity and political frustration. Electric streetcars started running in 1903, around the same time as the park's inauguration, and soon crisscrossed the center of the city. Routes connected popular spots like Shinbashi Station, Ginza, Asakusa, and Ueno Park, each line identifiable by the specific color of its trams. This new way of getting around the city worried rickshaw pullers, who saw it as an economic threat to their livelihood. And riding the streetcar was expensive for many Tokyoites, even more so after a 25 percent transport tax was added to the base fare during the Russo-Japanese

War. Together with tax increases to finance the war effort and inflation, people felt squeezed. So when the terms of the peace treaty were announced, weariness with financial hardship hardened into resentment toward a government that demanded personal sacrifices without providing any reprieve or delivering much national gain. Criticisms of government indifference toward people's struggles were heightened by suspicions of corruption and greed, as rumors spread about the cozy and lucrative relationship between the home minister, members of his political party on the Tokyo City Council, and streetcar companies.[14]

The anti-government and anti-treaty ire that drove the Hibiya protesters was shared across class lines, even as those who channeled their political convictions into acts of violence were largely young, male laborers. The protest in Hibiya Park was organized by journalists, lawyers, professors, and politicians who voiced their concerns in speeches to large political gatherings and mobilized compatriots through activist groups. Most of the rioters were laborers of various occupations; there were the rickshaw pullers and factory hands whom the government feared as unruly, as well as shopkeepers and shop workers, construction workers, students, artisans and apprentices, and transport workers. Almost all of the people who took to the streets were men, as women were subject to legal prohibitions on various forms of political participation, including attending and speaking at public rallies. And many of the rioters were Tokyoites who lived in areas of the city, such as Shitaya, with relatively high percentages of tenement housing. All told, most of the tens of thousands of people who claimed Hibiya Park and the streets of the capital for the public were the common people of the city. From their viewpoint, the government had forsaken the shared will of the people – and the emperor – by accepting humiliating peace terms. Assembling to express their disappointment with the treaty, the protesters

103

appropriated the symbolic power and legitimacy of the emperor, offered their full-throated support for imperialism and empire, demanded government by and for the people, and sought expanded popular participation in the nation's political life.

In expressing enthusiasm for an imperialist war, the protesters encouraged and justified continued expansion of the Japanese Empire. The era of popular violence ushered in by the Hibiya riot coincided with the intensification of Japan's imperial project, fueled by victory in the Russo-Japanese War. Having emerged from the war with control of southern Manchuria, Japan began to take an increasingly interventionist tack toward China. And having established a protectorate in Korea, Japan went on to annex Korea as a colony in 1910. For the next thirty-five years, a Japanese colonial government would rule the Korean peninsula, including the colonial capital of Seoul.

After the demonstration in 1905, Hibiya Park and other public spaces in the capital continued to be used for popular protests. On eight more occasions, Tokyoites expressed their political discontent through mass violence; six of those instances originated as rallies in Hibiya Park which escalated into physical attacks on policemen, streetcar drivers, police boxes, police stations, streetcars, and government offices. Tens of thousands of people participated in these demonstrations against the government, bureaucracy, and cabinet on issues ranging from increases in taxes and tram fares to foreign policy on China. Other protests began outside of the parliament building or in Ueno Park, but Hibiya had burnished its reputation as the public's space for mass rallies. By August 1918, when protesters across the country decried a spike in rice prices and government culpability for exacerbating inflation, demonstrators in the capital could call on an established script for where and how to express their grievances. During the four days of the "rice riots," thousands of people gathered in

Hibiya Park, as well as Ueno and Asakusa Parks, where they clashed with police and then proceeded out of the gates, fanning out into the city to attack rice merchants, police boxes, and streetcars. Stones were thrown at company offices (of banks and insurance firms), larger buildings (such as theaters and cinemas), and elegant restaurants (including those serving Western cuisine), and at the glass doors and windows of adjacent storefronts along the main streets of neighborhoods such as Ginza and Asakusa. Targeted too were cars and the Yoshiwara red-light district, visible examples of the privileges and pleasures available only to the wealthy.[15] While protesters in 1905 had focused on their exclusion from the halls of political power, those in 1918 also resented their exclusion from the ranks of the nouveau riche. Like the tens of thousands of Tokyoites before them, demonstrators voiced their desire for political and economic inclusion by taking to parks and streets, acting in and upon the physical spaces of the city.

• ● •

Politics took a different form and had a different valence for immigrants who inhabited less visible spaces in the city. In the years leading up to 1905, students, intellectuals, and exiles from across Asia were drawn to the used bookshops, restaurants, and classrooms of Tokyo. For many émigrés from Qing China, British India, Spanish and American Colonial Philippines, and French Indochina, the modern nation of Japan served as a model for how to resist Western colonialism, revive a monarchy, industrialize, and become a non-Western military power. Although the surge of nationalism in the wake of the Russo-Japanese War dampened and complicated admiration for victorious Japan, the imperial capital of Tokyo continued to nourish the hopes of those who sought to reclaim countries lost to colonialism and realize a brighter future for Asian nations.

Japanese colonialism couldn't be so conveniently elided or explained by the growing number of Korean immigrants in the city who faced the widespread perception that they were dangerous interlopers on Japanese soil. After the annexation of Korea, the "resident Korean" or "Zainichi Korean" population in Japan skyrocketed from around 2,500 in 1911 to about 40,000 in 1920. The Japanese colonial government's agricultural policies swelled the ranks of the impoverished and landless on the peninsula who needed work, and the economic boom sparked by the outbreak of World War I created demand in the Japanese metropole for inexpensive labor in mines, textile mills, foundries, shipyards, and construction. In a political atmosphere swirling with democratic, revolutionary, and radical leftist ideas, Korean immigrants were increasingly viewed with suspicion by the Japanese state and public as potentially subversive colonial subjects. Even before annexation, the image of untrustworthy Koreans had been fueled by Korean students in Tokyo protesting degrading depictions of the Korean king and calling for Korean independence. Then in 1919, the March First movement in the colony that started with a declaration of independence in colonial Seoul heightened fears of a disruptive Korean minority. Although some Japanese progressives hailed the March First movement as part of a wave of democratic politics, other Tokyoites became more deeply concerned about disorderly colonial subjects in their midst.[16]

· ● ·

The political commitments pulsing through the streets of Tokyo in the early twentieth century were shot through with tensions and contradictions – democratic, imperialist, anti-colonial, chauvinist, and nationalist. The cacophony of political tones included the popular protesters who vocally supported democracy, emperor, and empire; expatriate revolutionaries who denounced imperialism;

and resident Koreans who navigated the bigotry of Japanese colonizers.

At the same time, a certain broadening of political ideas and participation did signal a palpable shift in these decades, particularly in the political lives of male Japanese citizens. While the government continued to clutch the reins of power, the popular energies of tens of thousands of demonstrators and activists in the public spaces of the capital tempered the state's centripetal pull and opened the door to mass popular politics. For a protester who stood shoulder to shoulder with fellow citizens in Hibiya Park to assert their demands and rights, the notion that political views could be aired so publicly must have felt empowering. And the realization that protests could topple government leaders must have been stunning. In one vivid illustration of what popular action could accomplish, in 1918 the rice riots provoked the resignation of the prime minister (with an elite military pedigree) and his cabinet (of career bureaucrats). As many protesters had demanded, the next prime minister and almost all of the subsequent cabinet ministers were not bureaucrats or oligarchic protégés but elected politicians who were members of political parties. Over the next several years, the democratizing spirit endured, animating the movement for universal (male) suffrage. In the city's public spaces, often Hibiya or Ueno Park, dozens of large political meetings and rallies were held, each drawing hundreds to tens of thousands of protesters calling for expansion of the franchise. They were able to celebrate the fruits of their labor in 1925 when a universal male suffrage law passed, granting men over the age of twenty-five the right to vote. This was not an unqualified achievement; the law imposed some voting restrictions and was accompanied by another law that curtailed freedom of expression. But the arc of political life seemed to bend toward ever-broader participation.

By the mid-1920s, democratic reformers and popular activists had helped birth and shape the country's constitution, two-party political system, cabinet composed of party politicians, and enfranchisement of male citizens. Strides were also made by activist women, who had pressured lawmakers to overturn the legal prohibition on women attending political meetings and rallies, and mobilized suffragists to press for the vote and full political rights for women.[17] In these decades, there was a certain sense of openness and optimism, a belief that political conflict could improve the lives of the nation's citizens. And this political vitality resonated with a flourishing urban culture to sustain and remake the cosmopolitan city.

6

Tokyo Modern: Destruction and Reconstruction of the Cosmopolitan City

JUST before noon on the first day of September 1923, as Tokyoites slurped noodles at a pushcart, worked on the factory line, rode the streetcar, caught a movie, and busied themselves at home on a cloudless Saturday, the ground beneath them suddenly shook with tremendous, violent force. As the earth rippled and rumbled, buildings across the city swayed, strained, and crumbled, punctuating the air with creaks and bangs. One young teenager, the future filmmaker Kurosawa Akira, tried to take cover with a friend and watched, stunned, as "before our eyes, the two storehouses belonging to the pawnshop started shedding their skins. They shuddered and shook off their roof tiles and then let go of their thick walls. In an instant they were skeletons of wooden frame."[1] When the convulsions stopped, a momentary silence was quickly broken by people rushing to find loved ones and secure essentials. Survivors of the initial quake were then stalked by fire, which fed on gas leaking from broken lines, charcoal that had been lit to make lunch, and debris from crumpled buildings. As aftershocks persisted, the narrow roads, alleys, and bridges of the low city became packed with Tokyoites, belongings in tow, as they tried to escape the flames that consumed the eastern sections of the capital.[2]

Amidst the dislocation, unfounded rumors began to swirl among citizens of Tokyo and Yokohama that resident Koreans were committing all manner of crimes, from starting fires and poisoning wells to murdering Japanese women and children. Fearing and capitalizing on these falsehoods, thousands of neighborhood vigilante groups formed in the name of protecting Japanese communities from Korean attacks, many arming themselves with iron pipes, clubs, bamboo spears, axes, hoes, saws, and swords. Fueled by a potent mix of prejudice against colonized subjects, anxiety about competing for jobs with a growing number of Korean immigrants, and an impulse to exert superiority over those even weaker than themselves, the vigilante groups were also incited by soldiers and police officers who confirmed slanderous tales of Korean treachery and legitimized the use of force against Koreans. In the aftermath of the earthquake, an estimated 6,000 Koreans were massacred by Japanese citizens.[3]

Buffeted by a 7.9 magnitude earthquake, fires that raged for three days, and more than a thousand aftershocks over ten days, much of the Kanto region lay devastated. In Tokyo, over 45 percent of the land had been razed. And around 140,000 people were dead or missing. Looking out over what remained of the low city, Kurosawa observed a "burned landscape [that] for as far as the eye could see had a brownish red color ... It looked like a red desert. Amid this expanse of nauseating redness lay every kind of corpse imaginable."[4] About 65 percent of the houses in Tokyo were deemed uninhabitable, leaving well over half of Tokyoites homeless. About 7,000 factories had been destroyed. And the unemployment rate skyrocketed to 45 percent; 59 percent among men. With so many people displaced, the open spaces of the city became shantytowns for refugees (see Figure 6.1). Temporary barracks and tents filled the Imperial Palace Plaza, the grounds of Meiji Shrine, and Ueno and Hibiya Parks, which soon reeked of garbage and human waste. Even months later, at the end of the year, over 120,000 people were still taking shelter in barracks.[5] Reflecting on

Figure 6.1 Survivors of the Great Kanto earthquake on the Imperial Palace grounds. Tōkyōshi, ed., *Tōkyō shinsairoku,* vol. 5 (Tokyo: Tōkyō shiyakusho, 1924), 14. Courtesy of the Tokyo Metropolitan Archives.

what soon became known as the Great Kanto earthquake, the Buddhist writer and social critic Takashima Beihō lamented, "The big city of Tokyo . . . at the zenith of its prosperity burned down and melted away over two days and three nights."[6]

• ● •

After the fires had quieted and the ash had settled, it became stunningly clear that the neighborhoods in the eastern half of Tokyo had been ravaged with particular ferocity. The crowded wards of the low city (Honjo, Fukagawa, Kyōbashi, Nihonbashi, and Asakusa) suffered many more casualties than their wealthier counterparts to the west in the high city. Packed densely with people, factories, and wooden homes, and with little open space to serve as firebreaks, these areas were especially susceptible to

人 形 町 通 の り 燒 け 野 原 ⟨大正十二年九月一日 大震火災の実況⟩

Figure 6.2 The Ningyōchō neighborhood of the Nihonbashi ward in September 1923 after the Great Kanto earthquake. *Taishō jūninen kugatsu tsuitachi daishin kasai no jikkyō*, 1923. Courtesy of the Tokyo Metropolitan Library.

the rapid spread of flames (see Figure 6.2). And the maze of narrow roads and alleys, a legacy of Tokugawa efforts to protect their capital and castle from attack, hindered escape from burning neighborhoods.[7]

When elite bureaucrats, urban planners, and commentators surveyed the razed city, many saw an opportunity to remake Tokyo into the thoroughly modern capital of their dreams. More than in 1868, when the early Meiji government set up shop in Tokyo, or even in 1872, when fire paved the way for the construction of Ginza Bricktown, government leaders could aspire to a wholesale transformation of the city. "Now," wrote the prominent politician Wakatsuki Reijirō in late 1923, "we have the chance to make an almost brand new city."[8] The destruction of the low city, in particular, fueled optimism that Tokyo's problems – inadequate infrastructure, urban poverty, over-crowding, and lack of green space – could be overcome.[9]

While residents' interests, political opposition, and budget constraints moderated visions for a new Tokyo, elite-level efforts did ultimately improve the infrastructure in core areas of the city, laying the groundwork for decades of urban development. Public infrastructure projects were made possible through a process known as land reclamation, whereby the government appropriated all public and private land in an area, nullified existing property boundaries, and created new, smaller parcels that were assigned back to the private landowners. Around thirty square kilometers, or roughly half of today's Manhattan, was redesigned using this method. Created in these areas was a new network of roads, with major avenues like Shōwa-dōri and a series of auxiliary streets, most of which were widened, straightened, and paved. Almost all now had sidewalks. With better road transport, people began to move around the city in different ways, taking trams less frequently and opting instead to travel by bus. Key to mobility through this road system was the construction of hundreds of bridges, many of which were strikingly modern in their materials and design. Six major bridges across the Sumida River were built by the Home Ministry and became icons of modernity; five of them continue to stand today with their original shape. Even as the city's orientation increasingly turned toward the land and away from the water, canals were widened and deepened, and their embankments reinforced. Between roads, bridges, and canals, the improvement of transportation infrastructure claimed the largest share of reconstruction funds and was counted among its prime achievements.[10] Post-earthquake Tokyo had taken a step away from the labyrinth of oddly shaped plots, twisting roads, and cramped alleyways that had ensnared so many people in the fires of the low city.

More open space was also created in the reconstructed Tokyo to serve as both firebreaks and places for leisure. Even though there was still relatively little green space in the city, about 100 parks were built in the years after the earthquake, many of which continue to dot the landscape today. Most were small neighborhood affairs, and many were in the low city. These new parks were intended to slow the spread of fires. And in day-to-day life, the more than fifty that were next to primary schools were used by children as an extension of the playground on weekdays, and otherwise enjoyed by local residents.

Also concentrated in the eastern neighborhoods of the city were the institutions of a social welfare infrastructure. Pawnshops, employment agencies, public dining halls, inexpensive lodging houses, childcare facilities, women's workhouses, and public baths were created by the municipal government to support those most vulnerable after the earthquake.[11]

As the physical and social infrastructure of the city was modernized, the fate of different buildings in the earthquake was interpreted as a stark sign pointing architects and engineers to the materials for remaking Tokyo into a city of the future. Brick and stone, the symbols of Meiji-era modernization, had crumbled, reducing much of the Ginza area to rubble. The Anglo-Japanese masonry of the imposing Ueno Museum and the brick of the iconic Ryōunkaku, or twelve-story tower in Asakusa, did not fare well. In contrast, the office buildings in the Marunouchi district and the Imperial Hotel designed by Frank Lloyd Wright remained standing in a testament to the marvels of reinforced concrete. Much of the city was still rebuilt in wood. But several-story, concrete-framed structures also appeared, supplanting masonry and edging out American-style, steel-framed skyscrapers as new symbols of permanence and modernity.[12]

Ferroconcrete was also the material of choice for a new style of housing constructed after the earthquake: the urban apartment. Urban, concrete apartment buildings were designed by the Dōjunkai, or Mutual Prosperity Association, which was established in 1924 through donations to provide housing and work to earthquake victims. After erecting temporary wooden barracks just after the disaster, the Dōjunkai with its many young architects then turned to creating apartment complexes equipped with amenities such as municipal gas, trash chutes, and flush toilets. The fourteen Dōjunkai complexes in Tokyo included the mid-rise, ferroconcrete alternative to slum housing in Fukagawa, and a version for middle-class residents in Daikanyama and Aoyama. Many of the Dōjunkai projects had remarkably long lives – the last of the buildings weren't demolished until the early 2000s.[13] Perhaps most famous was the Aoyama complex, its modest, concrete presence increasingly conspicuous in the postwar era as fancy boutiques appeared around it and land values rose in this upscale Omotesandō area. Eventually, the Aoyama Dōjunkai buildings could no longer resist the forces of development. In 2003, the real estate firm Mori Building Company tore down most of the apartments to make way for the high-end retail and residential complex, Omotesandō Hills, demolishing these vestiges of post-earthquake Tokyo.

· ● ·

Even as reconstruction efforts focused on the devastated low city, the earthquake accelerated the shift of the capital's center of gravity westward toward the high city and to the burgeoning suburbs beyond. This move to the west as well as to the south had started around the turn of the century, as company executives and others of society's upper classes made their home in the peripheries. In the 1910s, the economic boom spurred by World

War I drew many newcomers to the city, driving up urban real estate prices, exacerbating crowding, and encouraging suburban development. The western edges of Tokyo, particularly the areas that are now Shinjuku, Shibuya, and Suginami wards, swelled with residents. Living in the suburbs and commuting into the city to work was a real possibility, thanks in large part to the westward extension of passenger rail lines, two of which continue to serve as vital commuter corridors. By the late 1910s, the Chūō Line linked Tokyo Station with Shinjuku and stopped at key stations along the way out to Hachiōji. And the Keiō Line connected Shinjuku with Hachiōji through a route a little further south.[14]

The destruction of homes and whole neighborhoods in the eastern core of the city hastened westward migration, as those displaced by the earthquake looked for new places to live and others decided to relocate to the suburbs. The immediate exodus of people seeking housing or jobs, and the sheer scale of life lost from the disaster, led to a drop in the population of Tokyo by over a quarter in the mid-1920s. By the early 1930s, the number of residents did climb back up, nearing pre-earthquake levels at over two million people. But the population in the suburbs came to outstrip that in the city, roughly doubling to almost three million people. In recognition of the tremendous expansion in the five counties surrounding Tokyo, in 1932 they were incorporated into a newly designated "Greater Tokyo." The original fifteen wards of the city grew to thirty-five (which included the creation of Shibuya and Yodobashi, later Shinjuku, wards) with a combined population of 6.8 million people.[15]

Most of the new suburbanites of the 1920s belonged to a burgeoning middle class of white-collar office workers who were seeking more affordable housing than they could find in the city. The kind of home that encapsulated their aspirations was a "culture house" – a broad term that came to mean any home designed for modern, cosmopolitan living, perhaps equipped with conveniences such as running water, gas fixtures, plate-glass windows, and electric appliances. Even though most suburbanites lived in three-room houses that were smaller than idealized models, the idea of the "culture house" transformed the home into an object of consumerist desire and one to be purchased rather than rented. The dream of such home ownership was fueled by planned suburbs that were few in number but influential in their visibility. Perhaps most famous was Den'en Chōfu, completed in August 1923 as an English-inspired, idyllic residential community or "garden city." Laid out in a radial pattern emanating from a railway station and central plaza, the large homes were a mix of architectural styles, some Victorian houses and some Arts and Crafts bungalows with elements reminiscent of samurai estates. With the opening of Den'en Chōfu just after the earthquake, those in the middle and upper-middle class could aspire to and even afford lives of cosmopolitan modernity.[16]

Although most suburbanites didn't quite experience this idealized life, they did establish new patterns of living and working. By the late 1920s, a white-collar salaryman, a reasonably educated man who worked for the government or a large company, might wake up in the morning in his suburban home and put on mass-produced clothes, pressed by his wife with an electric iron, while listening to the phonograph or radio. From one of the many neighborhoods clustered around railway stations, he could take the commuter line into Shinjuku, which – as a key terminal – was a hub for shopping and entertainment with department stores, movie theaters, and cafés.[17] At Shinjuku, he could transfer onto the Yamanote loop line and make his way to his office in the Marunouchi district in the center of the city. This lifestyle of a middle-class, suburban commuter would seem quite familiar to a twenty-first-century suburbanite living out their daily routine in contemporary Tokyo.

• ● •

The middle class, to which the salaryman and his wife belonged, propelled the emergence in the 1920s of a quintessentially modern city. This Tokyo grew out of its earlier self but was more consumerist and cosmopolitan than it had ever been. A flourishing urban consumer culture offered tantalizing opportunities for shopping, leisure, and entertainment. Chic and trendy places like the department store and the café became popular with the salarymen who poured into the city during the week, their wives who took the train in from the suburbs during the day, and young people with some money in their pockets. Even those who couldn't count themselves among the 10 percent of people who comprised the new middle class took in advertisements for consumer products and stories about enviable lifestyles in mass circulation newspapers and magazines that had an ever-growing audience. Women's magazines published patterns and diagrams so that readers of various backgrounds could sew and knit the latest styles or transform their kimono into Western clothes more in keeping with the times.[18] Many Tokyoites could watch a Hollywood film at a movie theater or see fashions on display at a department store.

Department stores weren't new in the 1920s. Prominent dry goods stores dating back to the Edo era, such as Mitsukoshi (formerly Echigoya) and Shirokiya, had reinvented themselves as modern emporiums over the previous two decades. Storegoers could browse items displayed in glass cases rather than requesting them from storage and choose from a wide array of goods including cosmetics, shoes, and bags. Starting in 1914, shoppers at the flagship Mitsukoshi department store in Nihonbashi stepped foot

118

into a new, reinforced concrete building equipped with elevators, escalators, heating, space for art exhibitions, and a dining room serving meals and sweet treats.[19]

After the earthquake, department stores adjusted to the pressing needs of Tokyoites, selling not just higher-end goods to higher-income customers but also daily necessities to more residents. And this shift in orientation toward a broader clientele persisted. After 1923, shoppers no longer had to take off their shoes at the entrance, so they could easily saunter in from the street. Passersby were also invited to stop and look at goods placed enticingly in large, plate-glass show windows, often framed with curtains. These displays beckoned pedestrians and gave birth to the new pastime of window shopping, which was widely enjoyed in Ginza by many, from youth to middle-class suburbanites, as part of an increasingly popular leisure activity dubbed *ginbura*, or "cruising the Ginza." In the dining rooms of Ginza department stores, customers no longer sat on *tatami*-mat floors but on chairs at Western-style tables, which was especially welcomed by middle-class working women.[20]

At the same time, department stores retained and enhanced their aura as a luxurious destination for a thoroughly modern experience. The buildings themselves were designed in the art deco style of the day. Once inside a department store, customers feasted their eyes on a large, light-filled space with high ceilings, wide aisles, mirrors, and colorful stained glass. A shining example was the Isetan department store, which relocated from the low city to the up-and-coming Shinjuku area after the earthquake. Completed in 1933, the new seven-story building was made of concrete and steel, and embellished with art deco motifs. Shoppers entered below elaborate bronze grillwork that reached skyward, through doors adorned with a bronze sunburst and peacocks, onto a floor of mosaic tile in a geometric pattern. At any major department store, customers could browse or shop. And they could attend a lecture or performance in the store's theater, relax in a beautifully furnished lounge, or go up to the rooftop to enjoy a Western-style garden, playground, zoo, or theme park. Most department stores also offered at least two restaurants serving a variety of international fare including Western-style sandwiches and burger steaks, and Chinese noodle soup (or ramen) and dumplings, as well as soba noodles and sushi.[21]

The department store not only offered cosmopolitan experiences to its customers, it also provided job opportunities to a growing number of young, educated, middle-class women. Among the occupations that could be pursued by middle-class women in the 1920s, from teacher to office worker, was added the department store "shop girl" or "department store girl." Female department store workers were most visible as sales clerks but also held positions as switchboard operators and account clerks. Less educated women might be hired as waitresses, escalator girls, or elevator girls. Women were first recruited as elevator operators late in the decade, replacing the men who initially held these positions. They drove the elevators using a handle connected to a motor controller. But they were most valued as young attractive employees who made customers feel comfortable stepping into a large moving cage and brought a touch of elegance to the department store experience. Providing and representing the kind of service that customers came to expect, elevator girls continued to be seen in department stores long after the advent of fully automatic elevators in the 1950s. Not only elevator girls but shop girls of all kinds became a fixture of the department store experience over the course of the 1920s. The percentage of women workers at Mitsukoshi increased from less than 20 percent in 1921 at the Nihonbashi flagship, to over 40 percent in 1930 at the newly opened Ginza branch, the especially high number reflecting the importance of women employees for promoting the characteristically classy reputation of Ginza department stores. In the 1930s, women would become both the primary employees and customers of department stores.[22]

Cafés also flourished in reconstructed Tokyo as purveyors and symbols of urban cosmopolitanism. The earliest cafés had appeared in the 1910s, catering mainly to artists and intellectuals as a place to enjoy Western foods and cocktails. In the 1920s, cafés, like department stores, broadened their appeal, enticing Tokyoites of various stripes but attracting in especially large numbers the office workers, government officials, and salespeople of the new middle class. After the earthquake, cafés proliferated "like bamboo shoots after a rain" in entertainment districts such as Asakusa and Shinjuku.[23] But it was Ginza that became home to the newest, glitziest, and largest cafés. While Asakusa offered the latest movies as well as musical revues, the district's cafés were seen as homier or grittier establishments with an older and less trendy clientele, presaging its eclipse by Ginza as the city's destination for novel entertainment. Shinjuku drew large crowds to its cafés but hadn't yet shaken the feeling of being on the outskirts, a waystation for commuting suburbanites. Ginza was fortunate to be in the center of the city and just south of the Marunouchi business district that was left relatively unscathed by the earthquake and bustled with office workers in search of evening entertainment before heading back home. In the 1920s, Ginza emerged as the premier district in the city for trendy pastimes and came to have so much cachet that new businesses in the suburbs had "Ginza" in their names and advertised themselves as having "Ginza-style" in order to appear cutting edge. By 1929, there were fifty cafés on Ginza's main street, more than double the twenty establishments in 1922, and that doesn't include the dozens of smaller cafés that dotted the back streets of the district.

Cafés were the place to enjoy a drink, listen to jazz, and soak in Western-style ambience. The newer and nicer cafés in Ginza were brightly lit on the outside by red and blue neon signs. On the inside, there were colorful stained-glass windows, and shiny materials such as stainless steel, aluminum, glass, and mirrors. The Ginza Palace, for example, was decorated with glass mosaic tiles, white glass, aluminum-plated pillars, and blue neon lights on the ceiling.

Enhancing the allure of the café, especially for men, was the café waitress – a young woman, paid entirely by tips, who poured drinks and chatted with her customers. The increasingly eroticized café waitress was distinctive to the post-earthquake café, which advertised service over food and drink as its primary attraction. Foregrounding the quality of its service, the Ginza Palace assigned one waitress to each male customer, so that no man would miss out on the seductive experience. It wasn't unusual for larger cafés like the Ginza Palace to employ over a hundred waitresses. And the popularity of their services along with the spread of cafés meant that the number of café waitresses in Tokyo more than doubled from roughly 7,000 women in the mid-1920s to around 18,000 in the early 1930s. The young women who worked as café waitresses generally came from poorer rural and urban families, and didn't have the skills or education for the new jobs open to middle-class women. Less physically taxing than work on a farm or in a factory, the café offered the possibility of a decent income and some degree of freedom. But aside from the few famed women at larger cafés, many waitresses didn't earn much, moved between establishments, and worked as prostitutes after hours. Glossing over the working lives of the women themselves, the popular image of the café waitress along with the café itself captured imaginations, eliciting a wide range of feelings from exhilaration to moral condemnation. Considered exciting by some and decadent by others, the café and the café waitress became contested symbols of urban cosmopolitan culture.[24]

Perhaps the most highly charged embodiment of post-earthquake modernity was the "modern girl," a young woman associated with trendy urban spaces from the department store and café to the dance hall. Like the modern girls that appeared in cities around the world, from the flapper of New York City to the *kallege ladki* of Bombay, the Japanese *modan gāru*, or *moga* for short, was immediately identifiable by her look. She had short, bobbed hair and cut a slim figure. She wore lipstick and rouge. And she flaunted the latest styles, sometimes a cloche hat, pearls, or stockings (see Figure 6.3). This fashionable *moga* was steeped in a lifestyle of consumption and leisure, often pictured shopping, driving, swimming, smoking, dancing, or drinking. While modern girls could be spotted in the city's streets, especially in areas such as Ginza, she was more a product of people's imaginations and anxieties – a "phantasm" created by marketers, journalists, social critics, intellectuals, and writers.[25] She appeared in advertisements for Shiseido cosmetics, Sapporo beer, Suntory wine, and the soft drink Calpis. She was criticized in articles as superficial and sexually promiscuous. And she was portrayed as a dangerously seductive character in fiction such as Tanizaki Jun'ichirō's *Chijin no ai*, or *A Fool's Love*, in which a consumerist, materialistic, sexually dissolute, and self-indulgent *moga* named Naomi breaks the salaryman with an unhealthy attachment to her. Men who were too enamored with the urban culture of Tokyo, Tanizaki warned, labored under the misguided notion that they could control the modern girl's impulses and appetites, and their own.[26] While she had a male counterpart in the modern boy, it was the modern girl who became the cultural lightening rod for debates about the future of a changing society – about the

Figure 6.3 Young women in modern girl fashion in the early 1930s. Photograph by the *Asahi Shinbun*, c. March 1932. Courtesy of Getty Images.

promises and threats of shifting roles for women, the pleasures and perils of consumerism, and the allures and dangers of cosmopolitan entertainment.

• ● •

In 1929, the popular song "Tokyo kōshinkyoku" or "Tokyo March" became a smash hit as consumers snatched up an unparalleled 150,000 copies of the record within just a few months of its release. With a melody at once catchy and melancholy, the song expressed the mix of emotions that could be elicited by Tokyo of the 1920s. Mentioned were the latest icons of urban modernity – from the cinema to the recently opened subway, from the "Maru Biru" office building in Marunouchi to the Ginza district. Together, they epitomized a city charged with excitement and laced with heartbreak. The soprano and rising star Satō Chiyako sang, "Dancing to jazz and drinking liqueur late into the night. In the morning, the dancer sheds her tears."[27] Intended to advertise the film *Tokyo March*, the song alluded to its romantic tale, a melodrama with a socioeconomic undercurrent about who could more easily access the glittery lifestyles of cosmopolitan Tokyo. Contrasted in the serialized story that inspired the film were two central characters – Sayuri, a modern girl from an upper-class family, and Michiyo, an orphan who worked at a factory until she was pressed into becoming a geisha in Ginza to make financial ends meet. The twists and turns of the plot mirrored the contradictions of this historical moment when a new white-collar middle class was entering the stage as the old middle-class of small shopkeepers and manufacturers still hovered in the scene, many people could see the latest cultural trends but didn't necessarily have the means to enjoy them, and the modern city was considered both culturally refined and suspect. As expressed in the opening lines of the film and story versions of *Tokyo March*: "Tokyo – the only truly modern city in the Orient. The center of Japan's culture, academy, cultivation, and art, as well as sin and depravity."[28] Revived and reconstructed, post-earthquake Tokyo pulsed with the desires and discontents of an urban consumer culture that was experienced, by many, largely as a dream.

As the 1920s turned into the 1930s and the country moved ever closer to fascism, the urban modernity of the post-earthquake years endured both because of and despite the ever-deepening commitment to war. The instigation of war with China contributed to an economic boom and further expansion of mass media that fueled middle-class lifestyles of consumption and leisure.

And, at the same time, the allure of urban culture persisted even as growing antagonism toward the Allied powers prompted government attempts to suffocate cosmopolitan culture. The Tokyo Metropolitan Police had already made its antipathy toward cafés and dance halls known in the late 1920s, when the commissioner vowed to "deal a devastating blow" to "the red lights and jazz world that pervade the capital."[29] Hundreds of waitresses and dancers had been arrested. After the outbreak of full-scale war with China in 1937, the Home Ministry condemned dance halls as "exert[ing] not a little bad influence on the nation's public morality" and labeled jazz "enemy music."[30] The government and local police harassed customers at dance halls, coffee shops, and cafés that played jazz. In 1940, the government announced a nationwide ban on dance halls; after Japan's attack on Pearl Harbor, all "enemy music," especially decadent jazz, was banned. And yet, enthusiasm for cosmopolitan entertainment persisted. Cafés turned off their Victrolas for a few days but then started playing their jazz favorites again, quietly at first, then more loudly.[31] So captivating was urban cosmopolitan culture that its allure was not snuffed out, even into the 1940s as cafés and dance halls were closed by government order, entertainment districts such as Ginza were reduced to ashes by Allied bombing, and the residents of the city adjusted to daily life amidst total war.

7

The Militarized City

O N October 19, 1937, at precisely 3 pm, Korean and Japanese residents of colonial Seoul bowed their heads in a Shinto ceremony to pray for auspicious favor in war. A few months earlier, in July, the Japanese military had provoked full-scale war in China in what would become known as the Second Sino-Japanese War or the Asia Pacific War. Now thoroughly on a war footing, the Japanese colonial government in Korea and the Japanese government at home employed fascist methods to mobilize support for war in the colonies as in the metropole, in the colonial capital of Seoul as in the imperial capital of Tokyo. The prayer event in Seoul was held atop South Mountain, or Namsan, at a Shinto complex of Japanese creation that looked out over the colonial city. This public performance of veneration for the emperor and empire was timed to coincide with rituals at Ise Shrine, in southeastern Japan, which was a sacred site dedicated to the Shinto deity Amaterasu, who in Japanese mythology was the goddess of the sun and progenitor of the imperial family. At the same moment on this afternoon, at Namsan as at shrines throughout the empire, colonial subjects and Japanese citizens made their prayers, participating in a simultaneous act of fealty to Japan's imperial war.

With the outbreak of the Asia Pacific War, Japanese efforts to mold Koreans into dutiful colonial subjects intensified, and Namsan became a site where the colonial regime sought to create active defenders of the empire and enthusiastic supporters of the war effort. In the last months of 1937, more than 500 military celebrations were held at Namsan. And in 1939, Japanese colonial officials erected an Imperial Subject Oath Tower about seventeen meters tall on the mountain at the base of Korea Shrine. Korea Shrine had been built in 1925 by the Japanese colonial regime to muffle the anticolonial sentiments of the March First movement, in which two million Koreans took to the streets in mass demonstrations for Korean national independence. Worship at Korea Shrine became mandatory for all able-bodied residents of Seoul with the start of the war. And the Imperial Subject Oath Tower came to serve as a repository for over a million oaths handwritten by Korean schoolchildren, who had also ponied up funds for the tower's construction. As the war waged on, it became increasingly difficult for Koreans to publicly resist participating in rituals at Namsan or in any other performances of loyalty to the Japanese wartime empire.

The coercive mechanisms for mobilizing people for total war in Seoul paralleled those in Tokyo. In both cities, the state organized all households into neighborhood patriotic associations, which became the vehicle through which the government conscripted labor, extracted contributions of money or materials like metals, and demanded appropriate wartime behavior from public acts of devotion to rationing.[1] For Korean housewife Yi Okpun, her neighborhood association and the inducement of food compelled her visits to Namsan. She recalled,

> Of course we had to go up to the shrine on Namsan ... The head of our neighborhood group was Japanese; that's why we had to do everything he said. If we didn't go, we didn't get any food ration. We didn't go alone. A whole group went – our

whole neighborhood cell, about ten households, you know.
Even with my babies, I had to take the streetcar, then walk all
the way up the hill. It was hard. We had to go up a lot, sometimes once a week, certainly two or three times a month.[2]

Along with the state, community organizations took up the cause
of societal mobilization. Neighborhood leaders, schoolteachers,
and company managers became "spiritual mobilizers" who collected donations for the army, urged residents to see off soldiers,
and surveilled the performance of rituals, like the daily bow
toward the Imperial Palace in Tokyo.

Although state and societal efforts to create wartime imperial subjects were similar in the colonies and the metropole, the
project of assimilating Koreans into the Japanese nation was pro-
foundly different in its effacement of Korean national sovereignty
and its attempted erasure of Korean identities. Invidious differences
had been inscribed into the very landscape of colonial Seoul as it was
shaped by the logics of Japanese nation-building that underlaid the
formation of Meiji-era Tokyo but were overlaid with colonial
dynamics of power. The colonial capital was essentially divided
into one area for Japanese settlers and another for Koreans, with
stark distinctions in architecture, street names, and the provision of
public utilities such as electricity, water, gas, and sewers. The
Japanese quarter displayed the characteristic signs of cosmopolitan
modernity, with a central shopping district that could easily have
been mistaken for Tokyo.[3] In wartime Tokyo, resident Koreans living
in "Korea towns" attempted to carry on with their daily lives as many
went through the motions of government compliance and resisted in
whatever ways they could. Recalling the conditions of a Korean
community in the city, Kim Chongjae observed, "Perhaps because
it was cut off from the world of the Japanese, here a simple and
abundant way of life prevailed, which was miles away from the

tension that pervaded Japan in the midst of the Pacific War. In particular, it was a completely different world at night. Then, there were illegally brewed *makkali* liquor and vegetables pickled with garlic and cayenne pepper."[4] Others, like this anonymous writer who sent a letter to a Japanese police chief, were more defiant: "Three of my relatives were murdered under your charge during the Great [Kanto] Earthquake. The time for revenge has come. With the next [American] air raid, three hundred comrades shall set fires throughout Tokyo and Yokohama and welcome our comrades from America."[5]

Even as people responded differently to the militarization of wartime life, public acts of patriotism were performed in visually symbolic sites of capital cities. In late April 1940, a group of almost thirty Korean students selected for a ten-day tour of Japan arrived in Tokyo. In front of the Imperial Palace, before the Nijūbashi bridge, they demonstrated respect for the emperor by bowing deeply, singing the national anthem, and reciting the imperial oath. As they visited government ministries and Yasukuni Shrine, dedicated to soldiers who had lost their lives in Japan's wars since 1868, the students were presented as exemplary colonial subjects. No notice was paid to how they, as Koreans, navigated the complexities and inequities of becoming imperial subjects or the contradictions of assimilating as colonized citizens.[6] From the vantage point of Tokyoites, the students' public acts of reverence and loyalty may have served as a reminder that the city had become much more than a national capital. In the crucible of the Asia Pacific War, Tokyo assumed spiritual, military, and political gravity as an exemplar of militarized mobilization in Japan's wartime empire.

• ● •

In the summer of 1938, to mark one full year of war against China, about 10,000 Tokyoites marched from Yasukuni Shrine to the Imperial Palace Plaza in a show of protecting the home front.[7] Organized by a major newspaper company, the procession was striking testimony to a city, like the nation and the empire, mobilized for war. Public support for Japan's military conflicts was not new, reaching back decades to the Sino-Japanese and Russo-Japanese Wars. More recently, the invasion of Manchuria in 1931 had fanned the flames of Imperial jingoism and war fever, propelled not just by the government but also by the media and its consumers (those who bought newspapers with stories of military heroism) and members of societal groups (those who belonged to associations for workers, businessmen, women, and neighborhood residents). But the Asia Pacific War was of a length and scale unprecedented for modern Japan. Over eight years, Japanese individuals perpetrated atrocious violence, contributed to the war effort, bore the burdens of militaristic zeal, and experienced devastating loss. Across thousands of miles, the wartime Japanese empire extended from Manchuria to Borneo, from Burma to the Marshall Islands. Staggering in its inescapability, total war conditioned all aspects of life.

The material and moral demands of the war precipitated changes to the physical spaces of Tokyo. Claims to land and buildings were fueled by the pressing need to equip fighting forces with weapons and supplies. Munitions factories and related heavy industry manufacturers sprouted up in great numbers, as the government spent close to 70 percent of the annual budget on military expenses by 1937. The army commandeered the popular horse racing venue for armaments production. And late in the war, some of the city's major theaters were converted into factories for the manufacture of balloon bombs, devised to float westward and wreak havoc on the Pacific Coast of the United States. The

collection of metals, to be melted down and turned into munitions, was mandated by law starting in the fall of 1941, and so the
city was stripped of signboards, stairs, gates, and bridge railings.
The Ginza district lost its traffic signals. Households contributed
their teapots, hibachi, and religious objects. Memorials to victims
of the Great Kanto earthquake were no more. And the bronze
statue in front of Shibuya Station of Hachikō, the dog glorified for
loyalty to his owner, was toppled. This symbol of fascist values,
distinct from its postwar reincarnation as a popular meeting spot
in front of a crowded train station, was called into service. So too
was the bronze statue before city hall commemorating Ōta Dōkan,
founder of Edo.[8] While metals disappeared from city streets,
moral admonitions about the war effort appeared. On the front
of the large, art deco Nichigeki theater hung an immense painting
of fighting soldiers with the proclamation: "There will be no
stopping until victory."[9] Sizable paintings of American and
English flags on the sidewalk in front of department stores encouraged pedestrians to demonstrate their national allegiance by tread-
ing upon these symbols of the enemy. Exhortations to be frugal
and to divert all resources to the war effort were declared on large
billboards and banners displayed at intersections.[10] On the main
streets of the Ginza district, over a thousand posters clamored,
"Luxury is the enemy!"[11]

Expectations of moral rectitude were not just rhetorical
but altered the ways Tokyoites lived in their city. Spearheaded by
the government and animated by societal groups, anti-luxury
movements called on women to wear drab, loose-fitting work
pants known as *monpe* and men to don a simple outfit of khaki
pants, a shirt, and a cap. Cosmetics and perms for women were
banned by the government. To enforce such austerity, members
of the National Defense Women's Association stood watch on
street corners to reproach fashionably attired women. And by

1944, about half of the women in Ginza could be seen wearing *monpe*. When it came to finding entertainment and amusements in the city, many Tokyoites could frequent their favorite haunts for a time, but venues like movie houses and Kabuki theaters eventually began to close for lack of customers or, in the last years of the war, on the order of a government suspicious of diversions that carried the stench of the American enemy. Dance halls were condemned by spiritual mobilizers as both a trivial luxury and a cultural affront because of their association with jazz; they started to lose business and close up shop in 1939. The following year, their doors were shuttered by the government's nationwide ban on dance halls. Baseball continued to draw spectators until the college baseball federation discontinued intercollegiate games in keeping with a Ministry of Education order to prioritize military drills, and the government suspended all professional play in late 1944. Cafés and bars in Ginza continued to serve drinks until that same year, when the government closed the district's establishments, putting around 10,000 women out of work.

Daily life in militarized Tokyo entailed not just restraint and abstention from prewar pleasures but also active contribution to the war effort. Women of the National Defense Women's Association organized send-offs for soldiers, embroidered thousand-stitch belts for servicemen to wear in battle as an amulet, and compelled school-children to write letters to military men.[12] But for most people in the wartime city, their most substantial participation in the war was as conscripted labor. As adult men were drafted into military service, the government established a draft for workers to fill their shoes and keep the wheels of the war machine turning. About one million adult women across Japan were conscripted for work; in Tokyo, women became ticket collectors at train stations, bus conductors, and truck drivers. The one million or so men called into labor service were typically moved from their previous jobs into munitions production or other strategic industries. In the last few years of the war, three million schoolchildren above the third grade were drafted into munitions plants, including recent graduates from elementary schools in rural areas brought to factories in Tokyo as "industrial soldiers in the making."[13] From the continent, around one million Koreans and Chinese were conscripted to work in the metropole, laboring under harsh conditions in factories and mines.

The long arm of the government shaped other fundamental aspects of daily life, including how and what people could eat. By the summer of 1940, Tokyoites secured staples such as rice, soy sauce, miso, salt, and sugar through rations, which were typically meted out by neighborhood associations. Fish, meat, and cooking oil were soon added to that list. As food allotments shrank, the insufficiency of government rations compelled people to stand in line for whatever food could be found at stores or for rice gruel served by eateries. Seeking sustenance, many Tokyoites, mainly women and children, took the train out to the edges of the city or to neighboring prefectures to buy food straight from farmers. Those without the means to pay the high prices for increasingly scarce food found their bodies atrophying, becoming prone to exhaustion and illness.[14] As the empire's soldiers fought on, the tolls of the war for those on the home front grew heavier. And then the metropole, too, was consumed in the military conflagration that raged across the Asia Pacific.

• ● •

In late July 1945, Takahashi Aiko, the wife of a doctor, headed out to the low city to see for herself the physical destruction in the capital. Having not ventured into this area for some time, the resident of the upscale Hiroo area wrote in her diary just how stunned she was by the shattered state of her native city.[15]

> Tokyo has changed completely. Fires usually leave charred wood strewn about, but the air raids left completely burned-out remains that were gray with a faint red hue.
>
> Looking out over the gray plain, only concrete buildings survived, but they were hollowed out and rather pathetic structures. In the distance, fleecy white clouds floated in a cobalt blue sky above a distant forest. The devastation was so bad that I wondered whether I was really in the center of Tokyo. Since the city was, with the exception of a few government ministries, mostly wooden structures, it had been completely leveled. Many hundreds of years ago this area probably was an uninhabited plain like this, but what I saw seemed fantastic and like a dream.[16]

Staring out over the barren landscape, Takahashi confronted a Tokyo that bore scars of the empire's brutal war (see Figure 7.1).

Most devastating to the imperial capital and its residents was the American fire bombing in March 1945. Just after midnight on the tenth, pathfinder planes flew into the skies above Tokyo and dropped incendiary bombs on strategic points in the low city, lighting fiery beacons for the almost 300 B-29 bombers that proceeded to barrage this target area of thirty-one square kilometers and over one million residents. For two and a half hours, each B-29 flew low over its mark and released thousands of pounds of napalm, blanketing the buildings and people below with the jellied gasoline. Strong winds and wooden houses stoked a veritable firestorm that spread well beyond the designated bombing area. By dawn, an estimated 80,000 people, but likely upwards of 100,000 people, had been killed. Around 40,000 were injured, and one million were left homeless. Thirty-nine square kilometers of the city were destroyed. Especially hard hit were the low city wards of Fukagawa,

Figure 7.1 Men walking through rubble in war-torn Tokyo.
Photograph, c. 1945. Courtesy of JapanAirRaids.org.

Honjo, and Asakusa, which were dense with munitions factories
and flammable wooden houses.[17] As the journalist and critic
Kiyosawa Kiyoshi noted in his diary on March 10, "I hear that
Asakusa, Honjo, and Fukagawa are almost completely burned
out. Moreover, because of the violent wind, certain people who
entered air-raid shelters were overcome by smoke and their corpses
were lying here and there about the road. It was a horrifying sight,
truly unbearable to look at."[18] In the days and weeks after the air
raid, the city's parks became sites of temporary mass graves as well
as barrack-style housing for the displaced; others took shelter
beneath bridges or along rail lines. Meanwhile, about half of
Tokyo's factory workers ignored the pleas of government ministries
and didn't return to their jobs.

Immediately after the firebombing of Tokyo, its chief architect, General Curtis LeMay, ordered incendiary attacks on Nagoya, Osaka, and Kobe, signaling the strategic focus for the rest of the war on aerial bombardment of urban Japan. The B-29s returned to Tokyo in mid-April and late May, executing air raids that battered about forty-four square kilometers, including the administrative center of the city and the suburbs.

The losses borne by Tokyoites spoke not just to the intended impact of the US campaign to incinerate large swaths of Japan's cities but also to the Japanese military's abdication of responsibility for air defense. As early as April 1942, when over a dozen B-25 bombers led by Colonel James Doolittle were able to breach the air space above the capital, it was clear that the military couldn't protect the city from aerial attack. Air defense, then, was placed on the shoulders of Tokyoites and, for quite some time, was focused mainly on fire preparedness. Aside from the antiaircraft and machine guns that were installed in parks and on the rooftops of buildings, the government emphasized the need for households to be ready to fight fires. The Home Ministry expected water to be stored in bathtubs, buckets, rainwater tubs, and cisterns. And inspections were conducted by members of neighborhood associations to ensure that each household was equipped with fire hoses, fire extinguishers, fire dampers, buckets, a ladder, sand, and shovels, as well as steel helmets. Neighborhood associations also organized air-defense drills in which residents, largely women, practiced bucket relays to toss water on fires.[19]

By the summer of 1943, as the Japanese military lost ground and the empire's borders were pushed inward, fear of attacks on the main islands and demands for better air defense of the capital mounted. The governor-general of Tokyo, Ōdachi Shigeo, knew of American might from his time as mayor of occupied Singapore and took seriously the need to brace his city

137

for aerial bombardment. Readiness, for Ōdachi, entailed inculcating in people a willingness to sacrifice for the sake of the war. To illustrate the severity of the military situation and what would be required of Tokyoites, Ōdachi ordered the systematic slaughter of animals at the Ueno Zoo, from the lions Ali and Katarina to the popular elephants John, Tonky, and Wanri. Martyrs for the nation, he declared, would now be made on the home front.[20]

While steeling Tokyoites for impending hardships, the city also stepped up efforts to protect its residents. Although the government had already built evacuation compounds for the emperor and other political and military leaders, in July 1943 Ōdachi commanded each ward to establish Imperial Capital Air Defense Patriotic Associations charged with the construction of public air raid shelters. Throughout Tokyo, students, city workers, and members of neighborhood associations dug underground shelters in parks and other open spaces. By later in the year, neighborhood associations were recommending that individual households create their own shelters. Greater attention was also paid to conducting air raid drills. Neighborhood associations organized training exercises for their firefighting units, and the Tokyo Metropolitan Police rehearsed train stoppages with passenger duck-and-cover drills on the Yamanote loop line.

As the threat of aerial bombardment grew acute and the government began to acknowledge the need to remove certain people from endangered urban areas, evacuation figured more prominently in the lives of city dwellers. In Tokyo, evacuation meant both relocating people and clearing space for firebreaks. According to the city's "Plan to Evacuate Key Zones of the Imperial Capital," wide firebreaks were to be created in densely populated areas, close to rail and streetcar lines, and around strategic structures like munitions factories through "building evacuation," or the destruction of all buildings in a designated space. Around Shibuya Station, the Imperial Capital Evacuation Construction Brigade consisting of over half a million students, neighborhood association members, and carpenters demolished restaurants, cafés, movie theaters, and shops. Across the capital, the brigade destroyed over 50,000 structures, emptied about 100 square kilometers of space, and rendered around 60,000 families homeless. Less forceful was the evacuation of people out of the city, which was voluntary through the early part of 1944. A few hundred thousand Tokyoites, including around 77,000 children, vacated the capital and moved in with relatives who lived elsewhere, most likely in neighboring prefectures. But with Japan's loss of the Mariana Islands of Guam, Tinian, and Saipan in the summer of 1944, every major Japanese city came within range of American B-29 bombers, and the government instituted compulsory evacuation of schoolchildren. Over the next few months, around 225,000 children were sent in school units from Tokyo to temples and resorts in the countryside. By the end of the year, the government was encouraging others such as pregnant women, mothers with infants, and those over age sixty-five to leave urban areas.

For those who stayed in Tokyo, air raids became a regular part of daily life in late November 1944. When sirens sounded, Tokyoites grabbed their pre-packed rucksacks and headed to a shelter.[21] This routine frayed residents such as Yoshizawa Hisako, a native of Fukagawa ward in her late twenties, who noted in her diary,

> The fatigue brought on by the sleep deprivation caused by the air raids is leading to a brittle sort of self-interest that makes boarding and getting off trains frightening. Try as I might to remain calm, my nerves are on edge. Today, a friend who recently joined my company reported that her aunt doesn't

clean house much because she said, "If [the house] catches fire during an air raid, it won't matter." Recently, life in the capital has been 'day-to-day,' as they say.[22]

The incendiary bombing raid in March 1945 upended Tokyoites' wartime routines and laid bare the woeful insufficiency of their preparatory measures. As the bombs began to fall, the firefighting units of neighborhood associations attempted bucket relays to extinguish the fires, but these dismal efforts, like all others, were soon overwhelmed by the ferocity of the flames. In the face of such widespread destruction, the metropolitan government encouraged all nonessential personnel to leave the capital, and set up offices at Ueno, Tokyo, Shinagawa, and Shinjuku Stations where people could receive first aid, some food, and train tickets out of the city. By late April, over two million people had left the capital. Between the casualties from the air raids and those who evacuated, the population of Tokyo had shrunk by the end of the war to less than half of what it had been in early 1944.[23]

• • •

On September 2, 1945, over 400 B-29 bombers reappeared in the skies above Tokyo. This time, the planes were not instruments of destruction so much as triumphant symbols of American military might, flying over the USS *Missouri* as Japanese officials signed the documents of surrender ending the Asia Pacific War. The ceremony aboard the US battleship, anchored in Tokyo Bay, was replete with reminders of Japan's past follies and weaknesses. Fluttering on the *Missouri* was the United States flag that had been flying over the White House on the day that Pearl Harbor was attacked, as well as the thirty-one star flag that had been displayed on Commodore Matthew Perry's vessel when he sailed into Edo Bay in 1854.[24] In Tokyo and across the former Japanese empire, symbols of Japanese military ambition and power were discredited and diminished at the dawn of the postwar era. On Namsan, in postcolonial Seoul, the shrine complex was demolished, taken down by the hands of Shinto priests who wanted to remove and protect the deities in the face of Korean desires to, "Burn Korea Shrine and Seoul Shrine!"[25] In the coming years, Namsan would be transformed into a site of monuments to anti-Japanese nationalism.[26] On the deck of the *Missouri*, General Douglas MacArthur, head of the postwar US occupation of Japan as Supreme Commander for the Allied Powers, also turned toward the future. MacArthur expressed his hope that "a better world shall emerge out of the blood and carnage of the past – a world founded upon faith and understanding – a world dedicated to the dignity of man and the fulfillment of his most cherished wish – for freedom, tolerance and justice."[27]

The occupation's project of demilitarizing and democratizing Japan was based in Tokyo, which came to host about 25,000 American soldiers who helped remake parts of the capital in the image of an American city. The occupation's General Headquarters (GHQ) began by commandeering buildings in the Marunouchi business district for use as offices, and MacArthur himself decided to orchestrate the whole affair from the former Dai Ichi Mutual Insurance Building, just across from the Imperial Palace grounds (see Figure 7.2). In addition to office and government buildings, the occupiers claimed wharves, piers, storage facilities, hospitals, and airports, as well as part of the Tsukiji Central Wholesale Market, Sugamo Prison and Tokyo Prison, and all of the former Imperial Japanese Army bases. The Eighth Army, charged with the military occupation, assumed management of the railway system, including partial control of Tokyo, Ueno, and Shibaura Stations. For the entertainment of the troops, cultural venues such as cinemas, theaters, clubs, and stadiums

Figure 7.2 Strollers on the Imperial Palace grounds with the General Headquarters of the occupation in the backdrop. Photograph by Hayashi Tadahiko, *Occupation Soldiers Sightseeing in Tokyo with Japanese Women (Imperial Palace Plaza)*, 1946. From the series *Kasutori jidai*. Courtesy of DNPartcom and the Tokyo Photographic Art Museum.

were requisitioned. Perhaps most popular was the Ernie Pyle theater, previously the Takarazuka theater, which screened recent film releases, hosted beauty pageants, and staged plays like *Arsenic and Old Lace* and musical productions like *The Mikado*. To Americanize the physical space of the city, the English language was marshaled to rename both buildings and streets. Meiji Shrine Stadium became Nile Kinnick Stadium, the Nakahachi Gohan Building became the Economic Research Building, and the Ryōgoku Kokugikan sumo wrestling arena became Memorial Hall. The maze of streets, many of which didn't have names or signage, was made navigable by new designations – streets radiating outward from the Imperial Palace were named Avenues A to

Z, and those encircling it in concentric rings were numbered one through sixty. Prominent roads in the center of the city were given special names, like University and St. Luke's, and so Avenue A in front of the GHQ building was known as Tokyo Boulevard. English came to be seen on street and traffic signs, and on displays like the twelve-meter neon "Merry X'mas" that appeared annually on the front of the GHQ building.

The need to house the American officers and enlisted soldiers transformed the use and ownership of buildings in the capital, at least for the duration of the occupation. Enlisted men and women initially stayed in former Imperial Army troop barracks, and then in private and government buildings that were converted into lodgings. While officers were put up in the city's nicest hotels, dozens of the highest ranking were housed in private residences of upper-class Tokyoites. The homeowners were typically given a week to vacate the premises, and the Japanese government was expected to make sure that the fully furnished homes were equipped with linens, silverware, and an English-speaking staff of servants. Pressure for housing intensified when it was decided that officers, enlisted soldiers, and some civilian employees could invite their dependents to join them in Tokyo. To accommodate the influx of family members, GHQ requisitioned all Western-style houses with at least six rooms and within a forty-five-minute drive of the Imperial Palace. By early 1947, around 600 residences in the capital had been designated for occupation personnel; the homeowners kept the title but relinquished rights to their property during the occupation and were assisted by the Japanese government in their search for an alternative place to live.

The demand for family housing precipitated the construction of large residential communities, which had an enduring impact on the postwar landscape of Tokyo and the lifestyles of

Tokyoites. These housing complexes were recreations of American middle-class neighborhoods, built by the Japanese government which supplied the labor (from architects and engineers to carpenters and bricklayers) and materials (from lumber and cement to circuit breakers and insulated wire). GHQ also expected the Japanese government to provide most of the items considered standard in middle-class homes, including porcelain enamel sinks and tubs, water heaters, electric stoves, refrigerators, overstuffed armchairs, davenports, Venetian blinds, carpets, mattresses, bed frames, playpens and cribs, telephones, electric fans, and toasters, as well as ice buckets, rolling pins, magazine racks, and toilet paper holders. Provisioning the residences entailed a significant transfer of knowledge and technology from the Americans to Japanese manufacturers, who were unfamiliar with how to make many of these goods.

The middle-class lifestyle modeled by the American occupiers was epitomized by two of the dependent housing communities in the capital: Washington Heights and Grant Heights. Washington Heights, the largest complex yet built in Japan, rose up on ninety-two hectares in the Shibuya ward on what was formerly the Yoyogi Parade Ground, just south of Meiji Shrine and two miles west of the Imperial Palace. In addition to the houses, the community included schools, a library, fire stations, gas stations, a chapel, movie theater, recreation hall, and shopping center with a dispensary, commissary, beauty parlors, and barber shops. Grant Heights was further out from the center of the city, on largely agricultural land that had been used by the Japanese Imperial Army as an airfield. Eighty construction companies employing well over 6,000 men built this vast complex of more than a thousand housing units for 5,600 Americans and 2,400 Japanese servants. By 1947, about 2,000 dependent families called Tokyo home, with most living in Washington Heights or Grant

Heights; by 1949, there were about 5,000 dependent housing units in the capital. In addition to the institutions and services of a self-contained community, each complex had post exchanges (PXs) that supplied goods from the United States, like cosmetics, clothing, canned goods, and frozen meat, as well as some American foods that were made in Tokyo. Coca-Cola bottling machines churned out hundreds of thousands of sodas a day, a factory at Keio University made tens of thousands of donuts daily, and the Morinaga Food Corporation produced well over 10,000 kilograms of candies and cookies a week.[28]

For most of the occupation period, an American-style, middle-class lifestyle was unimaginably distant from the day-to-day realities of most Tokyoites. Finding shelter was one immediate concern, as the wartime leveling of buildings for firebreaks and by air raids had destroyed over 1.5 million housing units. The Tokyo Metropolitan Government initially planned to build about 50,000 single-family barracks, each with two small rooms, a closet, an earthen floor for a kitchen area, and a semidetached toilet; but by the end of 1945, only 100 had actually been constructed. And 900 units were created by converting unlikely spaces, such as train cars, buses, and trolleys, into living quarters. As the demands of constructing complexes for occupation personnel mounted, it was difficult for the Japanese government to secure the materials, land, and labor necessary to provide emergency housing for its own citizens. Many Tokyoites took to living in air raid shelters or cobbled together wooden barracks with tin roofs, sometimes made out of flattened steel cans thrown out by the occupiers. In some districts of the city, areas dense with these temporary, rickety structures endured for years, into the 1960s. The upper-class families whose houses were requisitioned for use by high-ranking American officers took up residence in the servants' quarters or storage sheds on their property, dormitories in converted factories, and water craft on one of the city's canals. Others in search of housing moved to those residential areas in the western wards of the city that had been spared wartime destruction. This westward movement paralleled migration after the Great Kanto earthquake, but this postwar iteration didn't lead to much new construction, as many single-family houses came to accommodate multiple families.

Especially precarious were the many homeless people who took shelter in the city's public spaces, in the streets and parks and train stations. None was as crowded as Ueno Station, with an underground passageway that filled with thousands of destitute Tokyoites, among them many orphaned children, prostitutes, and unemployed veterans. And in largely circumscribed areas, where taxis and Japanese policemen would rather not go, shantytowns for resident Koreans with ramshackle sheds and no water or sewage systems stood until the late 1960s. Such Korean slums elicited the concern of occupation authorities only insofar as they were seen as a hotbed for communist activities. Little attention was paid to the high unemployment rate in the shantytowns whose residents worked as laborers, collected pieces of metal to sell, and engaged in business activity, including of the black-market variety. Life in Korean shantytowns was made more insecure by the liminal political status of resident Koreans, who were deprived by the postwar Japanese government of their de facto Japanese citizenship as subjects of the Japanese empire and rendered stateless persons until 1965, or 1981 if they identified as North Korean, making them ineligible for national health insurance, unemployment benefits, or any other state welfare program.

The exigencies of daily life during the occupation propelled the establishment of black markets which cropped up in the war-torn spaces of the city. A backbone of the capital's economic life, these open-air markets offered food, construction materials, and other necessities to Tokyoites, if at exorbitant prices. Often situated near train stations, their prime location was especially convenient for commuting customers and for farmers, who came into the city to sell their produce above official, government-set prices. For enterprising individuals, the black markets were an opportunity to earn some money. Most vendors started out selling food, like soup or steamed potatoes; some then moved up to clothing and then metal pots or watches. As long as stall operators registered their business with the police and navigated their relationship with local gangs which controlled most of the black markets, they stood a chance of making ends meet. In the early years of the occupation, an estimated 75,000 vendors set up shop at over 200 markets in districts around the capital, from Asakusa to Ginza to Shinjuku.[29]

While black markets were largely ephemeral, fading from the city as food rationing ended and the economy improved in the early 1950s, some left a unique imprint on their corner of the city. In the Kanda ward, the ten or so stalls that specialized in electric goods, such as radios, were the beginning of what became the now iconic Akihabara Electric Town. In the Shibuya ward, home to the Washington Heights complex, the market's specialty of selling used American clothing was a precursor to the district's characteristic cultivation of trendy and edgy fashion. And in Ueno, the hundreds of stalls that extended southward from the station selling peanuts, dried squid, noodles, tobacco, alcohol, and other sundry items endured into the postwar and continues to draw shoppers as the bustling, open-air market Ameyokochō, named after its signature potato candy, or *ame*, which was one of the few sweets that could be found in late 1940s Tokyo.[30]

With most Tokyoites consumed by making it through each day, the Japanese government scrambling to accommodate the occupiers, and GHQ focused on demilitarizing and

Figure 7.3 The plaza in front of Shibuya Station after the war, with a statue of Hachikō. Photograph by Tanuma Takeyoshi, 1948. Courtesy of Tanuma Takeyoshi.

democratizing a defeated Japan, the physical reconstruction of the capital received little attention (see Figure 7.3). This was not the time nor the circumstance for creating grand designs for a new or reformed city, or imagining a Tokyo of the future. Rebuilding meant repairing infrastructure, the roads and railways and electricity networks, so that the city could function.[31] And because the bones of the capital had been sound, its fundamental structure was altered little in the immediate postwar years. Meaningful changes to the landscape of the city would have to wait.

• • •

Well after the occupation ended in April 1952, physical reminders of Japan's loss and the preeminence of American military might lingered in the postwar city. Over 200 US military facilities remained throughout Tokyo, granted use of Japanese land by a security treaty concluded between the two countries. Some of these areas were small, just enough for a communications tower; others were sizeable military bases. Tachikawa Air Base, in western Tokyo, continued to be used by US forces until Governor Minobe Ryōkichi negotiated its return to the city in the late 1970s, when over 160 hectares of the land was converted into the largest park in the metropolis, Shōwa Memorial Park. Another of the large military bases, Yokota Air Base, is one of the seven US military facilities currently operating in Tokyo and serves as the headquarters of the US Forces Japan and the Fifth Air Force.

As part of the process of reclaiming the capital, two of the possessions that the Japanese and Tokyo governments sought repeatedly for return were the communities of Washington Heights and Grant Heights. In 1962, two years before the Tokyo Olympics, the United States acquiesced to handing back part of Washington Heights, which became the grounds for Yoyogi National Gymnasium. Just two months before the games, the rest of the complex reverted to the city and was quickly turned into housing for the athletes. After the Olympics, the Tokyo Metropolitan Government took down the housing units and created a large greenspace, Yoyogi Park. Grant Heights was given back to the city later, in the mid-1970s, and was turned into Hikarigaoka, the largest apartment development in Tokyo, with about 40,000 residents.[32]

One of the most captivating and enduring legacies of the occupation was the model it displayed, for all Tokyoites to see, of an American-style, middle-class life. As the Japanese economy pulled back from the brink of depression and began to recover in the early 1950s, the day-to-day became less desperate for many as food rationing ended, clothing and basic household items became more available, and the need to shop at black markets abated. Gradually, Tokyoites could turn away from the difficult past, look toward the future, and imagine what it might be like to enjoy the kind of wealth and material abundance that had been exhibited by the American victors and occupiers.[33] This aspiration for affluent, middle-class lifestyles, and the alliance forged between Japan and the United States through and beyond the occupation, guided the transformation of Tokyo from an occupied city to a revitalized postwar city. Yet what faded in this transition were memories of its recent, complicated history as the capital of a vast and violent empire.

8

Dreams and Disappointments

O N an otherwise ordinary morning in September 1960, the residents of a multistory apartment complex called Hibarigaoka woke up anticipating an extraordinary event: Crown Prince Akihito and Princess Michiko were coming to visit their homes. Excitement surrounded the young couple who exemplified the possibilities of a seemingly new, postwar era. Everyone could aspire to a brighter future, they appeared to suggest, even as they enjoyed uniquely privileged pedigrees, he the eldest son of Emperor Hirohito and she the daughter of a wealthy industrialist. With an air less of rarefied monarchy than royal celebrity, Akihito and Michiko had entranced people across the country a year earlier with their media sensation of a wedding. In the months leading up to the ceremony, weeklies and television shows inspired fascination with how the twenty-five-year-old crown prince and his fiancée, the first commoner to marry into the imperial family, were brought together not by familial arrangement but by love, in what was dubbed the "romance of the century."[1] The newly wedded couple's procession through central Tokyo in a horse-drawn carriage was watched in person by half a million onlookers who lined the almost nine kilometer route, and on television by an estimated fifteen million people. After the wedding, Michiko and Akihito distanced them-selves from the oppressive gaze of the imperial in-laws and established their own household, turning away from a multigenerational family structure and becoming instead an iconic nuclear family. Symbolizing postwar peace and progress, the imperial couple toured Hibarigaoka, smiling as they saw firsthand the coveted apartments of this planned community in the western suburbs of Tokyo (see Figure 8.1). Just opened in the previous year, the reinforced concrete buildings were home to the residents of more than 2,500 units, who also enjoyed the park, baseball field, tennis courts, elementary school, supermarket, post office, and more, all on the grounds of the Hibarigaoka complex. Akihito and Michiko were shown the apartment of an advertising executive and his family, a two bedroom unit with an eat-in

Figure 8.1 Crown Prince Akihito and Crown Princess Michiko visiting the Hibarigaoka apartment complex in September 1960. Photograph by the *Asahi Shinbun*, September 6, 1960. Courtesy of Getty Images.

kitchen that the princess complimented as "conveniently designed, healthy, and bright."[2] While imperial tours of the prewar period had been of weapons and troops, this postwar version was of modern kitchens and prosperous families. To capture and share this celebration of the domestic everyday, photographs were published of the imperial couple standing on an apartment balcony, surrounded by neighbors who had, as instructed, left their laundry hanging on the line to show the crown prince, princess, and rest of the country their comfortable "life as it really was."[3] Akihito and Michiko's visit to Hibarigaoka reinforced their image as imperial figures fit for the postwar era and encouraged all to dream of a middle-class life.[4]

In 1960, the residents of the Hibarigaoka apartments were among the earliest generation of Tokyoites to experience a taste of the postwar, middle-class dream. In their postwar iteration, middle-class lifestyles had elements resonant with their 1920s predecessors in the embrace of urbanism, cosmopolitanism, and consumerism. But they carried the symbolic weight of successfully overcoming the hardships of defeat and occupation, and achieving high rates of economic growth. Also in the late 1950s, unlike the 1920s, middle-class living was starting to become a majority experience. As Tokyo recovered from wartime poverty and remodernized its infrastructure, middle-class lifestyles started to come within grasp of more and more city dwellers. In the same year that Akihito and Michiko graced the lifestyles in Hibarigaoka with their imperial visit, the prime minister Ikeda Hayato announced his plan to double the gross national income in ten years, with the stated goal of raising standards of living. Over the late 1950s and 1960s, the economy did average double-digit growth rates, household incomes climbed, high school graduation rates rose, and the suburbs expanded.[5] In this time of burgeoning prosperity, a powerful middle-class ideal took firm root, propagating the allure of a nuclear family with a husband who worked a white-collar job, a wife who ran the home, and income enough to both consume material goods and save toward the purchase of a house. Owning certain consumer durables became an especially potent marker of middle-classness, as electric appliance companies marketed their products from rice cookers to washing machines as hallmarks of a bright new life. And as individual consumption grew, so too did consumer ambitions. The desire in the late 1950s to own the "three treasures" (washing machine, vacuum cleaner, refrigerator) or the "three S's" (*senpūki* or electric fan, *sentakki* or washing machine, *suihanki* or electric rice cooker) extended, by the mid-1960s, to the "three C's" (car, color television set, air conditioner). In 1960, about 55 percent of urbanites owned a television; by 1964, that number had jumped to 94 percent.[6] At the vanguard of the countrywide embrace and achievement of middle-class aspirations, Tokyoites spurred the re-emergence of the capital as the engine and emblem of national progress.

• • •

The selection of Tokyo as the host city for the 1964 Olympics provided the nation with an unparalleled opportunity to realize and demonstrate its postwar rebirth as a remodernized, peaceful, and prosperous Japan. There was much to prove. Having forfeited the 1940 Tokyo Olympics because of its war with China and then been banned from the 1948 Games, and having lost a bid to host in 1960, Japan needed to show that it deserved to be welcomed back into the international community as a full-fledged partner in cultural, diplomatic, and economic affairs. To illustrate how far the country had come from its darkest days of imperialism and fascism, the organizers of the 1964 Games highlighted the postwar nation's economic and technological achievements, and downplayed its militarist history. Only selective reference was made to the war, in ways that elided Japan's colonial and wartime violence and amplified the universalizing theme of peace.[7] Efforts to project the image of a peaceful and unified nation also paved over the country's most recent history of political activism and conflict. Only a few years earlier, in 1960, hundreds of thousands of people took to the streets of Tokyo in mass protests against the government's renewal of Japan's security treaty with the United States. With the Olympics, as with its promise of economic growth, the government performed a skilled sleight of hand, distracting people's attention away from political schisms and toward national advancement and achievement.[8]

If Tokyo was to showcase the nation's postwar evolution, it would have to look and function like a modern city. In the view of Tokyo governor and International Olympic Committee member Azuma Ryōtarō, the games were a chance to build the capital anew. Of highest priority was upgrading infrastructure, which had been hastily and shoddily repaired after the war. Many of these improvement projects were already planned or underway before the Olympic announcement, but the pace of construction quickened sharply to ensure completion before the curtain rose on the host city.[9]

Particularly transformative for how people moved through the physical landscape of the capital was the development of transportation infrastructure, which consumed roughly three-quarters of the metropolitan government's spending in preparation for the Olympics. The cityscape was extended upward with the construction of an elevated expressway system that wound in and around central Tokyo (see Figure 8.2). Over thirty-one kilometers long and hoisted, at points, about forty meters into the air, the imposing expressway cast shadows over buildings, canals, and parks. Most infamously, part of the Metropolitan Expressway was built directly over the iconic Nihonbashi bridge, which remains

Figure 8.2 Tokyoites enjoying the expressway before its opening. Photograph by Tanuma Takeyoshi, 1962. Courtesy of Tanuma Takeyoshi.

under its suffocating cover to this day (see Figure 8.3). But the massive highways ensured that visitors could travel quickly between their hotels and Olympic venues, avoiding entrapment in traffic snarls. In another effort to ease congestion, around 138 kilometers of new roads were built that linked the main Olympic facilities and also connected western Tokyo where they were clustered, to the city center with its key spots and attractions such as Tokyo Station and Ginza. While much vehicular traffic was raised skyward, some rail transport enhanced mobility below ground. A new subway line, the Hibiya line, was completed just

Figure 8.3 Construction of the Metropolitan Expressway over the Nihonbashi bridge. Photograph by the *Asahi Shinbun*, June 13, 1963. Courtesy of Getty Images.

weeks before the opening ceremonies, bringing the total number in operation up to four. And the unveiling of the *shinkansen*, or bullet train, necessitated the relocation of stores at its Tokyo Station terminus underground. Below railway stations throughout the center of the capital, passageways and shopping areas would be created to keep people moving through the multiple layers of the city's expanding transportation network.[10]

Impressive innovations in transportation helped convey the image that Japan had more than recovered from the physical destruction of the war and was rapidly developing into a technological powerhouse. A cutting-edge monorail, then the longest in the world, was inaugurated less than a month before the games to shuttle travelers between Haneda Airport and central

Tokyo. Though it let passengers off at a somewhat inconvenient station on the Yamanote loop line, and still today ends there at Hamamatsuchō, the technologically advanced Tokyo Monorail helped form visitors' first impressions of the host city.[11] For the international audience that experienced the Tokyo games on television, advances in media technology furthered the image of a state-of-the-art Japan. These Olympics were the first to be broadcast live, and in color, via satellite. Television viewers were also introduced to slow-motion playbacks and uninterrupted coverage of the marathon by some seventy cameras. One British reporter went so far as to dub the games the "'Science Fiction' Olympics."[12]

The sleekest and shiniest symbol of an ultramodern Japan was the Tōkaidō *shinkansen* which, not unlike the Tōkaidō road of early modern times, snaked along the coast between the Kanto and Kansai regions. What distinguished the *shinkansen* was its futuristic aesthetic and sheer speed (see Figure 8.4). Heralded as the world's fastest train when it debuted just nine days before the opening ceremonies, the *shinkansen* smoothly rocketed passengers between Tokyo and Osaka at maximum speeds of around 200 kilometers per hour. The trip, which took six hours and forty minutes on the standard train, was cut to four hours by the bullet train, and then to just over three hours in 1965. The technological feat of the *shinkansen* was covered and experienced by media from around the world who were already in Tokyo for the games. And in the months and years that followed, the new possibility of a day trip between Tokyo and Osaka shrank perceptions of space, birthing the idea that the two cities might be thought of as part of one urban network, a Tōkaidō megalopolis.[13]

While certain transportation projects forwarded an image of a nation at the leading edge of modern development, other infrastructure improvements were compelled by the fear that Japan would otherwise be revealed as "backward" and

Figure 8.4 A *shinkansen* on a test run pulls into Tokyo Station. Photograph by the *Asahi Shinbun*, July 15, 1964. Courtesy of Getty Images.

"uncivilized." Particularly concerning was the capital's inadequate management of garbage and human excrement, which could endanger both public health and the city's reputation. The Ministry of Health and Welfare worried about the games taking place during the peak months for infectious diseases such as Japanese encephalitis and dysentery, and urged the adoption of more hygienic practices of waste disposal to avert sickening the country's foreign guests. To address this challenge, the Tokyo Metropolitan Government phased out the use of large wooden garbage boxes, which were prone to catching fire, smelling, and breeding mosquitos and flies, and promoted their replacement with plastic garbage containers. In one newspaper advertisement from 1962, the plastics manufacturer Sekisui Chemical touted the virtues of its polyethylene garbage container, which would make "Dirty Tokyo" a thing of the past so that there could be an "Olympics in a town without garbage boxes, in a pretty Tokyo!"[14] The metropolitan government also made household garbage pickup more efficient and frequent by introducing scheduled trash collection, whereby each household would bring its refuse to a specific place at a specific time to meet the garbage truck. During the games themselves, sanitation drivers made their rounds in the early morning so that any signs of garbage would be kept out of sight.

To keep any evidence of human waste from public view, the city undertook the repair and construction of sewers. In 1960, only 21 percent of the capital was on a sewer system; most excrement was pumped from each household by a truck, transported to the outskirts of the city, and used as fertilizer. Some was just dumped untreated into local waters, at a time when the Sumida River, notoriously polluted with all manner of household and industrial effluent, stank of ammonia and hydrogen sulfide. To lessen the chance of any embarrassment, sewer construction was intense in the western parts of the city and Shibuya ward in particular, where foreign visitors would gather. By the time of the games, the portion of Shibuya on a sewer system had soared from a mere 3 percent in 1959 to 60 percent.[15]

The comprehensive, multifaceted campaign to clean and beautify the host city extended well beyond the improvement of waste management systems. To encourage civilized comportment, the metropolitan government launched a Beautification of the Capital movement that included calls for Tokyoites to refrain from public urination and spitting, and to pick up dog feces. In addition, the tenth of every month in the years leading up to the games was designated Metropolitan Beautification Day. On one such day in January 1964, about two million residents, from students to members of town assemblies and women's associations, mobilized to clean the streets of Tokyo. During the games, beautification efforts extended to the removal of mendicant and homeless people from the center of the city.[16]

The modernity of the capital was also projected by buildings that were designed and erected for the Olympics. A shiny new broadcasting center for the national network NHK arose in Shibuya, within view of many Olympic sites. And the upscale Hotel New Otani began welcoming guests in 1964 as the tallest building in the city at seventeen floors.[17] Most strikingly innovative was the Yoyogi National Gymnasium, born from the creative vision of acclaimed architect Tange Kenzō. Home to swimming and other events during the games, the arena was draped with a dramatic curved roof suspended by cables using a bridge-like structure never before attempted on a building of this size. An engineering and aesthetic marvel at the time, the now iconic gymnasium evokes the layered contours of a Japanese pagoda in thoroughly modernist form. Another notable, if less imaginative, Olympic venue was the Nippon Budōkan, an octagonal building with a curved roof reminiscent of both a historic Buddhist temple and Mount Fuji. This modern structure of concrete and steel, constructed on ground that had been a base of the Imperial Guards, hosted the debut of judo as an Olympic sport as well as exhibitions of kendo (fencing), kyūdō (archery), and sumo (wrestling). With both its aesthetics and events, the Nippon Budōkan subtly reminded spectators that these were the first Olympics in Asia, while the display of martial skills turned pure pastimes reinforced the idea of a peaceful, postwar Japan.[18]

Perhaps no aspect of the Olympics recast Japan and its wartime history as visibly and remarkably as the opening ceremonies. Into the National Stadium, in the outer gardens of Meiji Shrine, were welcomed more than 5,000 athletes from more than ninety countries by an audience of 75,000 spectators. The start of the games was officially proclaimed not by the prime minister but by Emperor Hirohito, the former leader of the wartime empire appearing in robes of a pacified, ceremonial figure. To further whitewash the nation's colonial and wartime history, the final torchbearer was Sakai Yoshinori, a runner born on August 6, 1945, in Hiroshima prefecture shortly after the dropping of the atomic bomb. The torch, which had been making its way from Greece through a dozen Asian countries as well as US-occupied Okinawa, was carried up the stadium steps by "Atom Boy" who lit the Olympic cauldron with a flame symbolizing international unity and friendship.[19] In a final flourish, a bevy of doves was released into the sky. (This romantic gesture was deflated by the realities wrought by thousands of uncaged pigeons flapping above people's heads.)

All of the attention and resources poured into those areas of the city most visible to Olympic guests helped shift the vital heart of Tokyo westward, and exacerbated the disparities between a redeveloped high city and an underdeveloped low city. While infrastructure in eastern wards was allowed to languish, the areas of Shibuya and Shinjuku, where many Olympic venues were clustered, flourished in subsequent decades as commercial and cultural centers. The district of Harajuku in Shibuya ward, for instance, capitalized on a cosmopolitan atmosphere animated first by the American presence at the Washington Heights housing complex and then by the concentration of media companies, shops, and nightspots spurred by the Olympics. To this day, the impact of the games remains visible in the diversity of youth cultures, trendy fashions, and enthusiastic consumerism that enliven the Shibuya area. Beyond Tokyo itself, the construction of infrastructure, accommodations, and venues in the neighboring prefectures of Saitama, Chiba, and Kanagawa for events such as yacht racing, canoeing, and cycling expanded the city outward and reinforced the emerging identity of a Tokyo metropolitan region.[20]

• • •

When Crown Prince Akihito and Princess Michiko toured Hibarigaoka in 1960, the apartment complex, or *danchi*, was fast becoming an object of desire not just for the housing it provided but also for the way of living that it promised. Newly designed and constructed, *danchi* tantalized upwardly mobile families with a middle-class life that was still beyond the reach of many Tokyoites. The concrete buildings, exceptionally resistant to fire, offered comfort and security to those haunted by memories of wartime bombing. Reassuring, too, were the steel doors intended to prevent the spread of flames. Each unit was also outfitted with amenities, including electricity and flush toilets, and fixtures such as stainless steel sinks, which were increasingly considered necessities for modern living. And the space and configuration of the apartments encouraged domestic lifestyles that revolved around the nuclear family. The relatively small size of a residence didn't leave room for extended family members, liberating young couples from their in-laws. And each unit's private bathroom, attached balcony, and dedicated bedrooms allowed for some privacy between immediate family members and from the community outside of its locking metal doors.[21]

In the late 1950s and early 1960s, the association of *danchi* with middle-class life was solidified by the profile of its residents, who were mainly white-collar families of relative wealth who considered *danchi* residence a stepping stone to home ownership. At a time when urban housing markets were still plagued by shortages, aspiring residents had to demonstrate that they met the income requirements to be entered into a lottery for a unit. Compared to Tokyoites as a whole, those families who were fortunate enough to secure an apartment tended to be smaller, with husbands who were younger and more highly educated. And *danchi*-dwelling housewives reportedly spent less time on housework than their *danchi*-less counterparts. *Danchi* families were also more likely to own electric goods, the rice cookers, washing machines, and refrigerators that were the talismans of middle-class living. Further enhancing the cachet of *danchi* life was the scarcity of units. When the state-sponsored Japan Housing Corporation (JHC) was building the Hibarigaoka complex, it was pioneering the construction of multistory apartment blocks, and its state-of-the-art *danchi* comprised a small fraction of available housing. With less than 1 percent of Japanese households actually residing in such housing, *danchi* life was discussed extensively and imagined romantically in the pages of magazines and newspapers as an enviable dream.[22]

Even though the modern apartment conceived and built by the JHC never assumed a large share of the housing market, its *danchi* units became a much emulated model for residences and for urban, middle-class lifestyles. By the 1970s, many people lived in multistory structures with concrete walls, whether built with public or private funds. Units replicated the configuration of JHC apartments, consisting of some number of bedrooms and an eat-in kitchen called a dining kitchen, or DK for short. It became standard to describe floor plans with the designation nDK, referring to the number of bedrooms and a dining kitchen (e.g., 2DK or 3DK). When the JHC began adding living rooms to their units to accommodate residents' acquisition of sofas, pianos, stereos, and more, another term was born: the nLDK, or the number of bedrooms, a living room, and a dining kitchen (e.g., 2LDK or 3LDK). Inside these spaces, the fixtures popularized by JHC *danchi* became conventional. By the mid-1970s, for example, almost three-quarters of kitchens were equipped with stainless steel sinks.

The JHC not only inspired a certain urban, middle-class life, but it also cultivated such a lifestyle in areas beyond the center of Tokyo. Pushed outward by rising land prices, the JHC purchased and developed large plots in the more affordable fringes, hoping to lure urbanites stung by skyrocketing housing costs out to the suburbs. In countryside locations distant from the city center, the JHC engineered the very creation of suburban communities. This typically involved building not just the apartments themselves but also extensive infrastructure including transportation, electricity, water, schools, post offices, and branches of the police, fire station, and city hall.[23] The sheer magnitude of these JHC projects expanded in the mid-1960s when pooled government monies and eased restrictions on development enabled the construction of mass public housing complexes known as "new towns." New towns emerged in the suburbs of Osaka and Nagoya. And in the Tokyo metropolitan region, three suburban communities were conceived in the 1960s: Chiba New Town in Chiba prefecture to the east, Kōhoku New Town in Kanagawa prefecture to the south, and Tama New Town to the west. Further out was a new town named Tsukuba Science City, in Ibaraki prefecture to the north. Tama New Town was one of the most ambitious of these such projects, spearheaded by the JHC and the Tokyo Metropolitan Government as well as the Tokyo Metropolitan Housing Supply Corporation. Planned by 1965 and opened in 1971, Tama New Town extended over 2,890 hectares and straddled four different cities of the Tokyo metropolis. It was organized into twenty-one neighborhoods, each intended to accommodate anywhere from 12,000 to 20,000 residents who would avail themselves of nearby shops, restaurants, clinics, banks, police boxes, post offices, and schools. The neighborhoods were grouped into six large districts, each with its own commuter rail station that anchored opportunities for consumption and leisure, from museums and amusement centers to department stores.

As aspects of urban life penetrated the farther reaches of the Tokyo metropolitan region, the suburbs came to be defined less by their particular patterns of daily life and more by their very location beyond the city center. In both the urban core and the suburban periphery, many people tended to live in small spaces and commute to work by train. Unlike what might be imagined of suburbs elsewhere, there was not a stark distinction between the kinds of housing in urban and suburban locales; there were neither blocks of towering apartment buildings in the city, nor rows of spacious houses with pristine lawns in the suburbs. Suburbanites lived in quarters as small as their city counterparts, with most residences of Tama New Town clocking in within the national average range of roughly forty to fifty-six square meters. Nor were city residents spared tiring commutes, able to walk to their workplaces. Opportunities to consume were not the reserve of the city, nor was the normalization of the nuclear family. There were similarities, too, in the patchwork character of the landscapes. It wasn't unusual in the city to find buildings of varied uses, types, heights, and prices intermingled in a single neighborhood. There was a suburban pastiche as well, though of a somewhat different composition, with modestly sized farms, undeveloped land, and small developments dotting the areas around planned communities such as the Hibarigaoka *danchi* and Tama New Town.[24] In the city and the suburbs, a widely shared middle-class lifestyle reflected the homogenizing urbanization of postwar Japan.

As a majority of people in Japan came to choose urban over rural living in the three decades after the end of the war, Tokyo experienced tremendous population growth, making it the unrivaled behemoth among the country's most populous urban regions. The very definition of the "Tokyo metropolitan region" was expansive, consisting of: the Tokyo metropolis or Tokyo prefecture (composed of the twenty-three wards at the center of the city plus more than two dozen other municipalities, mostly to the west) and three neighboring prefectures (Saitama to the north, Chiba to the east, and Kanagawa to the south). Even more extensive, if less frequently evoked, was the "capital region" which included the four additional prefectures of Gunma, Tochigi, Ibaraki, and Yamanashi.[25] Between 1945 and 1980, over nineteen million people moved to the Tokyo metropolitan region. By the mid-1980s, it was home to over thirty million people, or about a quarter of Japan's entire population.[26]

While millions of people were drawn to the Tokyo metropolitan region as a whole, growth was propelled by those who decided to move, not to the center of the city but to the suburbs. The number of new residents in central Tokyo peaked in the late 1950s, and the total population in the twenty-three wards declined after 1960. Over the next three decades, the places to which the largest number of people migrated were farther and farther away from the center of Tokyo. While in the early 1960s many people were moving to places about twenty to thirty kilometers outside of the city core, by the mid-1970s, that length had increased to forty to fifty kilometers. A white-collar worker who lived with his family this far out and worked in the city would have a fairly lengthy commute, traveling the rough equivalent of the distance from the US Capitol Building in Washington, D.C. to Annapolis, Maryland, or Grand Central Terminal in New York City to Edison, New Jersey.[27] This push outward was reflected in the rising population of the three metropolitan prefectures of Saitama, Chiba, and Kanagawa, which more than doubled from around 7.4 million residents in 1955 to about 15.4 million in 1975.[28]

This urbanization of suburban areas did not, however, come at the expense of central Tokyo. Many suburbanites had jobs in the twenty-three wards of the city, which expanded its labor force by some 2.6 million workers between 1955 and 1970. The city retained, even enhanced, its wealth and vitality – offering job opportunities, constructing office buildings, housing government agencies, and fostering commercial districts. Tokyo remained the capital of politics, commerce, media, and entertainment as the indispensable hub of work and play. The physical landscape of the city also grew, rising far into the sky for the first time in its long history. Advances in earthquake-resistant engineering enabled the construction of multistory buildings, even high-rises, that could bend to accommodate shaking ground and blustering typhoon winds. The completion of the Hotel New Otani in time for the Olympics was followed by the Kasumigaseki Building in 1968 which, at thirty-six stories, was the city's first office tower. Its height was soon topped by the World Trade Center, then the Keio Plaza Hotel, and, in 1974, by the Mitsui Building with fifty-five floors. From 1978 until 1992, the record for the tallest building in the city was held by the same engineering achievement: the Sunshine Building in Ikebukuro, constructed on the former site of a prison that had housed war criminals. A few miles to the south, in western Shinjuku, a cluster of a half dozen or so skyscrapers built over the course of the 1970s came to form the first high-rise profile in the city.[29]

• ● •

Even as the middle-class dream resonated deeply with many Tokyoites, the realities of everyday life began to tarnish its appeal. Criticisms of middle-class lifestyles had been expressed before. But by the late 1960s, frustration and disappointment set in as the distance between people's expectations and lived experiences seemed to widen. *Danchi* life was not immune from disillusionment; in the words of historian Laura Neitzel, "Once the life people 'longed for,' by the 1970s, the *danchi* would come to emblematize the life they *got*."[30] Urban-style housing in the city and in the suburbs was increasingly found to be too small. The roughly forty-five square meters of the average Tokyo residence, the tightest anywhere in the country, felt cramped, packed as it was with electric appliances, sofas, and dining room sets. As the suburbs expanded, residents also grew unhappy with how far they lived from the center of the city. Millions of people made long and exhausting commutes into and out of the city each workday, crammed into train cars where a seat was at a premium. While several hundred "pushers" had been hired by the national railway in the early 1960s, by the end of the decade, the white-gloved employees responsible for shoving passengers into seemingly full, rush hour trains became icons of the commuter's misery. Enduring a tiring commute to live in a suffocating space, some Tokyoites began to wonder if this was the comfortable middle-class life they had imagined.

Home ownership, the golden ticket of middle-classness, also began to seem quite costly. Those who wanted to purchase an affordable single-family house were pushed farther out from the city, adding to the length of their commute. Others who opted to buy condominiums, or *manshon*, in the city were spending less than they would on a typical house and dealing with relatively shorter commutes. But they were also resigned to living in what were essentially 2DK apartments that were pale imitations of JHC *danchi*, located in the less pricey, and less fashionable, neighborhoods of the city. Whether a house in the distant suburbs or a condo in the city, home ownership seemed to sap white-collar salaries, making some feel shackled to their office job. Others decided not to purchase a home at all, instead spending their money on rent, consumer goods, and leisure.[31]

A surge in the construction of *manshon* in the 1970s contributed to the concern that postwar middle-class lifestyles, and the high rate of economic growth that had fueled them, were causing pollution, or *kōgai*. The term *kōgai* was used frequently and defined broadly to refer not just to environmental pollution but also to anything that seemed to be eroding people's quality of life. When it came to *manshon*, part of the problem was their proliferation, spurred by changes that made home loans more readily available for the purchase of a condo in cities. By the early 1970s, the number of units built had increased tenfold over the past handful of years to reach 20,000 newly constructed residences a year. What was more, a revision of the building code in 1970 raised the height limit on buildings, giving birth to mid-rise and even high-rise *manshon*. These tall structures, along with imposing office buildings, created *kōgai* in the form of congestion and noise. And in areas of the city where they arose right next to low-rise residences, they obstructed breezes that had offered neighbors some respite on hot summer days and exposed them to intrusive gazes from above. Most offensive, the *manshon* and offices blocked nearby residences from direct sunlight. Considering the value placed on southern exposure and the necessity of sunlight for housework such as drying laundry and airing out bedding, the shadows cast by high-rises spurred a grassroots movement opposing their construction and calling for the protection of local residents' access to sunshine. Banding together in protest, citizens managed to mitigate this type of *kōgai* in a number of legal and political successes scored over the course of the 1970s. Perhaps most significant was the Supreme Court declaration in 1972 that a right to sunshine was guaranteed by the constitution, which ensured "minimum standards of wholesome and cultural living." In subsequent court cases, the legal right to sunshine was expanded, and violators were held liable for damages. The sunshine rights movement also won changes to zoning ordinances in Tokyo. And by 1976, all local governments were required by law to establish sunshine standards.[32]

A particularly noxious form of *kōgai*, for which Tokyo became notorious, was photochemical smog. The brownish haze created by the burning of fossil fuels and the increasing number of cars on the road began to attract attention in the late 1950s and early 1960s, in the early years of high economic growth (see Figure 8.5). During the Olympics, the metropolitan government constantly monitored smog levels and stood

Figure 8.5 Heavy smog darkens the city in the early afternoon. Photograph, December 24, 1964. Courtesy of Bettmann and Getty Images.

ready to issue a public health warning for athletes and visitors as well as Tokyoites.[33] But it was in the early 1970s that photochemical smog provoked more widespread concern as an issue plaguing urban residents. In the heat of the summer in 1970, thousands of Tokyoites reported experiencing eye irritation, sore throats, and other health effects, with some requiring hospitalization. And in another sign of the severity of the problem, in May of 1972, scores of students at a junior high school were affected, with many having trouble breathing, feeling dizzy, or losing sensation in their legs.[34] So polluted was the air in Tokyo that it received international attention. The head of the US Environmental Protection Agency spoke of the city's "world-class smog," and a *New York Times* article in 1971 identified the "soupy air of Tokyo" as one of the "seven pollution wonders of the world." Cherry trees were dying, views of Mount Fuji were obscured, and, "in the best tradition of devilish Oriental cleverness," Tokyoites were taking to wearing masks to protect themselves, the article reported, with a heavy dose of Orientalism.[35] Without such exoticism, environmental activists used the slogan "No More Tokyos!" when they marched as part of the first Earth Day in 1970 and at the groundbreaking United Nations Conference on the Human Environment in Stockholm in 1972.[36] Domestically, in Japan, grassroots protest movements against pollution of various kinds along with international disrepute and the worsening severity of environmental problems helped prompt the national government to propose, and the Diet or parliament to pass, fourteen laws establishing strict pollution regulations, including those intended to curb air pollution. At the level of the metropolitan government, the progressive Tokyo governor Minobe Ryōkichi attempted to increase the responsibility of businesses to prevent pollution and to set even tougher environmental protection standards.[37]

During his long tenure as governor, Minobe also tackled another kind of *kōgai* generated by the proliferation and normalization of middle-class lifestyles. In September 1971, Minobe stood before the Tokyo Metropolitan Assembly and declared a war on garbage. He explained that the amount of garbage discarded in the twenty-three wards had more than doubled over the past decade, that the surge in plastic waste was corroding incinerators, and that the almost fivefold increase in the disposal of large items such as electric home appliances and cars was quickly packing landfills. All of this garbage had turned landfills into havens for flies, mosquitoes, and rats, which infested bordering neighborhoods. And it was straining the city's waste management infrastructure. Minobe made no bones about his conclusion that this "garbage problem" was caused by the rapid economic growth that the country had been experiencing since the late 1950s. Following suit, the Tokyo Sanitation Bureau, which referred to garbage as "the third *kōgai*" after air and water pollution, clearly expressed its view that such abundant waste was the product of "an affluent, consuming lifestyle."[38] In the late 1960s and early 1970s, the realization dawned that mass production and mass consumption resulted in mass waste, that the goods which signaled the attainment of middle-class life ended up on the trash heap.

Also revealed by the accumulation of garbage was the unequal distribution of its environmental and social harms. Kōtō ward, in the low city, housed the massive Island of Dreams landfill in Tokyo Bay, which turned area neighborhoods into stomping grounds for pests. Residents also endured a constant parade of noisy and smelly garbage trucks through the streets of their ward, which was the site of two-thirds of the city's landfills. In the early 1970s, Kōtō waged a battle against freeloaders – the wealthier Suginami ward in particular – who shirked responsibility for disposing of their own garbage and assuming the costs of affluent middle-class living. While Kōtō's burden was somewhat lifted by Suginami's eventual concession to build its own incinerator, and while Minobe's efforts resulted in the construction of over a dozen incineration plants over the next twenty or so years, the material realities of mass consumerism persisted as a social and environmental challenge for the dense landscape and many residents of the Tokyo metropolis.[39]

• ● •

Even though middle-class life lost some of its sheen as the costs of rapid economic growth seemed to mount and imagined lives of comfort and leisure seemed to slip further away, the desire to belong to the middle class persisted as a defining element of a remodernized and urbanized postwar Japan. For both individuals and the nation, the attainment of middle-class lifestyles was emblematic of progress – a sign that the challenges of defeat and occupation had been surmounted, and that there had been not just recovery but growth. So powerful was the idea of middle-classness that by the mid-1960s, over 85 percent of respondents in a national survey conducted by the Prime Minister's Office identified as being part of some stratum of the middle class.[40] The significance of having achieved a middle-class life was made abundantly clear in 1973, when its foundations were tested by a series of shocks – the global oil crisis, skyrocketing inflation, and, as it turned out, the end to the era of high economic growth that had been enjoyed since 1955. In the face of these threats, people, mainly women, in Tokyo and elsewhere protested against the high price of goods, demanding transparency and accountability from corporations. As shortages brought home the limited nature of resources, grassroots recycling movements got off the ground. And many of these

174

efforts were framed and understood as attempts to defend and maintain middle-class lifestyles.

The urban life of consumption and leisure that many sought to preserve was not new to the postwar period. In the 1920s, white-collar Tokyoites had commuted from the western suburbs to work in offices in the city center and enjoy evenings in Ginza. But in the postwar period, middle-classness became a mass experience that transformed and left an indelible imprint on life in the capital. Tokyoites came to have the opportunity to move through more of the city by subway, to flush a toilet that whisked their waste away, to buy their groceries at supermarkets, to shop at department stores and a whole array of other establishments in districts such as Shibuya and Shinjuku in the western part of the city, to perhaps work on the thirtieth floor of an office building, and to travel to other parts of the country brought closer by the bullet train.

Over the course of the 1960s, the aspirations for the Olympics were largely realized. An urban, middle-class life became a majority experience. And Japan regained a place among industrialized, modernized, and "civilized" nations. By the late 1960s, Japan had the second largest economy in the world, and it weathered the financial tumult of the 1970s better than its economic counterparts. Buoyed by the nation's wealth and international standing, Tokyo was coming into its own as a preeminent global capital.

9

Global Capital

WHEN *Somehow, Crystal* hit bookstores in 1981, the novel created a splash with its unique depiction of this moment when living the high life felt more possible to more Tokyoites than ever before. The "crystal" of the title described a lifestyle free of worries and brimming with things that "somehow felt good."[1] For the young protagonist Yuri, what felt good was shopping and consuming. *Somehow, Crystal* is filled with her descriptions of where she goes and what she buys when the fancy strikes. At one point early in the novel, college student Yuri rattles off a list of Tokyo stores and cafés she frequents for her favorite sweets: "I buy cake at Lecomte in Roppongi or Aile D'or in Ginza. When I'm with friends from school, it's fun to go to Est in Roppongi or Cappucio in Nogizaka and eat a big American-style cake. When I'm with [my boyfriend] Jun'ichi we'd go a little upscale and try the pie at Reposer in Takagi-chō. When I go out at night for cake, I like to pair it with white wine at Chianti in Aoyama 3-chōme. On the way back I'd eat a large ice cream at Swensen's, a San Francisco-style shop."[2] Unusual in a work of fiction, this passage includes thirteen footnotes that provide further commentary from Yuri about these choice shops, locations, and treats. We learn that Aile D'or is a pricier pâtisserie, but well worth it; that more stores have recently been popping up in Nogizaka; and that her order at Swensen's is a parfait with eight flavors of ice cream, almonds, whipped cream, and cherries. The entire novel has over 400 such notes that were used, especially by younger readers, as a guide for what was fashionable to do and what was trendy to buy in Tokyo. Despite author Tanaka Yasuo's desire to critique a materialistic society, his work was understood by many as a celebration of spending money impulsively, even hedonistically.[3] Thin on plot, which loosely traced Yuri's romantic life over two short weeks, *Somehow, Crystal* was instead about how it felt to live in Yuri's Tokyo. In hindsight, Tanaka's work is remarkable for how presciently it conveyed the spirit of the decade to come – when money flowed freely, the world seemed to be Japan's oyster, and Tokyoites indulged in the city's overwhelming opportunities to consume.

Like *Somehow, Crystal*, the story of Tokyo in the 1980s doesn't have much of a plot. There are few new developments, twists and turns, or resolutions. If anything, longer term trends in the city and patterns of daily life were not fundamentally changed but were turbocharged in this decade by sheer economic force. Having weathered the global financial strains of the 1970s relatively well, Japan ushered in the new decade with a growing economy and unprecedented confidence in the nation's affluence. In the second half of the 1980s, as speculators fed an ever-expanding asset bubble, the Nikkei Index tripled, land prices doubled for the second time in a handful of years, and the Tokyo Stock Exchange became the largest in the world based on market capitalization. This was the era when those with deeper pockets bought luxury cars, joined expensive golf clubs, and drank sake glittering with gold flakes, and corporate employees entertained lavishly at restaurants, bars, and nightclubs on company expense accounts. Even those who were not especially affluent traveled to international destinations and enjoyed trips to resorts and theme parks, fueling tremendous growth in the leisure market. Young, single women working office jobs in the city spent their disposable income on the most recent fashions, dinners at gourmet restaurants, and the latest consumer electronics, such as the Sony Walkman. Corporations, too, went on a shopping spree. And much of what they bought leveraged their cultural capital. The Yasuda Fire and Marine Insurance Company purchased Vincent Van Gogh's "Sunflowers" at a Christie's auction in London for US$39.9 million; the Sony Corporation acquired CBS Records Group for $2 billion and Columbia Pictures Entertainment for $3.4 billion; Matsushita Electric Industrial Company (later Panasonic) bought the entertainment giant MCA for $6.6 billion; and Mitsubishi Estate Company gained control of Rockefeller Center in the heart of Manhattan for $1.4 billion.[4]

As money and goods circulated around the world with heightened intensity, the centripetal pull of Tokyo, which had been growing over centuries, was greatly amplified in a matter of years. Eclipsing the economic might and commercial prowess of Osaka, the capital was described by some as the center of a unipolar Japan. More and more, to speak of Tokyo was to speak of Japan. And metropolitan Tokyo became more than a national capital, assuming the ranks of a global capital as a nationally and internationally preeminent city, a vital node in an extensive web of transnational connections, a cultural force, and a financial powerhouse of stunning reach.

• • •

If you were one of the over two million people in the 1980s who traveled into the metropolis of Tokyo each weekday, you'd likely set out in the morning from your home to the nearest station and then spend around thirty to forty minutes on rush hour trains crisscrossing through an extensive railway network.[5] Like many Tokyo residents, those who streamed into the city during the day worked in a range of industries from services to manufacturing to finance. The Tokyo metropolitan area as a whole offered an array of jobs, boasting the highest concentration in the entire country of universities and colleges, cultural institutions, major newspapers, advertising firms, manufacturing company headquarters, small production factories, high-tech pilot plants, scientific research organizations, venture businesses, and banks. At the same time that Tokyo didn't lose as many manufacturing jobs as other major cities in the world, it also maintained its significance as the capital of national politics and emerged as a seat of global finance, a hub of media and information, and a center of high-tech innovation.[6] As the nation's predominant city, Tokyo was, by the end of the 1980s, London, New York, and Silicon Valley all wrapped up in one metropolitan area of over thirty million people.

While the capital had styled itself as the embodiment of national economic achievement since the Meiji years, the combination of a strong yen, corporate decisions, and government encouragement helped transform Tokyo of the 1980s into a global nerve center of economic activity and finance on a par with New York, London, Frankfurt, and Paris. Both the national and metropolitan governments spoke of turning Tokyo into a "world city" and promoted development plans to further concentrate economic functions like finance, media, and information services in the capital. In this decade, finance and services such as legal, accounting, and public relations were the fastest growing sectors of the economy in Tokyo, as in New York and London. By 1986, Tokyo was the world's foremost banking center measured in terms of cumulated assets.[7] The six big Japanese banks all had their headquarters in the capital, as did the major trading firms, or *sōgō shōsha*. Almost half of Japan's largest private companies had their head offices in the city; the next highest fraction, at a much smaller 14 percent, was in Osaka. Many firms from around the world, and especially those from the United States, the United Kingdom, and

West Germany, also chose to put down roots in Tokyo. Of the over 2,000 foreign companies in Japan, around 85 percent sited their offices in the capital. And more Fortune 500 firms were in Tokyo than any other city in the world.[8]

Economic activity also radiated outward from Tokyo, transcending the nation's borders. Most large Japanese corporations set up branch offices and subsidiaries in New York and London, and many also established a presence in cities such as San Francisco, Toronto, São Paulo, Frankfurt, and Zurich, as well as in other parts of Asia and the Pacific Rim, such as Hong Kong, Singapore, Jakarta, and Sydney. Manufacturers stepped up production in Southeast Asia, namely Malaysia, Thailand, and Vietnam, and then in China, while manufacturing companies in industries such as chemicals, electronics, automobiles, and shipbuilding increased their number of overseas subsidiaries. Japanese companies' direct foreign investment, or investment in assets outside of the country, which had been anemic in the 1960s and sporadic in the 1970s, skyrocketed in the mid-1980s to record levels.[9]

As the transnational movement of money intensified and company operations internationalized, the core area of Tokyo was elevated from a historic base for business and politics to a cutting-edge center of global finance. Particularly important were the wards of Chiyoda, Chūō, and Minato, home to the Marunouchi, Nihonbashi, Ginza, Roppongi, and Akasaka districts. Each weekday, these three wards alone drew in two million workers from other parts of the city and beyond to these prime stomping grounds for many Japanese and foreign firms. This concentration of global business functions in the city center was explicitly promoted by the national and metropolitan governments. Firms like Mitsubishi, that had created "One Block London" in Marunouchi around the turn of the century, continued to loom large in this district. The Mitsubishi Estate Company owned about 40 percent of the land and most of the high-rise office buildings in the area around Tokyo Station, earning billions of yen a month from its tenants. With echoes of the Meiji period, the conglomerate's presence also attracted related companies, such as foreign banks and securities firms, to this high-powered business district.[10]

The convergence of large businesses in central Tokyo fueled unprecedented demand for office space, which helped drive commercial property prices skyward. Also pushed upward by the shortage of office space and buoyed by speculation, land prices across Tokyo rose. In the center of the city, in the latter half of the decade, the average price of commercial real estate quadrupled. Average office rents in Tokyo were the highest of any major city in the world at roughly $1710 per square meter, compared to about $1,500 in London, $740 in Paris, and $550 in New York. This was the era when the approximately 7.5 square kilometers of land under the Imperial Palace was calculated to be worth more than all of the real estate in California, and the aggregate value of real estate in Tokyo outstripped that of the entire United States.[11]

• ● •

The transformation of Tokyo into a major player in world markets not only supercharged business activities and the price of space but also contributed to diversification and heterogeneity in the socioeconomic geography of the capital. In the bubble economy of the late 1980s, labor shortages in the manufacturing, construction, and service industries became acute, and many foreign workers immigrated to the country to work low-wage jobs. With this influx of migrant workers, the Tokyo metropolis came to have the largest number of registered foreign residents in Japan, edging out Osaka; the capital also became home to many unauthorized immigrants who stayed on after their visas had expired. Unlike the first postwar phase of immigration, consisting primarily of women from the Philippines, Thailand, South Korea, and Taiwan who were recruited into the entertainment and sex industries starting in the late 1970s, this second phase was largely men from countries such as Bangladesh, Pakistan, Iran, and the Philippines who took jobs that were conventionally and notoriously described as "dirty, dangerous, and difficult."[12] Such work was so plentiful in these years that one day laborer, Ōyama Shirō, would look back on the bubble era as "a golden age for us day laborers" who were able to subsist due to the many construction projects in the city. At the labor recruitment office in San'ya, a neighborhood with the capital's largest day laborer quarter, located north of Asakusa and near where the execution grounds and Yoshiwara pleasure quarters had been in the Tokugawa period, men like Ōyama could actually choose from among the job listings and decline the more arduous assignments during these economic boom years.[13]

In the 1990s, the composition of foreign workers in the Tokyo metropolitan area began to shift, spurred by the national government's creation of a new visa category for immigrants of Japanese descent, mainly from Brazil and Peru, who were permitted into the country to take low-wage jobs. The growing number of immigrants of Japanese descent tended to work in the factories of automobile and electronics companies or their subcontractors, located in the suburbs. There was also an uptick in immigrants, both women and men, from other countries in Asia, largely China and South Korea. Women continued to work in the entertainment and sex industries as well as in factories and the service sector, while men took a wider range of jobs in construction, manufacturing, and services, such as in hotels and restaurants. As labor pressures persisted, however abated, through the economic downturn of the 1990s, employers continued to rely on low-wage foreign workers. With the number of foreign residents in the metropolitan area reaching historical highs, the twenty-three wards of the metropolis became home to an increasing number of city dwellers from abroad even as the existing population declined, gently nudging Tokyo toward becoming a more multiethnic city.[14]

Those who immigrated to Tokyo in the late 1980s and 1990s lived in pockets around the city, establishing neighborhood communities within the metropolitan pastiche. There weren't large ethnic enclaves in Tokyo as there were in other major cities, in part because foreign residents, while growing in numbers, were still a modest fraction of Tokyoites; even accounting for unauthorized workers, immigrants were likely no more than 2 or 3 percent of the prefecture's population. American and European immigrants, with a labor status generally higher than low-wage workers from Asia or Latin America, could be found in the city's southwestern wards, near embassies and foreign company offices. Northeastern wards were home to more recent Chinese immigrants as well as Filipino workers and resident Koreans. Further to the south were both Chinese and Filipino neighborhoods. On the other side of the city, in the west, the Ikebukuro area experienced a sharp rise in the number of foreign residents in the late 1980s, many of whom were young Chinese men from mainland China, Taiwan, Laos, and Malaysia. In subsequent years, Ikebukuro was dotted with businesses aimed at serving its Chinese immigrant community.[15]

The area with the most registered foreigners in Tokyo, and in Japan as a whole, from the mid-1980s onward was Shinjuku – a ward that exemplified the increasingly variegated landscape of the metropolis. To the west of the labyrinthian Shinjuku Station in the heart of the ward, high-rise offices and hotels had risen in the 1970s and 1980s, creating a center of business and commerce. In 1991, the seat of city government was also brought to western Shinjuku with the unveiling of the new Tokyo Metropolitan Government Building, which featured a dramatic forty-eight story tower designed by Tange Kenzō to look like an electronics chip. To the east of Shinjuku Station were upscale department stores like Isetan, which had moved to this location after the Great Kanto earthquake, as well as Studio Alta, which opened in the 1980s and was best known for mounting on its building a large video monitor, the first of many such huge screens that would light up the city's major thoroughfares. The screen's most recent incarnation, still in the original location just opposite the station's east exit, continues to serve as a convenient spot to meet up with friends. Also nearby is Shinjuku Ni-chōme, a neighborhood where young Japanese prostitutes had serviced US soldiers during the occupation. By the 1970s, the area had transformed into the thriving mecca of gay nightlife which it remains today. In northern Shinjuku, the neighborhood of Ōkubo became home to resident Koreans and Taiwanese just after the war. In the early postwar decades, Ōkubo offered modest housing arrangements, small units in wooden tenements, to those workers, mostly young Asian women, who were employed in neighboring Kabukichō just to the south. Designated an entertainment area for American occupation forces just after the war, Kabukichō became by the 1980s a nightlife district filled with hostess clubs, bars, restaurants, massage parlors, movie houses, pachinko parlors, strip clubs, and more, many owned by resident Koreans. As a newer generation of Korean as well as some mainland Chinese immigrants moved into Ōkubo, a Korean community developed in the area and Korean churches, beauty salons, restaurants, and other services were established along the main street bordering Kabukichō and Ōkubo.[16]

Beyond Shinjuku, the metropolis was a sprawling patchwork of neighborhoods more than a city divided into large, socioeconomically distinct islands. Some of the poorest housing conditions could be found in wealthier central wards such as

Chūō and Minato, not far from shiny office buildings, upscale shops, and luxury hotels. And there were clusters of Tokyoites living in poverty not just in the least affluent wards of the low city but also further to the west, some in tenements without private bathrooms or kitchens. While the most economically challenged areas tended to be in the historically disadvantaged low city, wards such as Arakawa, Sumida, and Taitō were also particularly hard hit by the decline of the manufacturing industry in the 1980s. These particular wards, unlike others in the low city, also weren't located on Tokyo Bay so didn't benefit from the revitalization of the Tokyo waterfront.[17]

• ● •

The shifting fate of the waterfront mirrored the country's changing fortunes from the 1980s into the 1990s, as Tokyoites began to face an economic life at once affluent and stagnant, abundant and insecure. The national and metropolitan governments turned their attention to the waterfront in the mid-1980s as a way to alleviate the overcrowding of trains, general congestion, and shortage of office space which plagued the core wards of Tokyo. In 1987, the city came out with a plan to turn the former industrial areas along the waterfront into a "subcenter" for global telecommunications and information-related businesses, complete with ample office space and convention facilities, as well as some housing and leisure facilities. Known as the Tokyo Waterfront Subcenter, also called Tokyo Teleport Town or Odaiba (after the artillery batteries built there by the Tokugawa in the 1850s), this development was planned to be sited on over 440 hectares of reclaimed land in Tokyo Bay owned by the Tokyo Metropolitan Government, mostly in the low city's Kōtō ward.[18]

After the bubble burst and the economy stalled in the early 1990s, the need for a subcenter of businesses and office buildings dimmed, and greater emphasis was placed on creating a district for mixed uses. What took shape on this artificial land reflected the various, evolving interests of the project. The original "teleport" idea was exemplified by the Telecom Center, a steel and glass building for offices and telecommunication facilities as well as the headquarters of Fuji Television, a futuristic structure designed by Tange Kenzō with a dramatic spherical observation room constructed out of titanium panels. There was some housing, though the roughly 3,000 residents of Odaiba in the late 1990s were dwarfed by the working population of around 20,000 people.

Above all, this waterfront area became known, and successful, as a destination for leisure. A resort-like atmosphere was created by upscale hotels, a strip of beach, and public parks. Many sites offered visitors picturesque views of the bay and of Rainbow Bridge, the suspension bridge for the monorail, expressway, road, and pedestrian walkway that connected Odaiba with Minato ward to its west. With white towers illuminated in different colors at night, the bridge quickly became a scenic and much photographed Tokyo landmark. Odaiba could also be experienced as a theme park, with its small-scale Statue of Liberty celebrating Japan's relationship with France (see Figure 9.1); a Ferris wheel that was the tallest in the world until the London Eye opened shortly thereafter; entertainment centers with video games, karaoke, and bowling; and Venus Fort, a mall resembling an Italian town in Renaissance or Baroque style which opened just before the Venetian Resort in Las Vegas, featuring an ornate water fountain with six goddess statues as the centerpiece of an indoor piazza. Venus Fort was part of a shopping and entertainment complex called Palette Town, only one of a number of such malls in this "dreamscape of consumption."[19] There was also Decks Tokyo Beach, which included an indoor amusement park called Joypolis run by the video game company Sega, and two floors

Figure 9.1 Small-scale Statue of Liberty and the Fuji Television headquarters in Odaiba. Courtesy of Atlantide Phototravel, Corbis Documentary and Getty Images.

with shops and restaurants reminiscent of Hong Kong. Another mall, Aqua City, was distinguished by the number of foreign stores from Starbucks, Cinnabon, and Godiva, to Claire's, Swatch, and Coach. Even as the severity of the economic downturn set in over the course of the 1990s, the consumer's playground of Odaiba was extremely popular, attracting about thirty-one million visitors in 1999.[20]

While consumerist desires spanned the economically ebullient 1980s and the more restrained 1990s, the shift in moods across the two decades was marked. As a sense of uncertainty and insecurity began to descend over the 1990s, the city was jarred by shocking acts of violence. On a clear and crisp morning in March 1995, subway commuters and station workers were jolted out of their Monday routines. Their eyes hurt and watered, and vision blurred. They felt nauseous and vomited, grew drowsy and confused and weak, and had trouble breathing. Some lost consciousness. And thirteen people were killed. Thousands of Tokyoites became victims of the terrorist assault by members of the doomsday cult Aum Shinrikyō, who released sarin gas along three subway lines that converged on Kasumigaseki Station in the center of the city. In the weeks and months that followed, people tried to explain why the Aum movement, founded by its leader Asahara Shōkō in 1987, was attractive to so many, especially of younger generations. What, they asked, had gone wrong with Japan? A few years after the attack, writer Murakami Haruki observed in one of his rare non-fiction works, "One thing is for sure. Some strange malaise, some bitter aftertaste lingers on. We crane our necks and look around us, as if to ask: where did all *that* come from?"[21]

The attack epitomized and exacerbated feelings of anxiety, already stoked by the Hanshin earthquake in western Japan two months earlier as well as deepening realizations about the severity of the country's economic woes. The asset bubble had burst in 1990, as the Nikkei Index plummeted and land prices dropped. But it took several years before the underlying economy showed signs of serious illness. By the mid-1990s, it became clear that economic growth had stalled, and industrial production, construction starts, wholesale prices, and business and consumer confidence fell. Banks failed and major firms were restructured or went bankrupt, laying off workers.[22] As the bubble economy fizzled away, so too did the national confidence of the 1980s. Pessimism pervaded discussions of the future for the first time since the early 1970s, and many Tokyoites paid more attention to socioeconomic inequality and precarity in the city.

As the economy slumped into recession, the collapse of the asset bubble began to change the character of the city center. When the economy of Tokyo contracted and land values fell, the

188

demand for office space started to shrink and attention turned toward drawing residents back to the twenty-three wards of the city. To stem the tide of Tokyoites moving outward in search of housing that they could afford, private companies bought up land at deflated prices and built high-rise condominiums in the central wards and in locations, as along the waterfront, vacated by factory closures or moves offshore. Low land values also made the construction of less expensive housing possible. In the latter half of the 1990s, the greater availability of residential space along with the desire to live in the city rather than the more inconvenient suburbs, especially among dual income families without children, one-person households, and the elderly, drew an increasing number of residents to the twenty-three wards, including Chiyoda, Chūō, and Minato.[23]

The metropolitan government supported this migration of residents back into the city, encouraging the construction of high-rise residences as well as large, mixed-use complexes by private companies as a way to enhance the appeal of Tokyo and reinforce its global competitiveness in the twenty-first century. What had previously been public-private projects increasingly became private sector investments, spearheaded by large property management companies or the real estate division of conglomerates such as Mitsui or Mitsubishi.[24] A prime example of an influential private corporation is the Mori Building Company, a family-owned property management firm founded in the 1950s by Mori Taikichirō who, when he died in the early 1990s, was the wealthiest person in the world with an estimated net worth of $13 billion, twice that of Bill Gates at the time. Before his death, the company that he established and expanded had constructed over eighty buildings, including the Ark Hills complex that opened in Roppongi in 1986 with offices, apartments, shops, restaurants, a hotel, the Suntory concert hall, and a television studio. In the

1990s, the Mori Building Company was seemingly undeterred by its founder's passing and the economic downturn, taking on projects such as Venus Fort in Odaiba and Roppongi Hills. The Roppongi Hills development, opened in 2003, includes offices for financial, information technology, media, and law firms, as well as more than 800 upscale condo units, over 200 stores and restaurants, a luxury hotel, a movie theater, and the Mori Art Museum. Described by the Mori Building Company as "the largest ever private sector funded urban redevelopment project in Japan," Roppongi Hills required negotiations with more than 400 landowners for close to twenty years, generating friction and criticism along the way.[25] The ostensible motivation for this and all of the company's investments in the early 2000s was declared on the company's website: "Competition between cities is international – to revitalize Tokyo is to revitalize Japan . . . if Japan is to prosper in an age of globalization, its cities must attract residents, goods, finance and information from around the world."[26] Even as such expensive development projects incorporated more residences and retail than the office buildings of the 1980s, they continued to pour capital into, and gear their spaces toward, the more affluent central wards in the name of preserving the position and status of Tokyo as a global city.

• ● •

Early in *Somehow, Crystal,* Yuri details her night out at a club in Roppongi called Xanadu. She had sipped a Kahlúa milk and watched her friend Emiko with a guy outfitted in a shirt and pants from the Italian sportswear brand Marlboro and a belt by the French fashion house Lanvin, dancing slowly to songs by The Dramatics, Teddy Pendergrass, and Boz Scaggs. Yuri herself had been reaching toward her small Renoma bag for a Salem (the menthols that would later be manufactured by Japan Tobacco

International) when she was approached by a handsome guy wearing a Lacoste polo shirt.[27] That Yuri inhabited a Tokyo of cultural hybridity wasn't novel in the early 1980s. Tokyoites had long created and consumed pleasures with an international flair, from French haute cuisine and baseball starting in the late 1800s, to ramen and jazz in the early 1900s. Modern retail establishments had also been shaped by the adaptation of imported business models, be it the department store at the turn of the twentieth century, the café in the 1920s, or the supermarket in the 1950s. But from the 1980s onward, the sheer availability of such consumer goods, services, and leisure was stunning. It also came to be expected by middle-class consumers. Tokyoites drank wine from France, Italy, Australia, or California, wore clothes made in China or South Korea, and dined at restaurants serving Indian, Thai, Vietnamese, or Italian cuisine.[28] And over the course of the decade, an American import – the convenience store – proliferated, which, together with the already popular vending machine, made ubiquitous the opportunity to buy food or drink at any hour. Initially launched as joint ventures between US enterprises and Japanese companies, quite a few of today's major convenience store chains, such as 7-Eleven Japan and Lawson, got their start in the 1970s and then expanded by adjusting to the consumer desires of Japanese urbanites and promoting American-style business franchising. The first 7-Eleven in Tokyo opened in Kōtō ward in 1974. Then, over the next two decades, the number of convenience stores in Japan mushroomed – 2,000 convenience stores became a staggering 40,000, which turned close proximity to a 7-Eleven, Lawson, or Family Mart into a marker of urban living.[29]

Coupled with the intensification and diversification of global exchange, the excitement with which Japanese cultural exports were received in other parts of the world reached new heights in the 1980s and 1990s. At a time when Tokyo and Japan were increasingly seen as synonymous both in the capital and abroad, the product Hello Kitty was steadily winning global recognition as a Japanese pop culture phenomenon. Sanrio Company, the cat's parent, was reportedly named after the "San" of many California cities and "Rio" from the Spanish for river. Sanrio established its headquarters in Tokyo in 1973 and gave birth to Hello Kitty the following year. It then created a full-fledged life story for the fictional character: Kitty, a member of the White family, was born and lived in London with her parents, grandparents, and twin sister Mimmy, and dated her boyfriend Dear Daniel. Hello Kitty became a global commodity when she debuted in American and European markets in the late 1970s and Asia in 1990. First attaining cult status in Japan, even inspiring the creation of the theme park Sanrio Puroland in the Tama New Town development of suburban Tokyo in 1990, Hello Kitty capitalized on years of strategic expansion abroad to rocket to global fame in the late 1990s. Having cultivated a loyal fan base, especially among girls and young women, Hello Kitty would go on to serve as UNICEF's Global Special Friend of Children, participate in balloon form in the Macy's Thanksgiving Day Parade, assume the role of Japan Tourism Ambassador to Taiwan and South Korea, and collaborate with Lady Gaga for the singer's Kitty-themed photo shoot. By the 2000s, Hello Kitty had solidified her stature as a global icon of cute (see Figure 9.2).[30]

Like other elements of modern culture, from art to religion, Japanese cuisine had traveled beyond the nation's borders long before the late twentieth century. About a hundred years earlier, Japanese food made its way to the United States together with Japanese emigrants. The first Japanese-owned restaurant that served Japanese food opened in San Francisco in 1887 and was then followed by another in the Chinatown neighborhood of Los

Figure 9.2 Balloons of Hello Kitty and friends on Odaiba with the Rainbow Bridge in the backdrop, promoting a Green Tokyo through urban tree-planting. Photograph, February 7, 2010. Courtesy of Andia, Universal Images Group, and Getty Images.

Angeles. In the postwar era, familiarity with Japanese food beyond the Japanese American community was promoted by Aoki Hiroaki, known in the United States as Rocky Aoki, who inaugurated the first Benihana, in New York City, in the mid-1960s. Aoki introduced American diners to *teppanyaki*, a theatrical experience first devised by a Japanese restaurant owner catering to occupation soldiers, in which meat, shellfish, and vegetables are cooked on a steel griddle before patrons' eyes. By the 1980s, Benihana and its counterpart in Germany, Daitokai, proved to be such hits that *teppanyaki* restaurants sprang up across the United States and Europe. At the same time, Japan's rapidly expanding business relationships in the United States and Europe gave rise to communities of Japanese expatriates who yearned for food and restaurants from back home, and Japanese restaurateurs were happy to meet that demand. Also propelling the acceptance of Japanese cuisine abroad were higher-end Japanese chefs who would become international culinary celebrities; entrepreneurs such as Matsuhisa Nobuyuki who opened his first restaurant, in Beverly Hills, in 1987. In the early 1990s, he debuted in New York City his signature restaurant, Nobu, that would go on to inspire a global chain.

Dovetailing with the growing appeal of Japanese food was the popularization of sushi in particular. Sushi, including the hand-formed *nigirizushi* which first took off in early 1800s Edo, became an upmarket and cosmopolitan food of choice in the United States in the 1970s and 1980s. In the 1990s, sushi became a staple for take-out and in supermarkets as standard American fare. In Europe, the sushi boom of the late 1990s was driven by *kaitenzushi*, or restaurants where the sushi rotates around a counter on a conveyor belt. Especially trendy in London, *kaitenzushi* was given a boost by hip spots such as the now global chain, YO! Sushi. In a kind of cultural feedback loop, the *kaitenzushi* craze abroad helped improve the image of conveyor-belt sushi in Japan. With working-class origins in the late 1950s and a reputation for serving utilitarian sushi made of low-quality fish, *kaitenzushi* remade itself in 1990s Japan with some places becoming more family friendly as well as wallet friendly, and others styling themselves after their fashionable European counterparts and welcoming diners in chic areas of Tokyo.[31] As sushi became an iconic food at once global and Japanese, it's little wonder that in 2014, Prime Minister Abe Shinzō welcomed President Barack Obama to Tokyo with dinner at the renowned three-Michelin-star sushi restaurant Sukiyabashi Jirō.

• ● •

Even as much of the exuberance of the 1980s dissipated and daily life seemed increasingly fragile in what would become known as the "lost decade" of the 1990s, Tokyo was still enmeshed in global relationships as the capital of what was still one of the largest economies in the world. Many Tokyoites may have moderated their buying habits and aspirations in the 1990s, but they were still very much consumers in a thoroughly consumerist society. In a time of stagnant affluence, those walking through Ginza could now shop at Louis Vuitton, or at the flagship of the global fast-fashion juggernaut Uniqlo. Also thriving like Uniqlo despite the economic downturn was Muji, the Japanese retailer of household goods, clothes, and food that opened its first outlet in Tokyo in the early 1980s then expanded abroad in the 1990s and 2000s, building a global presence with several hundred stores in locations from China to the United Arab Emirates.[32] As the period of economic anemia wore on, Tokyoites adjusted to changed realities and started to look beyond financial might as the defining element of the capital's global image and identity in the twenty-first century.

10

Past and Present

AT the closing ceremony of the Rio Summer Games in 2016, Tokyo stepped into the Olympic limelight as the next host and teased the world with an artfully choreographed preview of all that Tokyo 2020 would be. As a fusion of city and nation, Tokyo presented its curated image to a global audience, revealing how it wanted to be seen, and how it wanted to see itself, at this expectant moment. The production opened with the red rising sun of the Japanese flag coming into focus on the stadium floor, encircled by women in all white gliding on personal transporters and wearing geometric costumes inspired by origami, as a choir sang the Japanese national anthem with its lyrics from the tenth century and melody from the early Meiji period. Blending historical elements with futuristic technology and aesthetics, the live performance then transitioned seamlessly into an upbeat prerecorded video featuring various athletes getting ready for the games against the backdrop of Tokyo icons. A gymnast flew through the air in the large intersection at Shibuya, a swimmer kept pace with an aerodynamic bullet train, a pole vaulter catapulted over the recently erected Tokyo Skytree and then the Rainbow Bridge, hurdlers cleared Tokyo Station, and a gymnast balanced atop the Kabukiza theater in Ginza. Interspersed throughout were Japanese pop culture icons – Pac-Man and his four ghost adversaries (Blinky, Pinky, Inky, and Clyde) of video game fame;

soccer-loving Ōzora Tsubasa from manga, anime, and video games; the robot cat Doraemon and four human kids (Nobita, Shizuka, Gian, and Suneo) from manga and anime; and Hello Kitty sporting a cheerleading uniform and yellow pompoms. To highlight the association between the nation and its popular culture, a red ball evoking the rising sun was passed from athletes into the hands of Prime Minister Abe Shinzō who, realizing that he's running late for an appearance in Rio, transforms into an animated Mario, the mustachioed Italian plumber created by the Japanese video game giant Nintendo. Abe-as-cartoon-Mario in his signature red cap and blue overalls dashes through the city and meets up with Doraemon, who conveniently provides a device to tunnel through the earth. In the segment's most buzzworthy and memorable moment, Abe makes a surprising appearance in Rio in the flesh – the prime minister rises out of a huge green sewer pipe in the middle of Maracanã stadium to the video game's power-up sound effect, dressed as Mario (see Figure 10.1). What was presented as quintessential Tokyo was the political leader of Japan draped in the garb of a fictional Italian plumber dreamed up by a multinational Japanese corporation and sold as a product to consumers worldwide. The creative director of this Olympic spot, Sasaki Hiroshi, drew on his considerable experience in advertising to foreground Mario and Doraemon as Japan's premier ambassadors and promote an image of Tokyo as at once historical and cutting edge. Reminding the world that Tokyo is "a cool place," said Sasaki, would "boost Japan's brand."[1]

Over half a century after the 1964 Olympic Games, the capital had much less to prove in the lead up to Tokyo 2020. This time, the burden wasn't to demonstrate national rehabilitation from imperialism, fascism, and war, but regional healing from the earthquake and tsunami in northeast Japan in March 2011 and from the ensuing nuclear calamity. Often called the Great

Figure 10.1 Prime Minister Abe Shinzō appearing as Mario at the closing ceremony of the Rio Olympic Games. Photograph by David Ramos, August 21, 2016. Courtesy of Getty Images.

East Japan earthquake, or 3.11, the triple disasters of the strongest recorded earthquake in Japan, destructive tsunami waves, and meltdown of nuclear reactors at the Fukushima Daiichi Nuclear Power Plant may have constituted the most devastating catastrophe of the postwar era. But from the vantage point of the national government in Tokyo, which was physically and psychologically distant from the most affected Tōhoku region, 3.11 was something that could and needed to be spun in the context of the Olympics. So Tokyo 2020 was dubbed the "Recovery and Reconstruction Games," billed as an opportunity to inspire the disasters' victims and used to show that the capital, at least, had made it through the worst. When Prime Minister Abe celebrated the selection of Tokyo as the host city in 2013, he insisted to the International Olympic Committee and potential Olympic participants that all was fine: "Some may have concerns about

Fukushima. Let me assure you, the situation is under control."[2] Abe had to acknowledge the hardships of 3.11, but he could also pivot attention toward Japan's reputation and status in the 2000s as a democratic, affluent, and thoroughly modern country and full-fledged member of the international community of nations. Tokyo had not been the command center of a war or any other military conflict for about seven decades. The city had built the world's largest rail network, with well over a hundred different lines shuttling more than forty million passengers across the metropolis each day. Several million people passed through Shinjuku Station alone, making it the busiest train station in the world. Technological advances had enabled the construction of thousands of earthquake-resistant skyscrapers higher than the Hotel New Otani of 1964, propelling the skyline upward and turning Tokyo into one of the world's tallest cities. The capital was also an established tourist destination, attracting four times more visitors than it had a handful of years earlier, in part through its aura of cultural cool. As a global culinary mecca, Tokyo has boasted more Michelin-starred restaurants than Paris and New York combined, and far more restaurants per capita than other major cities from Paris and London to Taipei and Shanghai. Tokyo's culinary reputation has been helped by the doubling of Japanese restaurants outside of the country, and UNESCO's designation of Japanese cuisine, or *washoku*, as "intangible cultural heritage."[3] The 2020 Olympics were not about remaking the reputation of an ascendant city but reminding a global audience of Tokyo's technological sophistication, sleek aesthetics, and cultural creativity. Tokyo 2020 was to be an opportunity for the host to trumpet its present and envision its future as a world-class, cosmopolitan city.

• ● •

Mario hadn't always seemed Japanese. When Nintendo debuted its *Mario Bros.* arcade game in 1983, the characters of Mario and Luigi were among many around that time who were not widely recognized as Japanese creations by global consumers. Joining the twin plumbers was Donkey Kong, also from Nintendo; Pac-Man from the video game company Namco; the transforming robots made by the toy manufacturer Takara which, through a deal with the American toymaker Hasbro, would become the Transformers; and the Mighty Morphin Power Rangers, who were originally from the *Super Sentai* series produced by the Tōei Company with the merchandise distributed by the toy company Bandai. Nor did consumer electronics, such as the VCRs from Panasonic, Sony, and JVC, or the Sony Walkman, project a particularly Japanese identity. But in the 1990s, as the economy sank into recession, cultural goods continued to cross national borders, media conglomerates globalized, and Japanese creative industries producing video and computer games, anime, manga, music, and fashion enjoyed growing enthusiasm for their exports.[4]

What really helped ignite the idea of Japan's cultural cool in the early 2000s was a catchy phrase coined by the American journalist Douglas McGray. In a 2002 article, McGray suggested that Japan was well on its way to becoming a cultural superpower, that the nation could remain influential in the world despite its economic anemia through its "Gross National Cool."[5] The possibility that Japan might leverage its growing cultural influence into a kind of soft power had already been considered by Japanese scholars, but the notion was given life by clever wording from an American voice. Various government ministries, excited by the prospect of Japan maintaining its global prestige and reviving its economy, embraced McGray's take on their country's future and began to draw up policies to promote cultural goods stamped with the "cool Japan" brand. As part of this effort, the prime minister established in 2002 the Strategic Council on Intellectual Property to foster innovation not just in manufacturing but also in fields such as design, music, movies, animation, and game software by protecting intellectual property. And the importance of burnishing Japan's image was explicitly framed as an international relations concern by the prime minister's Council for the Promotion of Cultural Diplomacy as well as the Ministry of Foreign Affairs. While many government institutions took up the call to foreground popular culture and culture more broadly, it was the Ministry of Economy, Trade and Industry, or METI, that spearheaded efforts to convert cultural cool into thriving, revenue-generating industries. The Cool Japan Promotion Office was set up by METI in 2010 to enhance the global competitiveness of cultural content creators and nurture potential growth industries. And such initiatives received a financial infusion in 2013, when the Cabinet Secretariat established the Council for the Promotion of Cool Japan with a budget of fifty billion yen, or roughly 500 million dollars.[6] The Cool Japan Strategy crafted by METI included its Creative Tokyo Project whereby over a hundred shopping districts, industries, nonprofit organizations, and local governments were brought together to "introduce the appeal of Tokyo" so as to boost tourism and consumption. Among the events organized was a fashion show on the main street in Ginza featuring Japanese denim. Models flaunted denim jeans, jackets, dresses, and kimono produced by well-known designers and fashion students, strutting down a denim catwalk in the heart of the upscale shopping district.[7] METI also sponsored the 100 Tokyo website which, as its tagline aptly suggests, highlights "creative venues, products and people in Tokyo."[8] Along with articles about creatives and a list of events, visitors could scroll through a list of a hundred places and things in the city deemed cool, from the public bathhouse Tsubameyu in Ueno to the girls' fashion boutique Bubbles in Harajuku, lacquer glass paperweights to balloons in unusual shapes, the restaurant Onigiri Asakusa Yadoroku specializing in rice balls to the Robot Restaurant in Kabukichō.

Such government efforts gave weight to the idea of Japanese cool, even though it was difficult to define what was particularly "Japanese" and what was especially "cool" about the marketed cultural goods. Much like the city of Tokyo itself, there wasn't anything irreducibly or essentially Japanese about an array of cultural products replete with different and often contradictory meanings; they could be cute, violent, banal, provocative, serious, whimsical, celebratory, and critical, sometimes claiming authenticity and sometimes embracing hybridity. Even within a single medium, there was considerable diversity in aesthetics and thematic concerns. Taking anime as an example, one of the early films popular with a global audience was Ōtomo Katsuhiro's *Akira*, known for its detailed and realistic rendering of a dystopian, post-apocalyptic Tokyo. Distinctly different were anime series for children, which themselves ran the gamut from *Doraemon*, about the cartoonish robot cat from the future, to *Dragon Ball Z*, with the extraterrestrial Goku who defends the earth, and *Sailor Moon*, whose protagonist is a schoolgirl who transforms into a sexy soldier to fight evil. For both younger and older audiences was Miyazaki Hayao's *Spirited Away*, whose release coincided with the buzz generated by McGray's article. Miyazaki's dreamlike evocation of a magical world was, among other things, a critique of materialism and consumption, not least for its environmental costs. In this way, Miyazaki was similar to contemporary artist Murakami Takashi, whose Superflat theory and artwork are a commentary on the emptiness of consumerism. The work of both men has often been cited as exemplifying Japanese cultural cool, despite their criticisms of the societal and economic forces propelling the Cool Japan strategy. Although Murakami was vocal about his dislike of the government's initiatives, his Superflat art was widely seen as defining a Japanese pop cultural aesthetic. And for his part, Miyazaki and Studio Ghibli, which he co-founded, made iconic films from *My Neighbor Totoro* to *Princess Mononoke*. Upon its release, *Spirited Away* became the highest grossing film ever in Japan, edging out James Cameron's *Titanic*. It drew in audiences across Asia, reaping ticket sales in places such as South Korea; it also earned international distinction with a top prize at the Berlin International Film Festival, the first animated feature so recognized, as well as an Academy Award for best animated film.[9]

The various images and associations that could be layered onto cultural products was exemplified by shifting perceptions of the Akihabara area of Tokyo. Known for much of the postwar period as Electric Town because of its many stores specializing in consumer electronics, from home appliances to personal computers, Akihabara was reimagined in the early 2000s as a neighborhood that does more than sell electronic goods but also spearheads technological innovation. Tokyo governor Ishihara Shintarō launched a redevelopment project to turn the area into a global information technology center, which fueled the construction of the Akihabara Daibiru skyscraper, the Akihabara UDX office complex, and an express rail line connecting the district with a research hub in the Tsukuba suburbs. At the same time, on the margins of the redevelopment zone, small and mid-sized stores selling anime, manga, and computer games flourished and turned the edges of the neighborhood into a mecca for *otaku*, or fans, even obsessives, of such cultural products. In the context of the Cool Japan efforts, the meaning of *otaku*, and the reputation of Akihabara, became ambiguous. On the one hand, the negative connotations of *otaku* as social misfits of the sort that joined the

Aum Shinrikyō cult began to fade as anime, manga, and computer games assumed a brighter sheen. Some, such as artist Murakami Takashi, celebrated *otaku* as drivers of cultural innovation and creativity. In Akihabara, festive celebrations of anime and manga by fans, such as role-players in costume, spilled out into the streets, particularly its main drag which was closed to traffic on Sundays. On the other hand, there was increased scrutiny of *otaku* who were considered by the local police, some politicians, and others as strange or weird for their politics or niche, subcultural fascinations. Complicated views of *otaku* could also be found abroad, where a vague notion of *otaku* culture was associated positively with anime-inspired films such as *Kill Bill: Volume 1*, *The Matrix*, and *The Animatrix*. At the same time, Americans and others not Japanese who were too enamored with Japanese popular culture, and anime and manga in particular, were referred to by the derogatory term "weeaboo." So-called "weeaboos" were even parodied on the American comedy show *Saturday Night Live* in a skit titled, "J-Pop America Funtime Now!"[10]

Despite the diversity and complexity of Japanese popular culture, the Cool Japan project was quite successful in convincing consumers that there was something quintessentially Japanese about the nation's cultural exports. Or, at least, the government's initiatives helped make audiences aware of the Japanese origins of what they were enjoying. Anime and manga, widely recognized as Japanese in creation, surged in popularity in the 2000s. Measured in terms of sales, the $75 million earned by both genres together in the mid-1990s shot up to $200 million by manga alone in 2006, and $2.7 billion by anime in 2009. In the United States, anime films and series became available to more viewers through mainstream outlets, no longer found just on the Cartoon Network or dedicated sites such as Crunchyroll and Funimation but through streaming services such as Netflix and Hulu. In the United States as well as

Japan, the sale of anime-related licensed goods such as action figures and trading cards has also been lucrative, bringing in around $17 billion. In Asia, anime has also proved very popular as has J-Pop or Japanese popular music. Listeners have been drawn to J-Pop stars such as the female duo Puffy (better known in the United States as Puffy AmiYumi, so as to avoid copyright entanglements with the rapper Sean "Puffy" Combs).

The visibility of cultural products "made in Japan" has been amplified by the ease with which fictional characters have been adapted to multiple media. It's not unusual for an anime series to be based on a manga and spark the development of toys and video games. A classic case of a cross-media juggernaut is Pokémon, originally a game from the early 1990s for Nintendo's handheld Game Boy console in which creatures called pocket monsters inhabit a fantastical world. In the years since, Pokémon has not only migrated across game platforms, such as the recent augmented reality mobile game *Pokémon Go* and *Pokémon Legends: Arceus* for the Nintendo Switch, but its characters have also inspired toys, trading cards, an anime series broadcast in over fifty countries, and more than a dozen animated feature films. What started out as about 150 species of Pokémon has mushroomed into about 900, with the most famous being Pikachu, the yellow mouse-like creature with a lightning bolt tail whose likeness has appeared everywhere from the airplanes of the Japanese carrier All Nippon Airways to the Macy's Thanksgiving Day Parade.

In Asia, an uptick in the number of transnational collaborations has both contributed to cultural flows across borders and heightened awareness of an artist's nationality. One of the early, if relatively short-lived, K-Pop or Korean popular music partnerships was the group Y2K, known for having one South Korean and two Japanese singers who became pop culture idols in South

Korea. More recently, the K-pop girl group Twice, with three Japanese performers among its nine members, has produced albums with songs in Korean, Japanese, and occasionally, English, which have been hugely popular in South Korea, Japan, and beyond. There have also been crossovers in multiple directions with television shows and films, including the casting of the famous Japanese actor and personality Kimura Takuya in Hong Kong director Wong Kar Wai's international co-production, *2046*.[11]

Even as the Cool Japan campaign lost some of its steam, the Japanese origins of global cultural phenomena haven't gone unnoticed, perpetuating the generally positive association of Japan with a vague sense of cultural cool. In 2020, as more people found themselves in search of entertainment during the COVID-19 pandemic, Nintendo sold thirty-one million copies worldwide of its video game *Animal Crossing: New Horizons*. And the world's highest grossing film of the year was Sotozaki Haruo's anime feature with the unwieldy title, *Demon Slayer: Kimetsu no Yaiba – The Movie: Mugen Train*. Based on a manga and written as a sequel to an anime television series, the fantasy action film unseated *Spirited Away* as the top-grossing film in Japanese history and became the rare non-Hollywood film to head the list of worldwide box office hits.[12]

• ● •

When Prime Minister Abe rose into Maracanã stadium as Mario, he was calling upon a carefully curated repertoire of globally recognized pop culture symbols to marry the Olympics, and Tokyo, with Japanese cool. In the lead-up to the summer of 2020, the marketing of the games highlighted the host's particular brand of cultural and technological ingenuity. The official Olympic and Paralympic mascots, Miraitowa and Someity, resembled futuristic manga and anime characters when they were drawn and were more cute in their costumed versions. Created by illustrator and character designer Taniguchi Ryō, the mascots were endowed with superpowers; Miraitowa could travel anywhere instantaneously, and Someity could communicate telepathically.[13] And, as part of the Tokyo 2020 Robot Project, both mascots assumed the form of robots developed by the Toyota Motor Corporation to welcome guests with "an innovative 'hello'!"[14] Showcasing robots of various kinds was but one way that Tokyo intended to present itself as the "capital of the future."[15] Other technologies planned for use included a 5G mobile communications network from NTT DoCoMo in partnership with Intel, and phones provided to athletes by Samsung; autonomous cars from Nissan; 8K resolution television broadcasts by NHK; 40 terabyte hard drives from the TDK Corporation; seismic isolation bearings in some venues from Bridgestone; and surveillance capabilities including drones as well as facial recognition software from Panasonic, Atos, and NEC.[16]

By the time the curtain rose on the Olympics in July 2021, delayed a year by an ongoing global health crisis, the initial ambition for Tokyo to "present itself to the world as a role model for the twenty-first century city" had been virtually extinguished by the COVID-19 pandemic.[17] In the opening ceremony, in what has historically been a prime opportunity for the host to craft an image and narrative about itself before the world, there were moments hinting at the festive performance that might have been. The athletes entered the stadium to music from Japanese video games, from "Star Light Zone" of *Sonic the Hedgehog* and "Roto's Theme" of *Dragon Quest* to "Victory Fanfare" from *Final Fantasy*.[18] In the sky above the heads of the assembled athletes, almost 2,000 Intel drones put on a light show against the urban nightscape, capped off by an impressive rotating Earth intended to symbolize "global solidarity and unity in diversity."[19] In a nod to the 1964 Tokyo Olympics, doves were released, this time made of paper to avoid the unfortunate byproducts of live birds. And in a video set to a soundtrack of upbeat jazz, lights were literally turned on across Tokyo – at Olympic venues, Tokyo Tower, the Tokyo Skytree, Rainbow Bridge, Shibuya crossing, the Sensōji temple in Asakusa, the Kabukiza theater, and in skyscrapers across the city.

But any sense of celebration was eclipsed by the inescapable reality that the ceremony was taking place in a largely empty stadium amid an unrelenting, deadly pandemic. The very first shot of the ceremony was of a solitary athlete, the boxer and frontline nurse Tsubata Arisa, running on a treadmill. Her breathing heavy and labored, she sits down on the edge of the treadmill in exhaustion before gathering her strength and getting back up, a testament not just to the grit of athletes but also to the stamina of viewers feeling isolated and enervated. There was a moment of silence for all who had lost their lives, particularly to COVID. And members of the Edo Firemanship Preservation Association performed a work song dating back to the Tokugawa period, setting the scene for dancers dressed as carpenters, some of the essential workers of Edo, making the Olympic rings out of wood.[20]

References to the victims of 3.11 ultimately did not figure prominently in the opening ceremony of what was initially marketed as the recovery games. The sidelining of the triple disasters may have been due in part to the pandemic but was also consistent with the government's subordination of the country's northeast, or Tōhoku, region to the capital for over a decade, and with the marginalization of rural peripheries by the megacity of Tokyo for still longer. Some of the harshest criticisms of Tokyo hosting the games, and clothing them in the rhetoric of recovery, came from Tōhoku residents angered by the diversion of national resources

and attention away from reconstruction of the areas devastated by
the triple disasters and toward preparation of the capital for the
Olympics. As many of the almost 50,000 displaced survivors
hoped their towns would be rebuilt, the surge of construction in
Tokyo contributed to a roughly 30 percent rise in building costs.
Others pointed out the hypocrisy of the government touting
a green Olympics, when tainted water in Fukushima was being
dumped into the ocean, nuclear clean-up was estimated to take
decades and cost around 600 billion dollars, and there was talk of
building over twenty new coal-burning plants.[21] While the Tokyo
Metropolitan Government created videos with titles such as *See
You in Tokyo and Tōhoku 2020*, continuing a pattern of Tokyo
rhetorically appropriating Tōhoku for its own ends, the very fact
that the capital could host the games and tsunami-stricken areas
wanted for reconstruction underscored the widening chasm
between them. In the immediate aftermath of the disasters in
2011, those in Tokyo had experienced fears of radiation as they
learned of elevated levels of radioactive contamination at metropolitan water purification plants and in locally grown vegetables.[22]
But they did not suffer directly from the worst of the earthquake or
tsunami, and as time passed, Tokyoites were able to resume their
daily lives in a way that many Tōhoku residents, struggling with
loss and displacement, could not. If 3.11 is sidelined in a history of
Tokyo, it is because the "Great East Japan earthquake" was
a national calamity more in rhetoric than in lived experience.

The unevenness of the hardships inflicted in the aftermath of 3.11 was a poignant exemplification of the shadow that had
been cast across the nation's dwindling rural areas by the seemingly inexorable growth of the Tokyo metropolitan region. In the
2010s, as the population of Japan as a whole declined due to low
birth and immigration rates, the Tokyo metropolitan region
gained residents for a number of years before trailing off near

the end of the decade. Growth in the central wards of the city, in particular, likely received a boost from the heightened construction of residences and office space after Tokyo's selection as Olympic host.[23] When it came to the Olympic venues themselves, while they were scattered across the capital region and a few were located farther away in Hokkaido and in Tōhoku, many were sited around Tokyo Bay in the hopes that they would propel further development of the waterfront area not just for but also beyond the games.[24] Near Odaiba and the wholesale fish market in its new location of Toyosu, recently moved from Tsukiji, the Ariake Arena was designed to host volleyball matches during the games and other large events such as concerts thereafter. Operated by a consortium headed by the marketing and advertising giant Dentsū, the arena is one of the few Olympic venues projected to earn a profit in future years. Also built in the vicinity was the Olympic Village, on Harumi Island just north of Odaiba, consisting of about twenty new residential buildings for athletes and slated for conversion after the games into upscale condos for Tokyoites. On land sold by the Tokyo Metropolitan Government to a group of property companies led by the developer Mitsui Fudōsan, this complex known as Harumi Flag is expected to become a new district with schools, shopping, and access to transportation across the waterfront area, which was improved for the Olympics. Such projects for Tokyo 2020 didn't entail the destruction of existing neighborhoods or large-scale displacement of poorer Tokyoites but rather amplified the pre-Olympic trend of developing not so much the suburbs in the west as much as the center of the city to the east, especially those wards along the bay which drew upper-middle-class residents to its higher-end condominium complexes.[25]

Although many of the plans laid in the years leading up to 2020 envisioned a forward-looking Olympics and a hopeful future for Tokyo beyond the games, most of the aspirations and ambitions for the city were suffocated by the national government's sluggish response to the pandemic. Desperate to placate the business community by saving the Olympics, the Abe administration downplayed COVID-19 risks and responded slowly to the escalating crisis. While Abe was pilloried for his handling of the pandemic, Tokyo governor Koike Yuriko earned points for urging business shutdowns, telling Tokyoites to stay home, and communicating openly and frequently about outbreaks and countermeasures. As preparations for the Olympics forged ahead nonetheless, in the months just before their start in July 2021, vaccination rates were still low, Tokyo was placed under a state of emergency amid a spike in infections, and a significant majority of people across the country opposed holding the games, calling instead for the prioritization of public health. In what was popularly dubbed the "Pandemic Games," the subdued opening ceremony and the over 10,000 athletes competing in empty venues devoid of spectators weren't the only casualties. A surge in coronavirus cases began during the Olympics and continued through the Paralympics, in a wave that was the largest of the pandemic to date.[26]

· ● ·

Walking the streets and alleyways of Tokyo, or looking out across its vast urban landscape from high up in the Tokyo Metropolitan Government Building or the Tokyo Skytree, the imprint of the past on the contemporary city is visible everywhere to those familiar with its history. Fires, earthquakes, and war have wreaked more destruction on this city than most, but didn't erase what came before and have left their mark in how Edoites and Tokyoites chose time and again to rebuild their neighborhoods and lives in the capital.[27] Encircled by a moat and verdant gardens, the Imperial Palace still stands in the center of the city where Ōta Dōkan constructed his fortress and Tokugawa Ieyasu built his castle. These grounds no longer house the seat of political power, but the space remains inviolate. And the spiral that radiated outward from the castle in Tokugawa days can be gleaned in the layout of the modern city's main roads, with major intersections where strategic gates used to be. In the high city, or Yamanote, the footprint of daimyo estates underlies structures such as the Mitsui Club in Minato ward. A Baroque-style building from 1913 graced with both European Renaissance and Japanese gardens, the club reflects the Tokugawa-era practice of constructing daimyo compounds on flat pieces of land atop hills with a garden along the downward slope. Even as daimyo residences were converted into sites for government offices, military facilities, embassies, universities, and then luxury hotels, many retained the beautiful gardens of the former estates. And areas demarcated for lower-ranking samurai have endured as residential neighborhoods. In the low city, or Shitamachi, the lives of the merchants and artisans of Edo can be glimpsed in the low-rise wooden buildings, family-owned shops, and small-scale manufacturers that are still part of the contemporary urban tapestry. Tokyoites of today can also be reminded of the city's early modern substructure by the names of neighborhoods, streets, bridges, and train stations encountered regularly in day-to-day life – the Ōtemachi area and station are just east of the Ōtemon gate to Edo Castle; the Marunouchi district, long a hub of business and finance, is *maru no uchi*, or "inside the circle" of the outer moat; and the Akasaka-Mitsuke neighborhood and station to the southwest are near where a key watchtower, or *mitsuke*, once stood. Nagatachō is where the Nagata family lived; Ningyōchō was for shops selling dolls, or *ningyō*; Konyachō was for dyers, or *kon'ya*; and Kajichō for ironsmiths, or *kaji*.[28]

As various Tokyoites have tried to preserve or recreate fragments of the city's history, traces of the past have assumed new meanings, forged in the present and layered upon that which came before. In the Marunouchi district, the Mitsubishi conglomerate has selectively chosen what of the past to demolish and what to rebuild in order to project an image of a company that has long been on the cutting edge of business development and cultural sophistication. To evoke its embrace of civilization and progress in the Meiji years, the corporation of the twenty-first century harked back to its "One Block London" of red brick and stone by recreating its Ichigōkan Building. Originally completed in 1894 and torn down in 1968, the British-designed Mitsubishi Ichigōkan was reconstructed and opened as a museum of European art in 2010. The three-story, red-brick structure in the Queen Anne style now sits against the backdrop of a shiny new skyscraper housing Mitsubishi Corporation offices and displays exhibits that illustrate "the dynamism that modern cities generate in art" at this location exemplifying "modern Japan's engagement with the world."[29] In other instances, conveying Mitsubishi's modernity involved destruction of the past. The Marunouchi Building of the early 1920s which survived both the Great Kantō earthquake and wartime bombing was torn down in the late 1990s to be replaced by a gleaming office tower with only some architectural nods to the original. Like its predecessor, the new Marunouchi Building stands across a plaza from Tokyo Station. As part of redevelopment efforts in the 2010s, this open space at the gateway to Marunouchi was redesigned and Tokyo Station itself was restored and renovated, bridging the 1914 landmark, designated by the government as Important Cultural Property, with the business district of the twenty-first century.[30]

In areas of the low city, local wards and residents have encouraged over the past several decades a shift in the image of

Shitamachi from a tired and run-down quarter of the capital to a cultural repository for an older and somehow more "authentic" Tokyo. Municipal governments, merchants' associations, magazines, and guidebooks have promoted historic shops, products, landmarks, and events to attract tourists. And efforts have been made to preserve the "traditional" feel and character of neighborhoods. In the district of Kyōjima in the Sumida ward, new community housing included small parks and squares, and was intentionally constructed on a modest scale to coexist with wooden rowhouses and maintain the balance between commercial and residential buildings. The Taitō ward built the Shitamachi Museum, largely funded by donations, which features architectural reconstructions of merchants' shops, artisans' workshops, and the interior of tenements. Beyond the curated space of the museum, in neighborhoods such as Shitaya and Negishi, explorers could find merchant houses with their characteristic combination of a store and family residence as well as wooden rowhouses for artisans. Temples and shrines dot the area, as do houses with gates and a garden, reminiscent of samurai estates.

In the heart of the low city, the historic Nihonbashi bridge has been the focus of efforts to remake the past for the present. Originally designated as the zero point for early modern Japan's transportation network, the bridge was built of wood in 1603 and burned down some eight times during the Tokugawa period. The wooden bridge was replaced with a stone structure in the early Meiji years and then, in 1911, with the Renaissance-style, double-arched stone bridge we now see. But today's Nihonbashi bridge is an underwhelming sight, quite literally overshadowed by the Metropolitan Expressway constructed for the 1964 Olympics. The bridge also arches over a sleepy river in a modern city whose development of railways and roads gradually oriented its residents more toward land than water. Starting in the early 1980s, when many metropolitan development plans were bandied about, the Nihonbashi Preservation Society argued for the removal of the expressway but didn't get much traction until the early 2000s, when there was greater government attention to projects in places such as Seoul, Boston, and San Francisco to reroute overhead highways. For the shopkeepers, local business executives, and heads of longtime area enterprises such as the Mitsukoshi department store, restoring the bridge to its former glory was a matter not just of aesthetics but of leveraging Nihonbashi's Tokugawa-era history of bustling commercial activity and vibrant popular culture to project an image of vitality in the present. In 2011, on the centennial of the current bridge's inauguration, the preservation society organized a festival that included a fleet of wooden boats that once brought fish and produce to the market on the district's riverbank, a centenarian resident energetic enough to lead the parade, and displays of samurai weapons and hundred-year-old cars. But in a testament to the subjectivity of the past, other voices suggested that it was not the bridge but the expressway that would prove in time to be the more significant landmark, symbolizing an era of infrastructure construction.[31] At the root of debates about the future of the Nihonbashi bridge lie deeper questions about which past, and whose past, should be reinterpreted and celebrated in present-day Tokyo.

• • •

Almost five kilometers northeast of the Nihonbashi bridge, in the low city ward of Sumida, stands the most recent and dramatic addition to the capital's skyline: the Tokyo Skytree. Completed and opened to the public in 2012, the Skytree both reflects and marshals the past, connecting history with how the city wants to be seen in the present. At 634 meters tall, the tower is an emblem of technological advancement on at least a few fronts. It expanded digital terrestrial broadcasting for television, radio, and mobile phones, more than making up for the insufficiencies of the landmark Tokyo Tower built in 1958. And it boasts state-of-the-art seismic proofing capabilities. The Skytree is also a destination for consumption, leisure, and tourism, with the Tokyo Solamachi shopping and entertainment complex at the base of the tower. In Tokyo Solamachi, visitors will find hundreds of restaurants, cafés, and stores from souvenir shops to clothing boutiques, as well as the Sumida Aquarium and the Konica Minolta Planetarium Tenkū. The Skytree experience is marketed by the cute mascot Sorakara-chan, literally From the Sky-chan, a girl from the "pointy star" whose yellow hair is styled into a star shape. In a short film playing in the theater on the observation deck 350 meters up, Sorakara-chan introduces viewers to tourist destinations around Japan, together with Hello Kitty.[32]

The image of Tokyo as technologically innovative and culturally fun is furthered by links made between the Skytree and aspects of the region's past which are endowed with a contemporary aura of cool. The tower's "neo-futuristic design" was married with its color of "Skytree white," allegedly inspired by a pale blue that's an homage to the indigo dyers who lived and worked in this area of the low city.[33] At night, the tower is illuminated in a way that "connects past and present," with LEDs bathing the Skytree in one of three colors intended to represent an aspect of Edo: light blue for its spirit, purple for its elegant aesthetics, and a reddish orange for its bustle of activity.[34] Evocation of the Tokugawa period seems to have had some popular resonance; in the contest to name the tower, "Tokyo Skytree" barely edged out the runner-up: "Tokyo Edo Tower."[35] The historical connection made by the height of the tower reaches even further back in time. The decision to build the Skytree to 634 meters not only ensured that it would be the tallest tower in the world at the time of its construction but also referenced the Japanese reading of the numbers six-three-four as *mu-sa-shi*, or Musashi, the name of the province that encompassed all of today's Tokyo metropolis, Saitama prefecture, and northeast Kanagawa prefecture, from well over a thousand years ago.[36] In a nod to Musashi province, the 634 Musashi Sky Restaurant on the observation deck describes itself as specializing in a new "Tokyo cuisine" that conveys "the spirit and air of Shitamachi."[37] The high-end restaurant presents its dishes as a "fusion of Edo chic and the elegance of French cuisine," offering its own take on both a purported style from the Tokugawa period and a definition of cultural sophistication from the Meiji era.[38]

From the observation deck 350 meters in the sky, and a second 100 meters higher, you can appreciate the sheer scale of the city as it extends far into the distance. You can visualize how early modern Edo and modern Tokyo have grown ever outward and then upward. When you return to ground level, you'll notice how the capital has developed less as a city of cars and highways and more of trains and subways, less of drivers and more of walkers and bicyclers. You may ask what the construction of Tokyo Skytree Town has meant for visitors to, workers in, and residents of Sumida ward (see Figure 10.2). And in a sprawling urban landscape not known for its beauty, you'll be attuned to the legacies, both the remnants and the absences, of the city's extraordinary arc as a capital of the shogun's realm, a modern nation, and an empire, then a global capital in a particularly interconnected world. There are chain restaurants and local watering holes, smaller lots and larger footprints, green grocers and convenience stores, neighborhood street grids and winding alleyways, modest shops and upscale department stores, low-rise buildings of wood and high-rise structures

Figure 10.2 The Shitamachi neighborhood Yanaka with the Tokyo Skytree in the background. Photograph by John S. Lander, May 4, 2019. Courtesy of LightRocket and Getty Images.

of glass and steel. The excitement of this remarkable city is in perceptively seeing, empathetically knowing, and continually learning how the past is woven into the richly textured pastiche of contemporary Tokyo.

NOTES

Prologue

1 Kanno Shunsuke, *Kochizu de tanoshimu Kagurazaka sanpo: Edo jidai kara kawaranu rekishi aru michisuji o tadoru* (Tokyo: Takarajimasha, 2021), 11, 15, 18, 48; Jinnai Hidenobu, *Suito Tōkyō: Chikei to rekishi de yomitoku shitamachi, yamanote, kōgai* (Tokyo: Chikuma Shobō, 2020), 179–180.

2 Kanno, *Kochizu*, 2–5, 13; Heide Imai, *Tokyo Roji: The Diversity and Versatility of Alleys in a City in Transition* (Abingdon, UK: Routledge, 2018), 101, 103–104; Matsui Daisuke and Kubota Aya, "Kagurazaka kagai ni okeru machinami keikan no hen'yō to keikakuteki kadai," *Nihon kenchiku gakkai keikakukei ronbunshū* 77, no. 680 (October 2012): 2408.

3 Okamoto Satoshi, *EdoTOKYO naritachi no kyōkasho: Marunouchi, Ginza, Kagurazaka kara Tokyo o kaibō suru* (Kyoto: Tankōsha, 2018), 250–251, 260, 264–265; Matsui and Kubota, "Kagurazaka kagai," 2408, 2411–2413; Imai, *Tokyo Roji*, 103–104.

1 Founding the Shogun's Capital

1 Kodama Kōta and Sugiyama Hiroshi, *Tōkyō-to no rekishi* (Tokyo: Yamakawa Shuppansha, 1972 [1969]), 148, 150; Tōkyō Hyakunenshi Henshū Iinkai, ed., *Tōkyō hyakunenshi*, vol. 1 (Tokyo: Tōkyō-to, 1979), 445; Seitōsha Henshūbu, *Chizu to shashin de wakaru Edo, Tōkyō* (Tokyo: Seitōsha, 2020), 64–65; Morgan Pitelka, *Spectacular Accumulation: Material Culture, Tokugawa Ieyasu, and Samurai Sociability* (Honolulu: University of Hawai'i Press, 2015), 62–64.

2 Tōkyō Hyakunenshi Henshū Iinkai, *Tōkyō hyakunenshi*, 449–450; Takeo Yazaki, *Social Change and the City in Japan: From Earliest Times through the Industrial Revolution* (San Francisco: Japan Publications, 1968), 174.

3 Takeuchi Makoto, Koizumi Hiroshi, Ikegami Hiroko, Katō Takashi, and Fujino Atsushi, *Tōkyō-to no rekishi* (Tokyo: Yamakawa Shuppansha, 2015), 146; Kodama and Sugiyama, *Tōkyō-to no rekishi*, 148; Pitelka, *Spectacular Accumulation*, 63–64; James L. McClain and John M. Merriman, "Edo and Paris: Cities and Power," in *Edo and Paris: Urban Life and the State in the Early Modern Era*, ed. James L. McClain, John M. Merriman, and Ugawa Kaoru (Ithaca, NY: Cornell University Press, 1994), 13.

4 Naitō Akira, "Planning and Development of Early Edo," *Japan Echo* 14, no. 5 (1987): 30–31.

5 Takeuchi et al., *Tōkyō-to no rekishi*, 11–16, 22–29, 31, 34, 36, 43, 63–67; David Spafford, *A Sense of Place: The Political Landscape in Late Medieval Japan* (Boston: Brill, 2013), 3, 39–40.

6 Tōkyō Hyakunenshi Henshū Iinkai, *Tōkyō hyakunenshi*, 37–38, 383; Takeuchi et al., *Tōkyō-to no rekishi*, 79–80, 109–112, 133–136; Spafford, *Sense of Place*, 27, 83, 170, 172, 174, 235–236, 241, 245–247, 249, 268; Kodama and Sugiyama, *Tōkyō-to no rekishi*, 139–141, 145.

7 Tōkyō Hyakunenshi Henshū Iinkai, *Tōkyō hyakunenshi*, 40, 451–452; Takeuchi et al., *Tōkyō-to no rekishi*, 146–148; Beatrice M. Bodart-Bailey, "Urbanisation and the Nature of the Tokugawa Hegemony," in *Japanese Capitals in Historical Perspective: Place, Power and Memory in Kyoto, Edo and Tokyo*, ed. Nicolas Fiévé and Paul Waley (Abingdon, UK: RoutledgeCurzon, 2003), 105.

8 Pitelka, *Spectacular Accumulation*, 75–78.

9 Takeuchi et al., *Tōkyō-to no rekishi*, 148–149; Katō Takashi, "Edo in the Seventeenth Century: Aspects of Urban Development in a Segregated Society," *Urban History* 27, no. 2 (August 2000): 196; Amy Stanley, "Women in Cities and Towns," in *The Tokugawa World*, ed. Gary P. Leupp and De-min Tao (New York: Routledge, 2022), 233; Akira Naito, *Edo, The City That Became Tokyo: An Illustrated History*, trans. H. Mack Horton (Tokyo: Kodansha International, 2003), 38, 41, 43, 45, 58, 92; Yazaki, *Social Change*, 176; Tōkyō Hyakunenshi Henshū Iinkai, *Tōkyō hyakunenshi*, 477; Conrad Totman, *Green Archipelago: Forestry in Pre-Industrial Japan* (Berkeley: University of California Press, 1989), 52.

10 William H. Coaldrake, *Architecture and Authority in Japan* (London: Routledge, 1996), 132, 134; Naito, *Edo*, 34–35, 48, 50–51, 57, 60–61; Stanley, "Women in Cities and Towns," 233; Seitōsha Henshūbu, *Chizu to shashin*, 102–107; William H. Coaldrake, "Edo Architecture and Tokugawa Law,"

Monumenta Nipponica 36, no. 3 (Autumn 1981): 246–250; Naitō, "Planning and Development," 36–37.

11 Constantine Nomikos Vaporis, *Tour of Duty: Samurai, Military Service in Edo, and the Culture of Early Modern Japan* (Honolulu: University of Hawai'i Press), 1, 12–13, 103–104, 129, 131–133, 136, 173, 187; Takeuchi et al., *Tōkyō-to no rekishi*, 148.

12 Vaporis, *Tour of Duty*, 23, 27–32, 123, 126–127, 129, 173; Amy Stanley, "Labor and Migration in Tokugawa Japan: Moving People," in *The New Cambridge History of Japan*, vol. 2, *Early Modern Japan in Asia and the World, c. 1580–1877*, ed. David L. Howell (Cambridge: Cambridge University Press, 2024), 548.

13 Vaporis, *Tour of Duty*, 131–132; Stanley, "Women in Cities and Towns," 233–234; Seitōsha Henshūbu, *Chizu to shashin*, 70–71, 78–79; Takeuchi et al., *Tōkyō-to no rekishi*, 3–4, 151–152; Tōkyō Hyakunenshi Henshū Iinkai, *Tōkyō hyakunenshi*, 42; Naito, *Edo*, 77–79, 104–105.

14 Takeuchi et al., *Tōkyō-to no rekishi*, 152–153; Reiko Hayashi, "Provisioning Edo in the Early Eighteenth Century: The Pricing Policies of the Shogunate and the Crisis of 1733," in *Edo and Paris*, 214–215; Theodore C. Bestor, *Tsukiji: The Fish Market at the Center of the World* (Berkeley: University of California Press, 2004), 101–102; Naito, *Edo*, 72.

15 Amy Stanley, *Selling Women: Prostitution, Markets, and the Household in Early Modern Japan* (Berkeley: University of California Press, 2012), 45–49, 60.

16 Hayashi, "Provisioning Edo," 213–215, 217–218; Vaporis, *Tour of Duty*, 2–3, 166, 168; Katō, "Edo," 203; Naito, *Edo*, 70; Brett L. Walker, *Toxic Archipelago: A History of Industrial Disease in Japan* (Seattle: University of Washington Press, 2010), 32–33.

17 Hayashi, "Provisioning Edo," 214; Naito, *Edo*, 33, 68, 70; Constantine N. Vaporis, "Linking the Realm: The Gokaidō Highway Network in Early Modern Japan (1603–1868)," in *Highways, Byways, and Road Systems in the Pre-Modern World*, ed. Susan E. Alcock, John Bodel, and Richard J. A. Talbert (Hoboken, NJ: Wiley-Blackwell, 2012), 90–91, 94–95, 97–99; Naitō, "Planning and Development," 34; Takeuchi et al., *Tōkyō-to no rekishi*, 149–150; Tōkyō Hyakunenshi Henshū Iinkai, *Tōkyō hyakunenshi*, 522–523.

18 Ronald P. Toby, "Reopening the Question of Sakoku: Diplomacy in the Legitimation of the Tokugawa Bakufu," *Journal of Japanese Studies* 3, no. 2 (Summer 1977): 325–326, 330; Tashiro Kazui, "Foreign Relations During the Edo Period: Sakoku Reexamined," trans. Susan Downing Videen,

Journal of Japanese Studies 8, no. 2 (Summer 1982): 288–289; Walker, *Toxic Archipelago*, 77.

19 Naito, *Edo*, 105.

2 Becoming the City of Edoites

1 Satoko Shimazaki, *Edo Kabuki in Transition: From the Worlds of the Samurai to the Vengeful Female Ghost* (New York: Columbia University Press, 2016), 53–54; Watanabe Tamotsu, *Edo engekishi, jō* (Tokyo: Kōdansha, 2009), 229–232; Tove Björk, "The Ejima-Ikushima Scandal," in *Theatre Scandals: Social Dynamics of Turbulent Theatrical Events*, ed. Vicki Ann Cremona, Peter Eversmann, Bess Rowen, Anneli Saro, and Henri Schoenmakers (Leiden: Brill Rodopi, 2020), 123–124; Donald H. Shively, "The Social Environment of Tokugawa Kabuki," in *Studies in Kabuki: Its Acting, Music, and Historical Context* (Honolulu: University of Hawai'i Press, 1978), 29.

2 Shimazaki, *Edo Kabuki*, 54; Watanabe, *Edo engekishi*, 232–234; Shively, "Social Environment," 34; Gregory M. Pflugfelder, *Cartographies of Desire: Male-Male Sexuality in Japanese Discourse, 1600–1950* (Berkeley: University of California Press, 1999), 122; Björk, "Ejima-Ikushima Scandal," 137.

3 Watanabe, *Edo engekishi*, 235; Pflugfelder, *Cartographies of Desire*, 118, 122; Shimazaki, *Edo Kabuki*, 53–54, 91; Amy Stanley, "Adultery, Punishment, and Reconciliation in Tokugawa Japan," *Journal of Japanese Studies* 33, no. 2 (Summer 2007): 311, 314.

4 Amy Stanley, "Women in Cities and Towns," in *The Tokugawa World*, ed. Gary P. Leupp and De-min Tao (New York: Routledge, 2022), 233–234; Shimazaki, *Edo Kabuki*, 56; William H. Coaldrake, "Edo Architecture and Tokugawa Law," *Monumenta Nipponica* 36, no. 3 (Autumn 1981): 252.

5 Susan B. Hanley, *Everyday Things in Premodern Japan: The Hidden Legacy of Material Culture* (Berkeley: University of California Press, 1997), 105–106.

6 William W. Kelly, "Incendiary Actions: Fires and Firefighting in the Shogun's Capital and the People's City," in *Edo and Paris: Urban Life and the State in the Early Modern Era*, ed. James L. McClain, John M. Merriman, and Ugawa Kaoru (Ithaca, NY: Cornell University Press, 1994), 313, 328; Seitōsha Henshūbu, *Chizu to shashin de wakaru Edo, Tōkyō* (Tokyo: Seitōsha, 2020), 164.

7 Kelly, "Incendiary Actions," 310–311, 313; James L. McClain, "Edobashi: Power, Space, and Popular Culture in Edo," in *Edo and Paris*, 105–106;

Beatrice M. Bodart-Bailey, "Urbanisation and the Nature of the Tokugawa Hegemony," in *Japanese Capitals in Historical Perspective: Place, Power and Memory in Kyoto, Edo and Tokyo*, ed. Nicolas Fiévé and Paul Waley (Abingdon, UK: RoutledgeCurzon, 2003), 113; Coaldrake, "Edo Architecture and Tokugawa Law," 256.

8 Naitō Akira, "Planning and Development of Early Edo," *Japan Echo* 14, no. 5 (1987): 37–38; Akira Naito, *Edo, The City That Became Tokyo: An Illustrated History*, trans. H. Mack Horton (Tokyo: Kodansha International, 2003), 103, 162; Coaldrake, "Edo Architecture and Tokugawa Law," 252; Constantine Nomikos Vaporis, *Tour of Duty: Samurai, Military Service in Edo, and the Culture of Early Modern Japan* (Honolulu: University of Hawai'i Press), 132–133, 139; McClain, "Edobashi," 107.

9 Kevin Bond, "The 'Famous Places' of Japanese Buddhism: Representations of Urban Temple Life in Early Modern Guidebooks," *Studies in Religion* 43, no. 2 (2014): 230; Nam-Lin Hur, *Prayer and Play in Late Tokugawa Japan: Asakusa Sensōji and Edo Society* (Cambridge, MA: Harvard University Asia Center, 2000), 31–72.

10 Coaldrake, "Edo Architecture and Tokugawa Law," 252; Hanley, *Everyday Things*, 39–40, 126–127; Kelly, "Incendiary Actions," 313, 324–325.

11 McClain, "Edobashi," 107, 109, 111–127.

12 Kelly, "Incendiary Actions," 315–324; McClain, "Edobashi," 127.

13 Shimazaki, *Edo Kabuki*, 44–45, 47, 54–55; Shively, "Social Environment," 12, 14–16; Amy Stanley, *Stranger in the Shogun's City: A Japanese Woman and Her World* (New York: Scribner, 2020), 138.

14 Shively, "Social Environment," 14, 20, 23, 26–27, 35–46; Björk, "Ejima-Ikushima Scandal," 135, 139; Stanley, *Stranger in the Shogun's City*, 138; Pflugfelder, *Cartographies of Desire*, 112–115, 120–122, 137; Shimazaki, *Edo Kabuki*, 8, 18, 86–88.

15 Shimazaki, *Edo Kabuki*, 22–23, 46, 53–54, 56, 58–60, 66, 68, 88; Pflugfelder, *Cartographies of Desire*, 118, 137; Kelly, "Incendiary Actions," 313, 325, 327–328.

16 Shimazaki, *Edo Kabuki*, 2.

17 Marcia Yonemoto, *Mapping Early Modern Japan: Space, Place, and Culture in the Tokugawa Period (1603–1868)* (Berkeley: University of California Press, 2003), 4; Shimazaki, *Edo Kabuki*, 2, 12–15.

18 C. Andrew Gerstle, "Flowers of Edo: Eighteenth-Century Kabuki and Its Patrons," *Asian Theatre Journal* 4, no. 1 (Spring 1987): 64.

19 Gerstle, "Flowers of Edo," 53, 61, 64, 67; Shively, "Social Environment," 42; Shimazaki, *Edo Kabuki*, 91.

20 Shimazaki, *Edo Kabuki*, 32, 42.

3 Seismic Shocks

1 Frederic Trautmann, "Introduction," in William Heine, *With Perry to Japan: A Memoir by William Heine*, trans. Frederic Trautmann (Honolulu: University of Hawai'i Press, 1990), 11–12; Amy Stanley, *Stranger in the Shogun's City: A Japanese Woman and Her World* (New York: Scribner, 2020), 232; John W. Dower, "Black Ships & Samurai: Commodore Perry and the Opening of Japan (1853–1854)," Massachusetts Institute of Technology, Visualizing Cultures, 2008, 1-1, 3-1, http://visualizingcultures.mit.edu; Tōkyō Hyakunenshi Henshū Iinkai, ed., *Tōkyō hyakunenshi*, vol. 1 (Tokyo: Tōkyō-to, 1979), 1414, 1417; William Heine, *With Perry to Japan: A Memoir by William Heine*, trans. Frederic Trautmann (Honolulu: University of Hawai'i Press, 1990), 63; William Speiden Jr., *With Commodore Perry to Japan: The Journal of William Speiden Jr., 1852–1855*, vol. 1, ed. John A. Wolter, David A. Ranzan, and John J. McDonough (Annapolis, MD: Naval Institute Press, 2013), 67; M. William Steele, *Alternative Narratives in Modern Japanese History* (London: RoutledgeCurzon, 2003), 6.

2 Tōkyō Hyakunenshi Henshū Iinkai, *Tōkyō hyakunenshi*, 1417–1418; Takeuchi Makoto, Koizumi Hiroshi, Ikegami Hiroko, Katō Takashi, and Fujino Atsushi, *Tōkyō-to no rekishi* (Tokyo: Yamakawa Shuppansha, 2015), 293; Steele, *Alternative Narratives*, 6; Stanley, *Stranger in the Shogun's City*, 233.

3 Stanley, *Stranger in the Shogun's City*, 223–228; Trautmann, "Introduction," 12; Heine, *With Perry to Japan*, 64.

4 Stanley, *Stranger in the Shogun's City*, 232–233; Heine, *With Perry to Japan*, 73–74; Dower, "Black Ships & Samurai," 1–11.

5 "From Millard Fillmore, President of the United States of America, to His Imperial Majesty, the Emperor of Japan" (November 13, 1852); "From

Commodore Matthew C. Perry to His Imperial Majesty, the Emperor of Japan" (July 7, 1853).

6 Sugita Genpaku, *Dawn of Western Science in Japan*, trans. Matsumoto Ryōzō and Kiyooka Eiichi (1815; Tokyo: Hokuseido Press, 1969), 24–25, 27–29; Grant K. Goodman, *Japan and the Dutch, 1600–1853* (Richmond, UK: Curzon, 2000), 82; Daniel V. Botsman, *Punishment and Power in the Making of Modern Japan* (Princeton, NJ: Princeton University Press, 2013), 23–24.

7 Sugita, *Dawn of Western Science*, 30.

8 Sugita, *Dawn of Western Science*, 26–27, 30–32; Goodman, *Japan and the Dutch*, 77, 83–84, 119; Ogata Tomio, "Introduction," in *Dawn of Western Science*, x–xii.

9 Bob Tadashi Wakabayashi, *Anti-Foreignism and Western Learning in Early-Modern Japan: The New Theses of 1825* (Cambridge, MA: Council on East Asian Studies, Harvard University, 1986), 40, 41, 46–47.

10 Goodman, *Japan and the Dutch*, 216.

11 Goodman, *Japan and the Dutch*, 210, 216, 221.

12 Dower, "Black Ships & Samurai," 2-2-2-6, 3-5-3-6; Steele, *Alternative Narratives*, 4–6, 12–13; Peter Duus, ed., *The Japanese Discovery of America: A Brief History with Documents* (Boston: Bedford, 1997), 106–107.

13 Duus, *Japanese Discovery of America*, 108–109.

14 Dower, "Black Ships & Samurai," 5-8; Steele, *Alternative Narratives*, 9.

15 Steele, *Alternative Narratives*, 5–6.

16 Dower, "Black Ships & Samurai," 1-11, 3-1, 4-9, 7-1, 7-4, 7-7-7-10; Seitōsha Henshūbu, *Chizu to shashin de wakaru Edo, Tōkyō* (Tokyo: Seitōsha, 2020), 24–25; Heine, *With Perry to Japan*, 126.

17 Gregory Smits, *Seismic Japan: The Long History and Continuing Legacy of the Ansei Edo Earthquake* (Honolulu: University of Hawai'i Press, 2013), 2, 16, 104–105, 108, 113, 118, 146; Andrew Markus, "*Gesaku* Authors and the Ansei Earthquake of 1855," in *Studies in Modern Japanese Literature: Essays and Translations in Honor of Edwin McClellan*, ed. Dennis Washburn and Alan Tansman (Ann Arbor: Center for Japanese Studies, University of Michigan, 1997), 54; Takashi Miura, *Agents of World Renewal: The Rise of Yonaoshi Gods in Japan* (Honolulu: University of Hawai'i Press, 2019), 91–92; Gregory Smits, "Shaking Up Japan: Edo Society and the 1855 Catfish Picture Prints," *Journal of Social*

History 39, no. 4 (Summer 2006): 1045; Stanley, *Stranger in the Shogun's City*, 238; Takeuchi et al., *Tōkyō-to no rekishi*, 296.

18 Miura, *Agents of World Renewal*, 86–87, 92, 94–96, 99; Smits, *Seismic Japan*, 33, 35, 124–125, 170; Markus, "*Gesaku* Authors," 59.

19 Smits, *Seismic Japan*, 122–124.

20 Smits, *Seismic Japan*, 120–121.

21 Miura, *Agents of World Renewal*, 108; Smits, "Shaking Up Japan," 1047, 1050, 1068–1069; Smits, *Seismic Japan*, 149.

22 Steele, *Alternative Narratives*, 15–17.

23 Smits, *Seismic Japan*, 115, 127–128, 144, 146–147, 149–150, 168; Markus, "*Gesaku* Authors," 55; Stanley, *Stranger in the Shogun's City*, 238; Steele, *Alternative Narratives*, 15.

24 Gregory Clancey, *Earthquake Nation: The Cultural Politics of Japanese Seismicity, 1868–1930* (Berkeley: University of California Press, 2006), 130.

25 Smits, *Seismic Japan*, 167–168; Takeuchi et al., *Tōkyō-to no rekishi*, 296; Donald Keene, *Emperor of Japan: Meiji and His World, 1852–1912* (New York: Columbia University Press, 2002), 52–55, 59–62.

26 Anne Walthall, "Edo Riots," in *Edo and Paris: Urban Life and the State in the Early Modern Era*, ed. James L. McClain, John M. Merriman, and Ugawa Kaoru (Ithaca, NY: Cornell University Press, 1994), 419, 422; Henry D. Smith, "The Edo–Tokyo Transition: In Search of Common Ground," in *Japan in Transition: From Tokugawa to Meiji*, ed. Marius B. Jansen and Gilbert Rozman (Princeton, NJ: Princeton University Press, 1986), 347, 350; Takeuchi et al., *Tōkyō-to no rekishi*, 299–300.

27 Miura, *Agents of World Renewal*, 109–111, 127; Smits, *Seismic Japan*, 162–163.

28 Steele, *Alternative Narratives*, 62.

29 Steele, *Alternative Narratives*, 65, 68, 79–80.

30 Takeuchi et al., *Tōkyō-to no rekishi*, 306; Smith, "Edo–Tokyo Transition," 355.

31 Yokoyama Yuriko, *Edo Tōkyō no Meiji ishin* (Tokyo: Iwanami Shoten, 2018), 22–24; Steele, *Alternative Narratives*, 83–85; Keene, *Emperor of Japan*, 159–167; Ishizuka Hiromichi and Narita Ryūichi, *Tōkyō-to no hyakunen* (Tokyo: Yamakawa Shuppansha, 1986), 16; Stanley, *Stranger in the Shogun's City*, 243.

4 Modernizing the Nation's Capital

1 Tristan R. Grunow, "Empire by Design: Railways, Architecture, and Urban Planning in Tokyo, Taipei, and Seoul" (PhD diss., University of Oregon, 2014), 50; Kawasaki Fusagorō, *Bunmei kaika Tōkyō: Meiji Tōkyō shiwa* (Tokyo: Kōfūsha Shuppan, 1984), 127; Steven J. Ericson, *The Sound of the Whistle: Railroads and the State in Meiji Japan* (Cambridge, MA: Council on East Asian Studies, Harvard University, 1996), 54; Tristan R. Grunow, "Trains, Modernity, and State Formation in Meiji Japan," in *Trains, Culture, and Mobility: Riding the Rails*, ed. Benjamin Fraser and Steven D. Spalding (Lanham, MD: Lexington Books, 2012), 206; *Manchester Guardian*, December 27, 1872; *New York Times*, January 19, 1873.

2 Ericson, *Sound of the Whistle*, 54, 61–62, 66, 69.

3 Carol Gluck, *Japan's Modern Myths: Ideology in the Late Meiji Period* (Princeton, NJ: Princeton University Press, 1985), 163, 356 fn 28; Ericson, *Sound of the Whistle*, 30.

4 David L. Howell, *Geographies of Identity in Nineteenth-Century Japan* (Berkeley: University of California Press, 2005), 155–158; Gluck, *Japan's Modern Myths*, 78, 93, 101, 254; Grunow, "Trains, Modernity, and State Formation," 203.

5 André Sorensen, *The Making of Urban Japan: Cities and Planning from Edo to the Twenty-First Century* (London: Routledge, 2002), 61, 63; Jinnai Hidenobu, *Tokyo: A Spatial Anthropology* (Berkeley: University of California Press, 1995), 144.

6 Grunow, "Empire by Design," 21–22, 27–28; Grunow, "Trains, Modernity, and State Formation," 210.

7 Grunow, "Empire by Design," 22–23, 27–28, 48–49; Sorensen, *Making of Urban Japan*, 61; Jordan Sand, "Property in Two Fire Regimes: From Edo to Tokyo," in *Investing in the Early Modern Built Environment: Europeans, Asians, Settlers and Indigenous Societies*, ed. Carole Shammas (Leiden: Brill, 2012), 61; Ishizuka Hiromichi and Narita Ryūichi, *Tōkyō-to no hyakunen* (Tokyo: Yamakawa Shuppansha, 1986), 24–25; Tokyo Hyakunenshi Henshū Iinkai, ed., *Tōkyō hyakunenshi*, vol. 2 (Tokyo: Tōkyō-to, 1979), 120–121.

8 Grunow, "Trains, Modernity, and State Formation," 210; Grunow, "Empire by Design," 22, 61–63; Tristan R. Grunow, "Paving Power:

Western Urban Planning and Imperial Space from the Streets of Meiji Tokyo to Colonial Seoul," *Journal of Urban History* 42, no. 3 (2016): 511.

9 Woodblock print artists conventionally assumed a last name taken from the school to which they belonged and a first name that might include an element of their teacher's name. The designation "II" (second) or "III" (third) typically indicated the adoption of their teacher's artistic name (e.g., Utagawa Hiroshige III was a student of Utagawa Hiroshige). It was not unusual for an artist to change, or have multiple, names.

10 Tristan R. Grunow, "Ginza Bricktown and the Myth of Meiji Modernization," https://meijiat150dtr.arts.ubc.ca/essays/grunow/.

11 Grunow, "Ginza Bricktown"; Grunow, "Empire by Design," 22–24, 30, 68, 88, 91, 103–107; Matsuyama Megumi, *Toshi kūkan no Meiji ishin: Edo kara Tōkyō e no daitenkan* (Tokyo: Chikuma Shobō, 2019), 70, 72; Ishizuka and Narita, *Tōkyō-to no hyakunen*, 26; James L. Huffman, *Down and Out in Late Meiji Japan* (Honolulu: University of Hawai'i Press, 2018), 38; Sorensen, *Making of Urban Japan*, 62–63; Seitōsha Henshūbu, *Chizu to shashin de wakaru Edo, Tōkyō* (Tokyo: Seitōsha, 2020), 180–181.

12 Takashi Fujitani, *Splendid Monarchy: Power and Pageantry in Modern Japan* (Berkeley: University of California Press, 1996), 40, 66–71, 76–77, 79; Gregory Clancey, *Earthquake Nation: The Cultural Politics of Japanese Seismicity, 1868–1930* (Berkeley: University of California Press, 2006), 55–56; Sorensen, *Making of Urban Japan*, 65.

13 Kawasaki, *Bunmei kaika Tōkyō*, 306; Grunow, "Paving Power," 526; Seitōsha Henshūbu, *Chizu to shashin*, 176–177; Sorensen, *Making of Urban Japan*, 65.

14 Ishizuka and Narita, *Tōkyō-to no hyakunen*, 21–22; Huffman, *Down and Out*, 31, 48; Hiromichi Ishizuka, "The Slum Dwellings and the Urban Renewal Scheme in Tokyo," *Developing Economies* 19, no. 2 (1981): 172.

15 Sand, "Two Fire Regimes," 62–63, 65; Grunow, "Trains, Modernity, and State Formation," 211.

16 Huffman, *Down and Out*, 11–12, 28, 48; Kawasaki, *Bunmei kaika Tōkyō*, 298, 301–302; Ishizuka and Narita, *Tōkyō-to no hyakunen*, 34; Jinnai, *Tokyo*, 112; Andrew Gordon, *The Evolution of Labor Relations in Japan: Heavy Industry, 1853–1955* (Cambridge, MA: Council on East Asian Studies, Harvard University, 1985), 11.

17 Paul Waley, "From Flowers to Factories: A Peregrination through Changing Landscapes on the Edge of Tokyo," *Japan Forum* 22, nos. 3–4

(2010): 282, 293–294, 296, 302; E. Patricia Tsurumi, *Factory Girls: Women in the Thread Mills of Meiji Japan* (Princeton, NJ: Princeton University Press, 1990), 5, 108, 137–138, 140.

18 Huffman, *Down and Out*, 13–14, 36, 40–43, 85, 87; Ishizuka, "Slum Dwellings," 173–174, 181–183; Kawasaki, *Bunmei kaika Tōkyō*, 302; Ishizuka and Narita, *Tōkyō-to no hyakunen*, 27, 80–81.

19 Quote from the *Chōya shinbun* in Ericson, *Sound of the Whistle*, 69.

20 Ericson, *Sound of the Whistle*, 26, 28, 68–69, 93; Grunow, "Trains, Modernity, and State Formation," 205, 209.

21 Ericson, *Sound of the Whistle*, 66, 71–73; Jinnai, *Tokyo*, 144; Huffman, *Down and Out*, 69.

22 Barak Kushner, *Slurp! A Social and Culinary History of Ramen, Japan's Favorite Noodle Soup* (Boston: Global Oriental, 2012), 126–127; Huffman, *Down and Out*, 2; Ericson, *Sound of the Whistle*, 90–91.

23 Jamie Coates, "Ikebukuro In-between: Mobility and the Formation of the Yamanote's Heterotopic Borderland," *Japan Forum* 30, no. 2 (2018): 166–167; Mark Pendleton and Jamie Coates, "Thinking from the Yamanote: Space, Place and Mobility in Tokyo's Past and Present," *Japan Forum* 30, no. 2 (2018): 152–153.

24 Tōkyō Hyakunenshi Henshū Iinkai, *Tōkyō hyakunenshi*, 545–548; Huffman, *Down and Out*, 75–76, 82.

25 Grunow, "Trains, Modernity, and State Formation," 203, 213–216; Gluck, *Japan's Modern Myths*, 101, 247.

5 The Politics of Public Space

1 Quoted in Andrew Gordon, "The Crowd and Politics in Imperial Japan: Tokyo 1905–1918," *Past and Present* 121 (November 1988): 165.

2 Fujino Yūko, *Toshi to bōdō no minshūshi* (Tokyo: Yūhikaku, 2015), 35–44; Gordon, "Crowd and Politics," 141, 151, 158; Shumpei Okamoto, "The Emperor and the Crowd: The Historical Significance of the Hibiya Riot," in *Conflict in Modern Japanese History*, ed. Tetsuo Najita and J. Victor Koschmann (Princeton, NJ: Princeton University Press, 1982), 260–263; Thomas R. H. Havens, *Parkscapes: Green Spaces in Modern Japan* (Honolulu: University of Hawai'i Press, 2011), 44.

3 Fujino, *Toshi to bōdō*, 44–45, 241; Gordon, "Crowd and Politics," 142.

4 Havens, *Parkscapes*, 24-26; Paul Waley, "Parks and Landmarks: Planning the Eastern Capital along Western Lines," *Journal of Historical Geography* 31, no. 1 (2005): 7-8.

5 Takashi Fujitani, *Splendid Monarchy: Power and Pageantry in Modern Japan* (Berkeley: University of California Press, 1996), 79-81.

6 Fujitani, *Splendid Monarchy*, 107-110, 131-135.

7 Havens, *Parkscapes*, 25-26, 30, 46, 52; Edward Seidensticker, *Low City, High City: Tokyo from Edo to the Earthquake* (New York: Alfred A. Knopf, 1983), 124; Waley, "Parks and Landmarks," 4-5, 7-9; Ian Jared Miller, *The Nature of the Beasts: Empire and Exhibition at the Tokyo Imperial Zoo* (Berkeley: University of California Press, 2013), 37; Yoshimi Shun'ya, *Toshi no doramaturugī: Tōkyō, sakariba no shakaishi* (Tokyo: Kōbundō, 1987), 127-129; Angus Lockyer, "Japan at the Exhibition, 1867-1970" (PhD diss., Stanford University, 2000), 90-91, 93-94, 97, 102.

8 Havens, *Parkscapes*, 29-31; Yoshimi, *Toshi no doramaturugī*, 131-132; Donald Keene, *Emperor of Japan: Meiji and His World, 1852-1912* (New York: Columbia University Press, 2002), 317; Richard T. Chang, "General Grant's 1879 Visit to Japan," *Monumenta Nipponica* 24, no. 4 (1969): 388-389; Fujitani, *Splendid Monarchy*, 111; Okamoto, "Emperor and the Crowd," 274-275.

9 Miller, *Nature of the Beasts*, 2-4, 37-38, 82, 84; Havens, *Parkscapes*, 28, 30; Waley, "Parks and Landmarks," 9; Yoshimi, *Toshi no doramaturugī*, 132.

10 Havens, *Parkscapes*, 14, 40-42; Waley, "Parks and Landmarks," 11; Kawasaki Fusagorō, *Bunmei kaika Tokyo: Meiji Tokyo shiwa* (Tokyo: Kōfūsha Shuppan, 1984), 316-317.

11 Havens, *Parkscapes*, 40-41, 43-44; Maejima Yasuhiko, *Hibiya kōen: Nihon saisho no yōfū kokumin hiroba* (Tokyo: Kyōgakusha, 1980), 53-55, 65-66; Waley, "Parks and Landmarks," 4, 12-13; Taizo Fujimoto, *The Nightside of Japan* (Philadelphia, PA: T. Werner Laurie, 1914), 12.

12 Gordon, "Crowd and Politics," 167.

13 Gordon, "Crowd and Politics," 158.

14 Alisa Freedman, *Tokyo in Transit: Japanese Culture on the Rails and Road* (Stanford, CA: Stanford University Press, 2011), 35-37; Gordon, "Crowd and Politics," 159.

15 Fujino, *Toshi to bōdō*, 15-16, 24, 61-62, 65-66, 68-78, 242-244, 247-254; Gordon, "Crowd and Politics," 143, 148-152, 157, 161-162; Andrew Gordon,

Labor and Imperial Democracy in Prewar Japan (Berkeley: University of California Press, 1991), 35–36, 61–62; Ishizuka Hiromichi and Narita Ryūichi, *Tōkyō-to no hyakunen* (Tokyo: Yamakawa Shuppansha, 1986), 106–109; Michael Lewis, *Rioters and Citizens: Mass Protest in Imperial Japan* (Berkeley: University of California Press, 1990), 109, 111.

16 Tim Harper, *Underground Asia: Global Revolutionaries and the Assault on Empire* (Cambridge, MA: Belknap Press of Harvard University Press, 2021), 33–44; Jeffrey Paul Bayliss, *On the Margins of Empire: Buraku and Korean Identity in Prewar and Wartime Japan* (Cambridge, MA: Harvard University Asia Center, 2013), 107–110, 112–113, 122–133, 140–145.

17 Fujino, *Toshi to bōdō*, 105–109; Barbara Molony, "Women's Rights, Feminism, and Suffragism in Japan, 1870–1925," *Pacific Historical Review* 69, no. 4 (November 2000): 646, 649–650, 654–655, 660–661.

6 Tokyo Modern: Destruction and Reconstruction of the Cosmopolitan City

1 Kurosawa Akira, *Something Like an Autobiography*, trans. Audie E. Bock (New York: Vintage Books, 1983), 48.

2 J. Charles Schencking, *The Great Kantō Earthquake and the Chimera of National Reconstruction in Japan* (New York: Columbia University Press, 2013), 18–20, 24; Kurosawa, *Autobiography*, 47.

3 J. Michael Allen, "The Price of Identity: The 1923 Kantō Earthquake and Its Aftermath," *Korean Studies* 20 (1996): 66, 77; Fujino Yūko, *Toshi to bōdō no minshūshi* (Tokyo: Yūhikaku, 2015), 271–279, 291–293; Schencking, *Great Kantō Earthquake*, 26–29; Miriam Silverberg, *Erotic Grotesque Nonsense: The Mass Culture of Japanese Modern Times* (Berkeley: University of California Press, 2006), 41.

4 Kurosawa, *Autobiography*, 52.

5 Gennifer Weisenfeld, *Imaging Disaster: Tokyo and the Visual Culture of Japan's Great Earthquake of 1923* (Berkeley: University of California Press, 2012), 3; Schencking, *Great Kantō Earthquake*, 2, 18, 38–40, 69–70; André Sorensen, *The Making of Urban Japan: Cities and Planning from Edo to the Twenty-First Century* (London: Routledge, 2002), 125; Judith Vitale, "The Destruction and Rediscovery of Edo Castle: 'Picturesque Ruins', 'War Ruins'," *Japan Forum* 33, no. 1 (2021): 120–121.

6 Schencking, *Great Kantō Earthquake*, 2.

7 J. Charles Schencking, "Mapping Death and Destruction in 1923," in *Cartographic Japan: A History in Maps*, ed. Kären Wigen, Sugimoto Fumiko, and Cary Karacas (Chicago: University of Chicago Press, 2016), 151–154.

8 Wakatsuki Reijirō quoted in Schencking, *Great Kantō Earthquake*, 153.

9 Schencking, *Great Kantō Earthquake*, 154, 184; Jordan Sand, *House and Home in Modern Japan: Architecture, Domestic Space, and Bourgeois Culture, 1880–1930* (Cambridge, MA: Harvard University Asia Center 2003), 206–207.

10 Sorensen, *Making of Urban Japan*, 126–127, 129; André Sorensen, "Rebuilding Tokyo after the Great Kanto Earthquake," in *Cartographic Japan*, 156; Schencking, *Great Kantō Earthquake*, 185–186, 283–287, 303.

11 Jinnai Hidenobu, *Tokyo: A Spatial Anthropology*, trans. Kimiko Nishimura (Berkeley: University of California Press, 1995), 198; Schencking, *Great Kantō Earthquake*, 289–292; Sorensen, *Making of Urban Japan*, 129; Sorensen, "Rebuilding Tokyo," 156.

12 Gregory Clancey, *Earthquake Nation: The Cultural Politics of Japanese Seismicity, 1868–1930* (Berkeley: University of California Press, 2006), 213, 222; Sand, *House and Home*, 207–208.

13 Sorensen, *Making of Urban Japan*, 132–133; Trent E. Maxey, "At the Threshold of Modern Living: Tokyo in the 1920s and 1930s," in *Reinventing Tokyo: Japan's Largest City in the Artistic Imagination*, ed. Samuel C. Morse (Amherst, MA: Mead Art Museum, 2012), 33.

14 Sand, *House and Home*, 257; Gary D. Allinson, *Suburban Tokyo: A Comparative Study in Politics and Social Change* (Berkeley: University of California Press, 1979), 20–21, 23; Sorensen, *Making of Urban Japan*, 124.

15 James A. Fujii, "Intimate Alienation: Japanese Urban Rail and the Commodification of Urban Subjects," *differences: A Journal of Feminist Cultural Studies* 11, no. 2 (Summer 1999): 115; Yamaguchi Hiroshi, *Kōgai jūtaku no keifu: Tōkyō no den'en yūtopia* (Tokyo: Kajima Shuppankai, 1987), 34–35; Allinson, *Suburban Tokyo*, 50.

16 Sand, *House and Home*, 225–226, 237–238, 246, 253, 256, 262, 294; Elise K. Tipton, "The Café: Contested Space of Modernity in Interwar Japan," in *Being Modern in Japan: Culture and Society from the 1910s to the 1930s*, ed. Elise K. Tipton and John Clark (Honolulu: University of Hawai'i

Press, 2000), 124; Ken Tadashi Oshima, "Denenchōfu: Building the Garden City in Japan," *Journal of the Society of Architectural Historians* 55, no. 2 (June 1996): 145–146.

17 Henry D. Smith II, "Shinjuku 1931: A New Type of Urban Space," in *Cartographic Japan*, 160.

18 Barbara Sato, "Contesting Consumerisms in Mass Women's Magazines," *The Modern Girl around the World: Consumption, Modernity, and Globalization* (Durham, NC: Duke University Press, 2008), 271–272.

19 Yoshimi Shun'ya, *Toshi no doramaturugī: Tōkyō, sakariba no shakaishi* (Tokyo: Kōbundō, 1987), 233; Tomoko Tamari, "Modernization and the Department Store in Early Twentieth-Century Japan: Modern Girl and New Consumer Culture Lifestyles," in *Approaching Consumer Culture: Global Flows and Local Contexts*, ed. Evgenia Krasteva-Blagoeva (Cham, Switzerland: Springer International, 2018), 240; Yazaki Takeo, *Social Change and the City in Japan: From Earliest Times through the Industrial Revolution*, trans. David L. Swain (San Francisco: Japan Publications, 1968), 440.

20 Yoshimi, *Toshi no doramaturugī*, 224, 226; Tipton, "The Café," 123; Elise K. Tipton, "The Department Store: Producing Modernity in Interwar Japan," in *Rethinking Japanese Modernism*, ed. Roy Starrs (Boston: Brill, 2011), 441–442.

21 Tipton, "The Department Store," 438, 441–442; Katarzyna J. Cwiertka, "Eating the World: Restaurant Culture in Early Twentieth Century Japan," *European Journal of East Asian Studies* 2, no. 1 (2003): 107–108.

22 Elise K. Tipton, "Moving Up and Out: The 'Shop Girl' in Interwar Japan," in *Modern Girls on the Go: Gender, Mobility, and Labor in Japan*, ed. Alisa Freedman, Laura Miller, and Christine Reiko Yano (Stanford, CA: Stanford University Press, 2013), 21, 25, 30, 38; Laura Miller, "Elevator Girls Moving In and Out of the Box," in *Modern Girls on the Go*, 46, 48.

23 Tanizaki Jun'ichirō quoted in Edward Seidensticker, *Tokyo Rising: The City since the Great Earthquake* (Cambridge, MA: Harvard University Press, 1991), 57.

24 Tipton, "The Café," 119–125, 127–132; Yoshimi, *Toshi no doramaturugī*, 206, 222, 224–225; Silverberg, *Erotic Grotesque Nonsense*, 78; Maxey, "Threshold of Modern Living," 32.

25 Barbara Sato, *The New Japanese Woman: Modernity, Media, and Women in Interwar Japan* (Durham, NC: Duke University Press, 2003), 49.

26 Vera Mackie, "Sweat, Perfume, and Tobacco: The Ambivalent Labor of the Dancehall Girl," in *Modern Girls on the Go*, 71; Silverberg, *Erotic Grotesque Nonsense*, 53; Sato, *New Japanese Woman*, 46, 48–49, 56, 61–62.

27 Lyrics translated in Hiromu Nagahara, *Tokyo Boogie-Woogie: Japan's Pop Era and Its Discontents* (Cambridge, MA: Harvard University Press, 2017), 36. Original Japanese lyrics in Nagahara Hiromu, "'Tokyo kōshinkyoku' kara saguru 'ankūru' na Nihon no saihakken," in *Popyurā ongaku kara tou: Nihon bunka saikō*, ed. Tōya Mamoru (Tokyo: Serika Shobō, 2014), 184–185.

28 *Tokyo March* quoted in Nagahara, *Tokyo Boogie-Woogie*, 44. Nagahara, *Tokyo Boogie-Woogie*, 18, 34, 36, 43–44; Sand, *House and Home*, 210.

29 Commissioner Maruyama Tsurukichi quoted in Sheldon Garon, *Molding Japanese Minds: The State in Everyday Life* (Princeton, NJ: Princeton University Press, 1997), 107.

30 E. Taylor Atkins, *Blue Nippon: Authenticating Jazz in Japan* (Durham, NC: Duke University Press, 2001), 139; Andrew Gordon, "Consumption, Leisure and the Middle Class in Transwar Japan," *Social Science Japan Journal* 10, no. 1 (April 2007): 14.

31 Gordon, "Consumption, Leisure and the Middle Class," 8–9, 16; Atkins, *Blue Nippon*, 139.

7 The Militarized City

1 Todd A. Henry, *Assimilating Seoul: Japanese Rule and the Politics of Public Space in Colonial Korea, 1910–1945* (Berkeley: University of California Press, 2014), 1–2, 62, 66, 77, 82, 182–184, 200; Michael E. Robinson, *Korea's Twentieth-Century Odyssey: A Short History* (Honolulu: University of Hawai'i Press, 2007), 93–94, 96–97; Leo T. S. Ching, *Becoming "Japanese": Colonial Taiwan and the Politics of Identity Formation* (Berkeley: University of California Press, 2001), 126, 131–132.

2 Hildi Kang, *Under the Black Umbrella: Voices from Colonial Korea, 1910–1945* (Ithaca, NY: Cornell University Press, 2001), 113.

3 Jun Uchida, *Brokers of Empire: Japanese Settler Colonialism in Korea, 1876–1945* (Cambridge, MA: Harvard University Asia Center, 2011), 72–74, 355–356, 359–360, 362–363; Henry, *Assimilating Seoul*, 192, 194; Robinson, *Korea's Twentieth-Century Odyssey*, 79.

4   Kim Chongjae quoted in Jeffrey Paul Bayliss, *On the Margins of Empire: Buraku and Korean Identity in Prewar and Wartime Japan* (Cambridge, MA: Harvard University Asia Center, 2013), 332.

5   Anonymous letter writer quoted in Bayliss, *On the Margins of Empire*, 331.

6   Henry, *Assimilating Seoul*, 178–181; Ching, *Becoming "Japanese,"* 6.

7   Thomas R. H. Havens, *Valley of Darkness: The Japanese People and World War Two* (New York: Norton, 1978), 17.

8   Cary Lee Karacas, "Tokyo from the Fire: War, Occupation, and the Remaking of a Metropolis" (PhD diss., University of California, Berkeley, 2006), 27–28, 31–32; Edward Seidensticker, *Tokyo Rising: The City since the Great Earthquake* (Cambridge, MA: Harvard University Press, 1991), 134; Samuel Hideo Yamashita, *Daily Life in Wartime Japan, 1940–1945* (Lawrence: University Press of Kansas, 2015), 15; Aaron Herald Skabelund, *Empire of Dogs: Canines, Japan, and the Making of the Modern Imperial World* (Ithaca, NY: Cornell University Press, 2011), 87–89, 124.

9   Karacas, "Tokyo from the Fire," 38.

10   Karacas, "Tokyo from the Fire," 28–29; Owen Griffiths, "Need, Greed, and Protest in Japan's Black Market, 1938–1949," *Journal of Social History* 35, no. 4 (Summer 2002): 830.

11   Karacas, "Tokyo from the Fire," 28.

12   Griffiths, "Need, Greed, and Protest," 831; Yamashita, *Daily Life*, 13–14; Karacas, "Tokyo from the Fire," 25–27, 29; Seidensticker, *Tokyo Rising*, 134; E. Taylor Atkins, *Blue Nippon: Authenticating Jazz in Japan* (Durham, NC: Duke University Press, 2001), 140–141.

13   Karacas, "Tokyo from the Fire," 36.

14   Karacas, "Tokyo from the Fire," 36–37; Yamashita, *Daily Life*, 14, 16, 40–42, 44.

15   Samuel Hideo Yamashita, *Leaves from an Autumn of Emergencies: Selections from the Wartime Diaries of Ordinary Japanese* (Honolulu: University of Hawai'i Press, 2005), 161.

16   Yamashita, *Autumn of Emergencies*, 186.

17   Karacas, "Tokyo from the Fire," 57–58, 89, 90–92, 95–97; Robert M. Neer, *Napalm: An American Biography* (Cambridge, MA: Harvard University Press, 2013), 75–76; David Fedman and Cary Karacas, "A Cartographic Fade to Black: Mapping the Destruction of Urban Japan during World War II," *Journal of Historical Geography* 38, no. 3 (July 2012): 319–320.

18 Kiyosawa Kiyoshi, *A Diary of Darkness: The Wartime Diary of Kiyosawa Kiyoshi*, ed. Eugene Soviak and trans. Eugene Soviak and Kamiyama Tamie (Princeton, NJ: Princeton University Press, 2018), 326.

19 Thomas R. H. Havens, *Parkscapes: Green Spaces in Modern Japan* (Honolulu: University of Hawai'i Press, 2011), 113–114; Fedman and Karacas, "Cartographic Fade to Black," 320; Karacas, "Tokyo from the Fire," 58–62, 102, 104–105; Yamashita, *Autumn of Emergencies*, 166–167.

20 Ian Jared Miller, *The Nature of the Beasts: Empire and Exhibition at the Tokyo Imperial Zoo* (Berkeley: University of California Press, 2013), 120–122, 129–131.

21 Karacas, "Tokyo from the Fire," 64–65, 67, 70–74, 77–79, 81, 83.

22 Yamashita, *Autumn of Emergencies*, 194.

23 Karacas, "Tokyo from the Fire," 93, 101, 104–105, 191.

24 John W. Dower, *Embracing Defeat: Japan in the Wake of World War II* (New York: W. W. Norton, 1999), 40–41; Karacas, "Tokyo from the Fire," 112–113.

25 Henry, *Assimilating Seoul*, 206.

26 Henry, *Assimilating Seoul*, 207.

27 Douglas MacArthur quoted in Dower, *Embracing Defeat*, 41.

28 Cary Karacas, "The Occupied City," in *Cartographic Japan: A History in Maps*, ed. Kären Wigen, Fumiko Sugimoto, and Cary Karacas (Chicago: University of Chicago Press, 2016), 195, 197; Karacas, "Tokyo from the Fire," 116–117, 120, 122–123, 129–130, 142, 147–148, 153, 156–157, 162–164, 166, 169.

29 Karacas, "Tokyo from the Fire," 158, 195–196, 199–200, 202–207, 231–233, 243, 245; Sayaka Chatani, "Revisiting Korean Slums in Postwar Japan: Tongne and Hakkyo in the Zainichi Memoryscape," *Journal of Asian Studies* 80, no. 3 (August 2021): 587–588, 598; Bayliss, *On the Margins of Empire*, 381–382; Ishida Yorifusa, "Japanese Cities and Planning in the Reconstruction Period, 1945–55," in *Rebuilding Urban Japan after 1945*, ed. Carola Hein, Jeffry M. Diefendorf, and Ishida Yorifusa (New York: Palgrave Macmillan, 2003), 21; Carola Hein, "Rebuilding Japanese Cities after 1945," in *Rebuilding Urban Japan after 1945*, 3; Ichikawa Hiroo, "Reconstructing Tokyo: The Attempt to Transform a Metropolis," in *Rebuilding Urban Japan after 1945*, 54.

30 Griffiths, "Need, Greed, and Protest," 834, 849–850; Karacas, "Tokyo from the Fire," 239, 241–242, 245; Seidensticker, *Tokyo Rising*, 201–202.

31 Ichikawa, "Reconstructing Tokyo," 51; Hein, "Rebuilding Japanese Cities," 2–3; Ishida, "Japanese Cities and Planning," 19.

32 Karacas, "Tokyo from the Fire," 178, 180–183; Tokyo Metropolitan Government, Bureau of Urban Development, "US Military Facilities in Tokyo," www.toshiseibi.metro.tokyo.lg.jp/base_measures/english/etono kiti.htm.

33 Eiko Maruko Siniawer, *Waste: Consuming Postwar Japan* (Ithaca, NY: Cornell University Press, 2018), 39, 45.

8 Dreams and Disappointments

1 Quote from Yoshikuni Igarashi, *Japan, 1972: Visions of Masculinity in an Age of Mass Consumerism* (New York: Columbia University Press, 2021), 74.

2 Quote from Laura Neitzel, *The Life We Longed For: Danchi Housing and the Middle Class Dream in Postwar Japan* (Portland, ME: MerwinAsia, 2016), 97.

3 Quote from Neitzel, *Life We Longed For*, 97.

4 Simon Partner, *Assembled in Japan: Electrical Goods and the Making of the Japanese Consumer* (Berkeley: University of California Press, 1999), 173–175; Igarashi, *Japan, 1972*, 74, 79–80; Neitzel, *Life We Longed For*, 97.

5 Yoshimi Shun'ya, *Banpaku gensō: Sengo seiji no jubaku* (Tokyo: Chikuma Shobō, 2005), 11–13; Andrew Gordon, "The Short Happy Life of the Japanese Middle Class," in *Social Contracts Under Stress: The Middle Classes of America, Europe, and Japan at the Turn of the Century*, ed. Olivier Zunz, Leonard Schoppa, and Nobuhiro Hiwatari (New York: Russell Sage Foundation, 2002), 117–121; Eiko Maruko Siniawer, "'Toilet Paper Panic': Uncertainty and Insecurity in Early 1970s Japan," *American Historical Review* 126, no. 2 (June 2021): 534.

6 Eiko Maruko Siniawer, *Waste: Consuming Postwar Japan* (Ithaca, NY: Cornell University Press, 2018), 58–65; Partner, *Assembled in Japan*, 137–138, 140; Igarashi, *Japan, 1972*, 38–39.

7 Jessamyn R. Abel, "Japan's Sporting Diplomacy: The 1964 Tokyo Olympiad," *International History Review* 32, no. 2 (June 2012): 204, 206; Shimizu Satoshi, "Rebuilding the Japanese Nation at the 1964 Tokyo Olympics: The Torch Relay in Okinawa and Tokyo," in *The Olympics in East Asia: Nationalism, Regionalism, and Globalism on the Center Stage*

of World Sports, ed. William W. Kelly and Susan Brownell (New Haven, CT: Council on East Asian Studies, Yale University, 2011), 41.

8 Christian Tagsold, "Modernity and the Carnivalesque (Tokyo 1964)," in *Surveilling and Securing the Olympics: From Tokyo 1964 to London 2012 and Beyond*, ed. Vida Bajc (London: Palgrave Macmillan), 98; Igarashi Yoshikuni, *Bodies of Memory: Narratives of War in Postwar Japanese Culture, 1945–1970* (Princeton, NJ: Princeton University Press, 2000), 145.

9 Christian Tagsold, "Modernity, Space and National Representation at the Tokyo Olympics 1864," *Urban History* 37, no. 2 (August 2010): 290, 296; Abel, "Japan's Sporting Diplomacy," 211–212; Christian Tagsold, "Symbolic Transformation: The 1964 Tokyo Games Reconsidered," *Asia-Pacific Journal: Japan Focus* 18, no. 5 (March 2020): 1.

10 Bruce Suttmeier, "On the Road in Olympic-Era Tokyo," in *Cartographic Japan: A History in Maps*, ed. Kären Wigen, Fumiko Sugimoto, and Cary Karacas (Chicago: University of Chicago Press, 2016), 210–211; André Sorensen, *The Making of Urban Japan: Cities and Planning from Edo to the Twenty-First Century* (London: Routledge, 2002), 191–193; Takeuchi Makoto, Koizumi Hiroshi, Ikegami Hiroko, Katō Takashi, and Fujino Atsushi, *Tōkyō-to no rekishi* (Tokyo: Yamakawa Shuppansha, 2015), 341; Shimizu, "Rebuilding the Japanese Nation," 42; Jessamyn R. Abel, "The Power of a Line: How the Bullet Train Transformed Urban Space," *positions: asia critique* 27, no. 3 (August 2019): 538.

11 Sorensen, *Making of Urban Japan*, 191–192; Abel, "Japan's Sporting Diplomacy," 214; Tagsold, "Symbolic Transformation," 3.

12 *The Times*, October 26, 1964; Abel, "Japan's Sporting Diplomacy," 209–210, 216; Tagsold, "Symbolic Transformation," 5; Sandra Wilson, "Exhibiting a New Japan: The Tokyo Olympics of 1964 and Expo '70 in Osaka," *Historical Research* 85, no. 227 (February 2012): 177–178.

13 Abel, "Japan's Sporting Diplomacy," 214; Sandra Wilson, "Exhibiting a New Japan," 174; Christopher P. Hood, *Shinkansen: From Bullet Train to Symbol of Modern Japan* (New York: Routledge, 2006), 27–28; Abel, "Power of a Line," 543.

14 *Yomiuri shinbun*, July 12, 1962, quoted in Siniawer, *Waste*, 81.

15 Siniawer, *Waste*, 78–83; Igarashi, *Bodies of Memory*, 150–151; Jessamyn R. Abel, "When Athletes Are Diplomats: Competing for World Opinion at the Tokyo Olympiads," in *The East Asian Olympiads, 1934–2008:*

Building Bodies and Nations in Japan, Korea, and China, ed. William M. Tsutsui and Michael Baskett (Leiden: Brill, 2011), 60; Takeuchi et al., *Tōkyō-to no rekishi*, 339–340.

16 Siniawer, *Waste*, 83; Igarashi, *Bodies of Memory*, 148; Tagsold, "Modernity and the Carnivalesque," 100.

17 Tagsold, "Modernity, Space and National Representation," 296; Rafael Ivan Pazos Perez, "The Historical Development of the Tokyo Skyline: Timeline and Morphology," *Journal of Asian Architecture and Building Engineering* 13, no. 3 (September 2014): 611.

18 Abel, "Japan's Sporting Diplomacy," 212; Yoshimi Shun'ya, "1964 Tokyo Olympics as Post-War," trans. Samuel James Holden, *International Journal of Japanese Sociology* 28, no. 1 (March 2019): 81.

19 Abel, "Japan's Sporting Diplomacy," 206; Wilson, "Exhibiting a New Japan," 161–162; Tagsold, "Modernity, Space and National Representation," 298, 290; Tagsold, "Symbolic Transformation," 6; Shimizu, "Rebuilding the Japanese Nation," 47, 53.

20 Suttmeier, "On the Road," 211; Shimizu, "Rebuilding the Japanese Nation," 44; Takeuchi et al., *Tōkyō-to no rekishi*, 340; William O. Gardner, *The Metabolist Imagination: Visions of the City in Postwar Japanese Architecture and Science Fiction* (Minneapolis: University of Minnesota Press, 2020), 123–125; Tagsold, "Modernity, Space and National Representation," 299–300.

21 Neitzel, *Life We Longed For*, xiv, xv–xvi, 37; Ann Waswo, *Housing in Postwar Japan: A Social History* (New York: Routledge, 2002), 75.

22 Neitzel, *Life We Longed For*, xiv, 25–26, 51–52; Partner, *Assembled in Japan*, 177; Keizai Kikakuchō, *Shōwa 35 nendo kokumin seikatsu hakusho* (Tokyo: Ōkurashō Insatsukyoku, 1961), 137–145; Sorensen, *Making of Urban Japan*, 185.

23 Neitzel, *Life We Longed For*, xiv–xv, 24–25, 37, 43–45, 76.

24 Hiroyoshi Kano, "Tama New Town: The Growth of a New Residential Area in the Suburbs of Tokyo," in *Growing Metropolitan Suburbia: A Comparative Sociological Study on Tokyo and Jakarta*, ed. Hiroyoshi Kano (Jakarta: Yayasan Obor Indonesia, 2004), 134–135, 137–141; Sorensen, *Making of Urban Japan*, 185, 206–207; Andrew Scott and Eran Ben-Joseph, *ReNew Town: Adaptive Urbanism and the Low Carbon Community* (Abingdon, Oxon: Routledge, 2012), 19; Takeuchi et al., *Tokyo-to no rekishi*, 32–33; Neitzel, *Life We Longed For*, 52.

25 Tokyo Metropolitan Government, "Geography of Tokyo," https://www.metro.tokyo.lg.jp/ENGLISH/ABOUT/HISTORY/history02.htm.

26 Neitzel, *Life We Longed For*, 46; Ken'ichi Miyamoto, "Japanese Environmental Policy: Lessons from Experience and Remaining Problems," trans. Jeffrey E. Hanes, in *Japan at Nature's Edge: The Environmental Context of a Global Power*, ed. Ian Jared Miller, Julia Adeney Thomas, and Brett L. Walker (Honolulu: University of Hawai'i Press, 2013), 240.

27 Neitzel, *Life We Longed For*, 46; André Sorensen, "Building Suburbs in Japan: Continuous Unplanned Change on the Urban Fringe," *Town Planning Review* 72, no. 3 (July 2001): 250; Sorensen, *Making of Urban Japan*, 205.

28 "Population, Percent of Population and Index of Population for Each Prefecture: 1920 to 1975," *Population Census: 1975 Population Census*, www.e-stat.go.jp/en/stat-search/files?page=1&layout=datalist&tou kei=00200521&tstat=000001036406&cycle=0&tclass1=000001036897&t class2val=0.

29 Gary D. Allinson, *Suburban Tokyo: A Comparative Study in Politics and Social Change* (Berkeley: University of California Press, 1979), 149–150; Perez, "Tokyo Skyline," 611; Waswo, *Housing in Postwar Japan*, 117.

30 Neitzel, *Life We Longed For*, 78.

31 Waswo, *Housing in Postwar Japan*, 100, 102, 110, 115; Neitzel, *Life We Longed For*, xxv, 116, 123; Takeuchi et al., *Tōkyō-to no rekishi*, 340; Chauncy D. Harris, "The Urban and Industrial Transformation of Japan," *Geographical Review* 72, no. 1 (January 1982): 86–87.

32 André Sorensen, "Building World City Tokyo: Globalization and Conflict over Urban Space," *Annals of Regional Science* 37, no. 3 (August 2003): 524–525; Margaret A. McKean, *Environmental Protest and Citizen Politics in Japan* (Berkeley: University of California Press, 1981), 113–115; Waswo, *Housing in Postwar Japan*, 100, 118; Neitzel, *Life We Longed For*, 116–117.

33 Scott O'Bryan, "The Climatic Dilemmas of Built Environments: Tokyo, Heat Islands, and Urban Adaptation," in *Environment and Society in the Japanese Islands: From Prehistory to the Present*, ed. Bruce L. Batten and Philip C. Brown (Corvallis: Oregon State University Press, 2015), 237; *The Times of India*, September 18, 1964.

34 Yasuhei Homma, *Environmental Pollution in Japan: The Case of Tokyo* (Berkeley: Lawrence Berkeley Laboratory, University of California, 1972), 6, 9; Ōdaira Toshio and Fukuoka Saburō, "Tokyo no kōkagaku sumoggu no genjō," *Kankyō gijutsu* 1, no. 6 (1972): 27, 32; McKean, *Environmental Protest*, 117; *The Times of India*, May 28, 1972.

35 Richard Curtis and Dave Fisher, "The Seven Wonders of the Polluted World," *New York Times*, September 26, 1971.

36 Simon Andrew Avenell, *Transnational Japan in the Global Environmental Movement* (Honolulu: University of Hawai'i Press, 2017), 1–2.

37 Jeffrey Broadbent, *Environmental Politics in Japan: Networks of Power and Protest* (Cambridge: Cambridge University Press, 1998), 123; Miyamoto, "Japanese Environmental Policy," 233.

38 Siniawer, *Waste*, 102–103.

39 Siniawer, *Waste*, 77–78, 84–86, 93, 97–101; Tokue Shibata, "Land, Waste and Pollution: Challenging History in Creating a Sustainable Tokyo Metropolis," in *Sustainable Cities: Japanese Perspectives on Physical and Social Structures*, ed. Hidenori Tamagawa (Tokyo: United Nations University Press, 2006), 100–105; McKean, *Environmental Protest*, 102–108.

40 Naikaku Sōri Daijin Kanbō Kōhōshitsu, *Kokumin seikatsu ni kansuru seron chōsa* (Tokyo, 2000), https://survey.gov-online.go.jp/h11/kokumin/images/zu25.gif.

9 Global Capital

1 Tanaka Yasuo, *Somehow, Crystal*, trans. Christopher Smith (Kumamoto: Kurodahan Press, 2019), 82, 136.

2 Tanaka Yasuo, *Nantonaku, kurisutaru* (Tokyo: Kawade Shobō Shinsha, 1981), 31. The translation is an edited version of Tanaka, *Somehow, Crystal*, 30–33.

3 Norma Field, "Somehow: The Postmodern as Atmosphere," in *Postmodernism and Japan*, ed. Masao Miyoshi and Harry D. Harootunian (Durham, NC: Duke University Press, 1989), 170–172; Takahashi Gen'ichirō, "Introduction: Completely Unique," in *Somehow, Crystal*, 3–4; Eiko Maruko Siniawer, *Waste: Consuming Postwar Japan* (Ithaca, NY: Cornell University Press, 2018), 161.

4 R. Taggart Murphy, "Power Without Purpose: The Crisis of Japan's Global Financial Dominance," *Harvard Business Review* (March–April 1989); Nancy K. Stalker, *Japan: History and Culture from Classical to Cool* (Berkeley: University of California Press, 2018), 363–364; David Leheny, *The Rules of Play: National Identity and the Shaping of Japanese Leisure* (Ithaca, NY: Cornell University Press, 2018), 109.

5 Tokyo Metropolitan Government, "Tokyo's History, Geography, and Population: Population of Tokyo," www.metro.tokyo.lg.jp/ENGLISH/A BOUT/HISTORY/history03.htm; David Merriman, Toru Ohkawara, and Tsutomu Suzuki, "Excess Commuting in the Tokyo Metropolitan Area: Measurement and Policy Simulations," *Urban Studies* 32, no. 1 (February 1995): 71, 73, 78; Jeffrey E. Hanes, "From Megalopolis to Megaroporisu," *Journal of Urban History* 19, no. 2 (February 1993): 87.

6 Saskia Sassen, *The Global City: New York, London, Tokyo* (Princeton, NJ: Princeton University Press, 2001), 216–217; Kuniko Fujita, "A World City and Flexible Specialization: Restructuring of the Tokyo Metropolis," *International Journal of Urban and Regional Research* 15, no. 2 (June 1991): 273; Yasuo Masai, "Greater Tokyo as a Global City," in *Cities in a Global Society*, ed. Richard V. Knight and Gary Gappert (London: Sage Publications, 1989), 156–157; Kenichi Miyamoto, "Japan's World Cities: Osaka and Tokyo Compared," in *Japanese Cities in the World Economy*, ed. Kuniko Fujita and Richard Child Hill (Philadelphia, PA: Temple University Press, 1993), 68; Richard Child Hill and Kuniko Fujita, "Japanese Cities in the World Economy," in *Japanese Cities in the World Economy*, 9.

7 Mike Douglass, "The 'New' Tokyo Story: Restructuring Space and the Struggle for Place in a World City," in *Japanese Cities in the World Economy*, 90; Sassen, *Global City*, 11–12, 182, 215; Asato Saito, "Global City Formation in a Capitalist Developmental State: Tokyo and the Waterfront Sub-centre Project," *Urban Studies* 40, no. 2 (February 2003): 292; André Sorensen, "Building World City Tokyo: Globalization and Conflict over Urban Space," *Annals of Regional Science* 37, no. 3 (August 2003): 526.

8 Peter Rimmer, "Japan's World Cities: Tokyo, Osaka, Nagoya or Tokaido Megalopolis?" *Development and Change* 17, no. 1 (January 1986): 131, 134–135, 146; Kazutoshi Abe, "Status of Tokyo: Comparing Tokyo with Major Cities of the World," in *Tokyo as a Global City: New Geographical*

Perspectives, ed. Toshio Kikuchi and Toshihiko Sugai (Singapore: Springer, 2018), 320–321; Sassen, *Global City*, 166.

9 Takashi Machimura, "The Urban Restructuring Process in Tokyo in the 1980s: Transforming Tokyo into a World City," *International Journal of Urban and Regional Research* 16, no. 1 (March 1992): 116–117; Heidi Gottfried, "The Phoenix Rises: Tokyo's Origins as a Global City," *Critical Sociology* 44, no. 3 (May 2018): 423; Douglass, "'New' Tokyo Story," 89–90; Sassen, *Global City*, 187.

10 Hanes, "From Megalopolis to Megaroporisu," 87; Sassen, *Global City*, 166; Rimmer, "Japan's World Cities," 146; Gottfried, "Phoenix Rises," 430; Takashi Machimura, "Building a Capital for Emperor and Enterprise: The Changing Urban Meaning of Central Tokyo," in *Culture and the City in East Asia*, ed. Won Bae Kim, Mike Douglass, Sang-Chuel Choe, and Kong Chong Ho (Oxford: Clarendon Press, 1997), 161; Hill and Fujita, "Japanese Cities," 9.

11 Douglass, "'New' Tokyo Story," 97; Asato Saito and Andy Thornley, "Shifts in Tokyo's World City Status and the Urban Planning Response," *Urban Studies* 40, no. 4 (April 2003): 669; Roman Cybriwsky, *Tokyo: The Shogun's City at the Twenty-First Century* (Chichester, UK: Wiley, 1998), 105; Masai, "Greater Tokyo," 159; Hill and Fujita, "Japanese Cities," 9; Stalker, *Japan*, 366.

12 Takashi Machimura, "Local Settlement Patterns of Foreign Workers in Greater Tokyo: Growing Diversity and its Consequences," in *Japan and Global Migration: Foreign Workers and the Advent of a Multicultural Society*, ed. Mike Douglass and Glenda S. Roberts (New York: Routledge, 2000), 177–179; Erin Aeran Chung, *Immigration and Citizenship in Japan* (Cambridge: Cambridge University Press, 2010), 145, 149–151; Mike Douglass and Glenda S. Roberts, "Japan in a Global Age of Migration," in *Japan and Global Migration*, 6–8; Fujita, "World City," 278.

13 Ōyama Shirō, *A Man with No Talents: Memoirs of a Tokyo Day Laborer*, trans. Edward Fowler (Ithaca, NY: Cornell University Press, 2005), 17–18.

14 Petrice R. Flowers, "From Kokusaika to Tabunka Kyōsei: Global Norms, Discourses of Differences, and Multiculturalism in Japan," *Critical Asian Studies* 44, no. 4 (December 2012): 518; Douglass and Roberts, "Japan in a Global Age of Migration," 7–8, 12; Machimura, "Local Settlement Patterns," 178, 182–183.

15 Machimura, "Local Settlement Patterns," 178; Yoshiki Wakabayashi and Ryo Koizumi, "Spatial Patterns of Population Change in Central Tokyo since the Period of the Bubble Economy," in *Tokyo as a Global City*, 169, 171; Junko Tajima, "A Study of Asian Immigrants in Global City Tokyo," *Asian and Pacific Migration Journal* 9, no. 3 (September 2000): 357–358, 360–361.

16 Flowers, "From *Kokusaika* to *Tabunka Kyōsei*," 531–534; Cybriwsky, *Tokyo*, 153–155, 159–161; Thomas Baudinette, *Regimes of Desire: Young Gay Men, Media, and Masculinity in Tokyo* (Ann Arbor: University of Michigan Press, 2021), 33; Douglass and Roberts, "Japan in a Global Age of Migration," 13.

17 Sassen, *Global City*, 279, 283–284; Wakabayashi and Koizumi, "Spatial Patterns," 159; A. J. Jacobs, "Has Central Tokyo Experienced Uneven Development? An Examination of Tokyo's 23 Ku Relative to America's Largest Urban Centers," *Journal of Urban Affairs* 27, no. 5 (December 2005): 531, 537, 550; Nakabayashi Itsuki, "Socio-economic and Living Conditions of Tokyo's Inner-city," *Geographical Reports of Tokyo Metropolitan University* 22 (1987): 125–126.

18 Saito and Thornley, "Shifts in Tokyo's World City Status," 670; André Sorensen, "Subcentres and Satellite Cities: Tokyo's 20th Century Experience of Planned Polycentrism," *International Planning Studies* 6, no. 1 (February 2001): 18; Sorensen, "Building World City Tokyo," 527; Saito, "Global City Formation," 295.

19 Meiko Murayama and Gavin Parker, "Sustainable Leisure and Tourism Space Development in Post-Industrial Cities: The Case of Odaiba, Tokyo, Japan," in *Tourism, Culture, and Regeneration*, ed. Melanie K. Smith (Cambridge: CABI, 2006), 81.

20 Murayama and Parker, "Sustainable Leisure and Tourism Space Development," 74, 76–79; Saito, "Global City Formation," 299; Jacobs, "Central Tokyo," 548.

21 Haruki Murakami, *Underground*, trans. Alfred Birnbaum and Philip Gabriel (New York: Vintage International, 2000), 226.

22 David Leheny, *Think Global, Fear Local: Sex, Violence, and Anxiety in Contemporary Japan* (Ithaca, NY: Cornell University Press, 2018), 30–34, 38–42.

23 Saito and Thornley, "Shifts in Tokyo's World City Status," 673; Leheny, *Rules of Play*, 127; Hiroshi Matsubara, "Office Space Developers and the

Production of Place in the Central Area of Tōkyō," in *Shaping the Future of Metropolitan Regions in Japan and Germany: Governance, Institutions and Place in New Context*, ed. Thomas Feldhoff, Winfried Flüchter, and Uta Hohn (Duisburg: Universität Duisburg-Essen, 2005), 61; Sayaka Fujii, Junichiro Okata, and André Sorensen, "Inner-city Redevelopment in Tokyo: Conflicts over Urban Places, Planning Governance, and Neighborhoods," in *Living Cities in Japan: Citizens' Movements, Machizukuri and Local Environments*, ed. André Sorensen and Carolin Funck (New York: Routledge, 2007), 248–250; Wakabayashi and Koizumi, "Spatial Patterns," 157–158, 162, 164; Hiroshi Matsubara, "The Changing Spatial Economy and Cultural Industries in Tokyo," in *Tokyo as a Global City*, 238.

24 Saito and Thornley, "Shifts in Tokyo's World City Status," 675; Matjaž Uršič and Hide Imai, *Creativity in Tokyo: Revitalizing a Mature City* (Singapore: Palgrave Macmillan, 2020), 22; Wabakayashi and Koizumi, "Spatial Patterns," 158; Paul Waley, "Tokyo-as-World City: Reassessing the Role of Capital and the State in Urban Restructuring," *Urban Studies* 44, no. 8 (July 2007): 1486–1487.

25 *New York Times*, January 31, 1993; Cybriwsky, *Tokyo*, 126–127; Matsubara, "Office Space Developers," 66; Waley, "Tokyo-as-World City," 1479–1480; Mori Biru, ed., *Six Strata: Roppongi Hills Defined* (Tokyo: Heibonsha, 2006), n.p.

26 Sorensen, "Building World City Tokyo," 519.

27 Tanaka, *Somehow, Crystal*, 22–29; Tanaka, *Nantonaku, kurisutaru*, 21–28, 160.

28 John Clammer, "The Global and the Local: Gender, Class and the Internationalisation of Consumption in a Tokyo Neighborhood," in *Consumption and Material Culture in Contemporary Japan*, ed. Michael Ashkenazi and John Clammer (New York: Kegan Paul International, 2000), 269.

29 Gavin Hamilton Whitelaw, "Rice Ball Rivalries: Japanese Convenience Stores and the Appetite of Late Capitalism," in *Fast Food/Slow Food: The Cultural Economy of the Global Food System*, ed. Richard Wilk (Lanham, MD: AltaMira Press, 2006), 131, 134, 138; Theodore C. Bestor, "Kaiten-zushi and Konbini: Japanese Food Culture in the Age of Mechanical Reproduction," in *Fast Food/Slow Food*, 122; Seven-Eleven Japan, "History," www.sej.co.jp/company/en/history.html.

30 Christine Yano, *Pink Globalization: Hello Kitty's Trek across the Pacific* (Durham, NC: Duke University Press, 2013), 9, 15, 17, 269–271.

31 Eric C. Rath, *Oishii: The History of Sushi* (London: Reaktion Books, 2021), 91–98, 138–139, 157; Katarzyna J. Cwiertka, *Modern Japanese Cuisine: Food, Power, and National Identity* (London: Reaktion Books, 2006), 182–191, 194–197.

32 Stephanie Assmann, "Consumption of Fast Fashion in Japan: Local Brands and Global Environment," in *Consuming Life in Post-Bubble Japan*, ed. Katarzyna J. Cwiertka and Ewa Machotka (Amsterdam: Amsterdam University Press, 2018), 49–51, 58–59.

10 Past and Present

1 Ishii Masato, "Tokyo gorin 'yokokuhen' ni kometa messēji: Kuriēchibu direkutā, Sasaki Hiroshi," nippon.com (April 3, 2017). An English translation can be found at: www.nippon.com/en/people/e00112/?pnum=2. The closing ceremonies of the Rio Olympics can be viewed at: Olympics, "Rio 2016 Closing Ceremony Full HD Replay / Rio 2016 Olympic Games," www.youtube.com/watch?v=ssc5eLjLoMQ.

2 Abe Shinzō, "Presentation by Prime Minister Shinzo Abe at the 125th Session of the International Olympic Committee (IOC)," September 7, 2013, https://japan.kantei.go.jp/96_abe/statement/201309/07ioc_presenta tion_e.html.

3 Barbara Holthus, Isaac Gagné, Wolfram Manzenreiter, and Franz Waldenberger, "Understanding Japan through the Lens of Tokyo 2020," in *Japan Through the Lens of the Tokyo Olympics*, ed. Barbara Holthus, Isaac Gagné, Wolfram Manzenreiter, and Franz Waldenberger (New York: Routledge, 2020), 3–4; Alisa Freedman, *Tokyo in Transit: Japanese Culture on the Rails and Road* (Stanford, CA: Stanford University Press, 2011), 10; Grace Gonzalez Basurto, "Asian and Global? Japan and Tokyo's Cultural Branding Beyond the 2020 Olympic and Paralympic Games," in *Asian Cultural Flows: Cultural Policies, Creative Industries, and Media Consumers*, ed. Nobuko Kawashima and Hye-Kyung Lee (Singapore: Springer, 2018), 50; Nancy K. Stalker, *Japan: History and Culture from Classical to Cool* (Berkeley: University of California Press, 2018), 394; Pepi Ronalds, "The Ruptures of Rhetoric: Cool Japan, Tokyo 2020 and Post-3.11 Tohoku," *New Voices in Japanese Studies* 11 (2019): 41.

4 E. Taylor Atkins, *A History of Popular Culture in Japan: From the Seventeenth Century to the Present* (New York: Bloomsbury, 2017), 208; Michal Daliot-Bul, "Japan Brand Strategy: The Taming of 'Cool Japan' and the Challenges of Cultural Planning in a Postmodern Age," *Social Science Japan Journal* 12, no. 2 (Winter 2009): 247; Koichi Iwabuchi, *Recentering Globalization: Popular Culture and Japanese Transnationalism* (Durham, NC: Duke University Press, 2002), 29.

5 Douglas McGray, "Japan's Gross National Cool," *Foreign Policy* 130 (May–June 2002): 44–54.

6 David Leheny, "A Narrow Place to Cross Swords: Soft Power and the Politics of Japanese Popular Culture in East Asia," in *Beyond Japan: The Dynamics of East Asian Regionalism*, ed. Peter J. Katzenstein and Takashi Shiraishi (Ithaca, NY: Cornell University Press, 2018), 220–221, 227–228; Strategic Council on Intellectual Property, *Intellectual Property Policy Outline* (July 2002), https://japan.kantei.go.jp/policy/titeki/kettei/020703taikou_e.html; Daliot-Bul, "Japan Brand Strategy," 248, 250–251, 253; *Establishing Japan as a "Peaceful Nation of Cultural Exchange,"* https://japan.kantei.go.jp/policy/bunka/050711bunka_e.html; Koichi Iwabuchi, "Creative Industries and Cool Japan," in *Global Game Industries and Cultural Policy*, ed. Anthony Fung (Cham, Switzerland: Palgrave Macmillan, 2016), 35–36, 38–39.

7 Ministry of Economy, Trade and Industry, *Cool Japan Strategy (Modified Version of the Interim Report Submitted to the Cool Japan Advisory Council)* (September 2012), 2–5; *Japan Times*, March 25, 2012.

8 Ministry of Economy, Trade, and Industry, "100 Tokyo," http://100tokyo .jp/.

9 Atkins, *Popular Culture*, 228; Stalker, *Japan*, 381–382, 395; Susan Napier, *Miyazakiworld: A Life in Art* (New Haven, CT: Yale University Press, 2018), 195, 200; David Leheny, *Empire of Hope: The Sentimental Politics of Japanese Decline* (Ithaca, NY: Cornell University Press, 2018), 98; McGray, "Gross National Cool," 46.

10 Patrick W. Galbraith, "Akihabara: Promoting and Policing 'Otaku' in 'Cool Japan'," in *Introducing Japanese Popular Culture*, ed. Alisa Freedman and Toby Slade (New York: Routledge, 2018), 373–385; Atkins, *Popular Culture*, 204.

11 Stalker, *Japan*, 381–382, 388; Leheny, "Narrow Place to Cross Swords," 213–214; Iwabuchi, *Recentering Globalization*, 30, 207.

12 Matt Alt, "'Demon Slayer': The Viral Blockbuster from Japan," *New Yorker*, June 18, 2021, 2.

13 "Miraitowa and Someity: Tokyo 2020 Mascots Make Official Debut," htt ps://olympics.com/en/video/miraitowa-and-someity-tokyo-2020-mas cots-make-official-debut; "Tokyo 2020 Olympic Mascots: Meet Miraitowa and Someity," www.jrailpass.com/blog/tokyo-2020-olympics/mascots.

14 International Olympic Committee, "New Robots Unveiled for the Tokyo 2020 Games," https://olympics.com/ioc/news/new-robots-unveiled-for-tokyo-2020-games, July 22, 2019.

15 Tokyo Bid Committee quoted in Eva Kassens-Noor and Tatsuya Fukushige, "Olympic Technologies: Tokyo 2020 and Beyond," *Journal of Urban Technology* 25, no. 3 (July 2018): 85.

16 Kassens-Noor and Fukushige, "Olympic Technologies," 99; Franz Waldenberger, "The Olympic and Paralympic Games as a Technology Showcase," in *Japan Through the Lens of the Tokyo Olympics*, 136; International Olympic Committee, "Worldwide Olympic Partners Helping to Make Tokyo 2020 Most Innovative Olympic Games Ever," https://olympics.com/ioc/news/worldwide-olympic-partners-hel ping-to-make-tokyo-2020-most-innovative-olympic-games-ever, August 2, 2021.

17 Kōno Ichirō, chairman and CEO of the Tokyo 2016 Bid Committee, quoted in Kassens-Noor and Fukushige, "Olympic Technologies," 85.

18 "Olympics Ceremony Uses Music from Japanese Video Games," *The Mainichi*, July 23, 2021.

19 International Olympic Committee, "Spectacular Intel Drone Light Show Helps Bring Tokyo 2020 to Life," https://olympics.com/ioc/news/spectacu lar-intel-drone-light-show-helps-bring-tokyo-2020-to-life-1, July 24, 2021.

20 "Opening Ceremony," https://olympics.com/en/video/opening-cere mony-ceremony-tokyo-2020-replays.

21 Holthus et al., "Understanding Japan through the Lens of Tokyo 2020," 3; Isaac Gagné, "Tokyo 2020 from the Regional Sidelines," in *Japan Through the Lens of the Tokyo Olympics*, 119–120; Ronalds, "Ruptures of Rhetoric," 36; Jeff Kingston, "Tokyo's Diversity Olympics Dogged by Controversy," *Asia-Pacific Journal: Japan Focus* 18, issue 4, no. 3 (February 2020): 5.

22 Tokyo Metropolitan Government, "2020-nen: Tokyo to Tōhoku de aima-shou," www.youtube.com/watch?v=FCGjeY3meWU (2016); Leheny, *Empire of Hope*, 174–176; Tatsuhiro Kamisato, "Food and Water Contamination after

the Fukushima Nuclear Accident," in *Legacies of Fukushima: 3.11 in Context*, ed. Kyle Cleveland, Scott Gabriel Knowles, and Ryuma Shineha (Philadelphia, PA: University of Pennsylvania Press, 2021), 157, 160, 163.

23 Ralph Lützeler, "Tokyo 2020 and Neighborhood Transformation: Reworking the Entrepreneurial City," in *Japan Through the Lens of the Tokyo Olympics*, 41.

24 Olympic and Paralympic Games Tokyo 2020 Coordination Division, "Competition Venue Map (Wide Area Map)," www.2020games.metro.toky o.lg.jp/eng/taikaijyunbi/taikai/map/wide_map/index.html; Olympic and Paralympic Games Tokyo 2020 Coordination Division, "Competition Venue Map," www.2020games.metro.tokyo.lg.jp/eng/taikaijyunbi/taikai/ma p/index.html#tabOlympic.

25 "Post-Olympic Venues Confront Fate as White Elephants," *Nikkei Asia*, August 10, 2021; Lützeler, "Tokyo 2020," 43–45; Chikako Mori, "Social Housing and Urban Renewal in Tokyo: From Post-War Reconstruction to the 2020 Olympic Games," in *Social Housing and Urban Renewal: A Cross-National Perspective*, ed. Paul Watt and Peer Smets (Bingley, UK: Emerald Publishing, 2017), 296.

26 Jeff Kingston, "PM Abe's Floundering Pandemic Leadership," *Asia-Pacific Journal: Japan Focus* 18, issue 9, no. 2 (May 2020): 3, 6, 8; Gavan McCormack, "ORIPARA: Japan's Olympic and Paralympic Summer Games and Beyond," *Asia-Pacific Journal: Japan Focus* (August 2021): 1–2.

27 Jordan Sand, *Tokyo Vernacular: Common Spaces, Local Histories, Found Objects* (Berkeley: University of California Press, 2013), 2–3, 143.

28 Jinnai Hidenobu, *Suito Tōkyō: Chikei to rekishi de yomitoku Shitamachi, Yamanote, kōgai* (Tokyo: Chikuma Shobō, 2020), 193–194; Jinnai Hidenobu, "The Locus of My Study of Tokyo: From Building Typology to Spatial Anthropology and Eco-History," *Japan Architectural Review* 3, no 3 (July 2020): 274; Jinnai Hidenobu, *Tokyo: A Spatial Anthropology*, trans. Kimiko Nishimura (Berkeley: University of California Press, 1995), 13; Roman Cybriwsky, *Tokyo: The Shogun's City at the Twenty-First Century* (Chichester, UK: Wiley, 1998), 145–148.

29 Mitsubishi Ichigōkan Bijutsukan, *Mitsubishi Ichigokan Museum, Tokyo* (2015), 1.

30 Jiewon Song, *Global Tokyo: Heritage, Urban Redevelopment and the Transformation of Authenticity* (Singapore: Springer, 2020), 255,

257–258, 283, 285; Tokyo Station City Management Council, "Tokyo Station City: Marunouchi Station Building Highlights," www.tokyosta tioncity.com/en/learning/station_building/.

31 Sand, *Tokyo Vernacular*, 20–21, 84, 120, 145–150; Jinnai, *Suito Tōkyō*, 188; Jinnai, "Locus of My Study of Tokyo," 272–273; Theodore C. Bestor, "Rediscovering Shitamachi: Subculture, Class, and Tokyo's 'Traditional' Urbanism," in *The Cultural Meaning of Urban Space*, ed. Robert Rotenberg and Gary McDonogh (Westport, CT: Bergin & Garvey, 1993), 49, 53.

32 Tōbu Railway Company and Tōbu Tower Skytree Company, "Digital Terrestrial Broadcasting and the Role of Tokyo Skytree," www.tokyo-sk ytree.jp/en/about/tower/; Tōbu Railway Company and Tōbu Tower Skytree Company, "Find Japan," www.tokyo-skytree.jp/en/enjoy/findja pan/.

33 Tōbu Railway Company and Tōbu Tower Skytree Company, "Color Design," www.tokyo-skytree.jp/en/about/design/.

34 Tōbu Railway Company and Tōbu Tower Skytree Company, "Raichingu dezain," www.tokyo-skytree.jp/about/design/lighting.html.

35 Tōbu Tetsudō Kabushiki Gaisha and Shin Tokyo Tawā Kabushiki Gaisha, "Shin tawā no meishō ga kettei shita," June 10, 2008.

36 Tōbu Tetsudō Kabushiki Gaisha and Tōbu Tawā Sukaitsurī Kabushiki Gaisha, "Tokyo sukaitsurī no saikō takasa o 634m ni kettei shimashita," October 16, 2009.

37 Tōbu Railway Company and Tōbu Tower Skytree Company, "Kafe, resutoran," www.tokyo-skytree.jp/shop_restaurant/restaurant/index.ht ml#restaurant-top.

38 Tōbu Railway Company and Tōbu Tower Skytree Company, "634 Musashi Sky Restaurant," https://restaurant.tokyo-skytree.jp/restaur ant/.

INDEX

Made in the USA
Middletown, DE
10 February 2025

71106863R00170